The Yukon

A Travel Adventure Guide
By Dieter Reinmuth

ITMB Publishing Ltd.

Vancouver   London   Prague   Mexico City   Ha Noi

The Yukon
A Travel Adventure Guide
By Dieter Reinmuth

Published by:

ITMB Publishing Ltd.
345 West Broadway
Vancouver, B.C. Canada V5Y 1P8
tel: (604) 879-3621 fax: (604) 879-4521.

PRINTED IN CANADA by:
Kromar Printing Ltd.
Winnipeg, Manitoba, Canada.

First edition, 1997.

Canadian Cataloguing in Publication Data

Reinmuth, Dieter

Yukon Travel Adventure Guide

Includes bibliograhical references and index.

ISBN 1895907942

1. Yukon Territory - Guidebooks. 2. Outdoor Recreation - Yukon Territory - Guidebooks. I. Title.

FC4007.R456 1997   917.19'1043   C97-910377-0   F1091.R456 1997

This book is a first edition and we appreciate all comments. We have done our best to provide an up-to-date book. The author and the publisher do not accept any liability for incorrect information. Nor do we accept responsibility for any injury, death, financial loss or inconvenience that may occur while or because of using this guide book. However, we do wish to provide the most accurate information possible, so please forward all comments regarding errors, omissions and suggestions to the author Dieter Reinmuth, c/o the publisher, ITM, 345 West Broadway, Vancouver B.C. Canada V5Y 1P8.

Other travel adventure guides by ITM:
- *Prague and the Czech Republic (ISBN 1895907926)*
- *Alaska's Inside Passage Traveler (ISBN 0942297113)*
- *Northern California (ISBN 1895907969)*

Contents

Introduction

INTRODUCTION

This guidebook has been written with those in mind who will organize their own way to the North - may it be by Alaska Ferry; by plane, train or bus; by their own or a rental vehicle; or, and why not, by bicycle - or maybe a combination of all those mentioned above. For those with time, the trip north itself will be an adventure. Some tickets, especially if the vehicle is to go on the Alaska Marine Highway Ferry, need to be booked well in advance. Those starting their northern adventure in Whitehorse, the capital of the Yukon Territory, will find a wealth of accommodation particulars in this guide, from recreational vehicle parks to motels, wilderness lodges, campgrounds, hostels as well as addresses of all car, RV and canoe rental businesses and information about all transportation companies serving the Yukon.

A few words about the nature of guide books:

The hard reality about guide books is that some facts can be already out-of-date by the time they hit the store shelves. Writing and researching this book took more than a year, with new facts, new data, new businesses and new telephone numbers added until just a few days before the final printing. Reading these pages, you will notice the large number of businesses in the Yukon which burned to the ground during the summer of 1996. These businesses might or might not be rebuilt for the coming seasons, but others will burn down, cease operating or go bankrupt. Well - that is the nature of building with wood and/or running a business. Prices also will change and usually only in one direction - upwards! Some changes are on-going, such as the new regulations concerning the Chilkoot Trail. By 1998, the new fees, number of hikers allowed on the trail, and other regulations, may be cancelled, revised or added to - and that is the nature of government. Even the length of northern highways does not stay the same, as roads are almost constantly up-graded, levelled and, in the process, shortened. One quite drastic change occurred during the summer of 1996: until 1995 only one airline served Whitehorse from the south, but by 1996 three other airlines connected the rest of Canada with the Yukon. There might even be an international service from Frankfurt (Germany) to Whitehorse via Anchorage, starting in 1998. Maybe by 1999, we will be back to one airline - who knows!

I hope that most, if not all facts stated in this book, will remain unchanged, correct and true, helping you to organize your northern adventure with the least inconveniences. If things are found to be wrong, out-dated or plainly false, let me know - I am the guy who runs the hostel in Dawson City and there is no person easier to find than me. Or contact the publisher, ITMB Publishing, (ITM), 345 West Broadway, Vancouver, B.C. V5Y 1P8, tel. (604) 879-3621.

Picture this: you are relaxing on an Alaska bound ferry heading to Skagway; the most northern port in the Alaskan panhandle. A bike is tied on your vehicle, and the hiking boots are oiled and ready to go. In Skagway you park, take out your camping gear and start for a three to five day hiking trip along the Chilkoot Trail. You are following in the footsteps of tens of thousands of gold-seekers and adventurers who rushed towards the fabled gold fields of the Klondike in the years 1897-98. Having braved the trail, you return to your car for a short but spectacular drive to Whitehorse, where you can rent a canoe for a two week wilderness trip floating down the Yukon River toward Dawson City. Consider taking your bicycle with you in the canoe. It could be a tight fit, but river travellers have been spotted with bicycles on board and a log raft (there is a section in this book on how to get logs legally) might even accommodate a motorcycle.

Once you arrive in Dawson City, return the rented canoe, oil the chain of your bike and slowly drift off toward the Dempster Highway. This is a once-in-a-lifetime (and you want to do this bike trip only once!) 800 km biking trek over mountains and tundra, across the Arctic Circle to Inuvik on the delta of the Mackenzie River, the northernmost city in Canada.

You could hitch-hike, take the bus or fly back to Whitehorse, then drive back home along the long and lonely Alaska Highway. Does this scenario sound like your kind of holiday? Or would you prefer it to be a bit more down to earth and relaxing - like renting a car or an RV in Whitehorse to explore the many interesting side roads of the Territory, fish secluded lakes where your line might be the only one along its shores, or spend glorious days driving the splendour of the Dempster Highway.

This book provides detailed hiking tips and maps of the of the Yukon and its communities. It features a description of the Yukon River, including Alaska's Yukon River towns of Eagle and Circle. Also included is a kilometre by kilometre biking guide of the Dempster Highway and the lonely Canol Road, all the information you will need about every community in the Yukon, the Kluane National Park, all Territorial Parks, all Mackenzie River Delta communities in the NWT and all roads crisscrossing the region - paved or not - and many are not.

THE CLIMATE

It is well-known that winter in the Yukon can be very cold and very long, but few know that our summers can be incredibly hot. Not many visitors turn to the Yukon for their winter vacations, though more and more Europeans are doing just that. The value of clean, cold and unpolluted air in an unspoiled and uncrowded winter setting has its attractions, for example: crossing untrammeled valleys on cross-country skis, or being part of a small group of people on guided dog sled tours following in the footsteps of Jack London. Whitehorse, capital of the Yukon, offers a long list of winter fun and festivals. Smaller communities, such as Dawson City, have varied programs of winter related activities. All dates and kinds of winter activities Yukon-wide will be given in the appropriate sections of this book.

Of course, it is summer that draws the largest number of visitors from all over the world and those summers can be dry, hot and sweet but also tend to be rather short. The end of May still sees plenty of snow on most mountain tops and some lakes still carry ice. Most rivers will be open and running by the end of May, but broken up ice on the river banks might belie a possible daytime temperature of around 30°C. May 1995, was one of those hot ones, making many of the early visitors believe they had ended up in Mexico rather than Canada's North. Of course, nights can still be freezing and this extreme range of temperature can easily last to the end of June. July and up to the middle of August can be called our true summer, with warm to hot days and cool to warm nights.

Even if temperatures are not always in the high 20s in those three glorious summer months, 24 hours of daylight in most parts of the Yukon will give you so much more time to do that favourite thing of yours - like fishing, reading or watching the world turn. Sleep might fall a bit short on days when the sun only sets behind the hills by midnight and rises again a couple of hours later! By mid-August, some night has returned to all but the extreme northern parts of the Territory. It is a sign of colder months to come, but it also will shower the late summer visitor with an added attraction - the Northern Lights, the Aurora Borealis, those waves of multi-coloured lights dancing across the northern sky 90 to 140 km above the earth's surface. By the middle of August, those seemingly unending northern forests will change their colours into golden yellows and, lo and behold, mosquitoes grow a lot less aggressive as the temperature continues to drop. The first half of September can still be a lovely experience, with more wintery weather soon on its way. It might be interesting to note just how extreme the range of temperatures can be. The hottest recorded temperature reached 36.1°C (97°F) on June 14, 1969, in the community of Mayo. The coldest recorded temperature occurred in 1947 at Snag, -62.8°C (-81°).

PHYSICAL GEOGRAPHY

It is the Yukon River, of course, that gives this huge, largely unspoiled, land its name. The name "Yukon" possibly stems from the Ingalik (Deg Hit' an) language meaning great or clear river. John Bell, chief trader for the HBC (Hudson Bay Company), canoed down the Porcupine River, from the East, to reach the Yukon River in 1846. Natives his party met at the confluence of these two rivers told him this big river was the "Yukkhane", the "Diuke on" or the "Youkon". The Yukon River, at over 3000 km (1900 miles) - fifth largest in North America, can't be called "clear". It turns grey once the silt-laden White River dumps glacial run-off into it about 160 km (100 miles) south of Dawson City. There are plenty of clear water rivers left in the Yukon Territory - roughly 70 major rivers feed into the Yukon River. Most of them can be enjoyed by canoe, kayak, raft, skis or snowmobile, depending on the season.

This 482,000 square km (186,660 square miles) wedge-shaped Territory is tucked away in Canada's western-most corner, next to Alaska and touched by two large bodies of water: the Beaufort Sea of the Arctic Ocean in the far north, and the Gulf of Alaska in the Pacific Ocean to the south. Between these two oceans can be found some of the most varied and fascinating landscapes in North America. There are eight biogeoclimatic zones and 33 ecological districts ranging from Mount Logan, at 6050 m. (19,849 feet) the highest in Canada, to the largest non-polar ice fields in the world (located within the St. Elias Mountains), the world's second largest coastal mountain range. There is even a desert, tiny as it may be, near Carcross, and a northern Arctic coastal plain where polar bears and beluga whales roam and the summer sun shines 24 hours a day.

About half of the Territory is covered by forest. The Arctic Tundra to the north is dotted with as many lakes as there may be mosquitoes. Roughly 5% of the Yukon is covered with a permanent layer of ice; the remainder is taken by lakes, rivers, mountains and marshy wetland. The human presence in this vast expanse is so thinly spread that only a fraction of a person could be recorded for each square kilometre. Slightly over 32,000 people call the Yukon their home. The stark and beautiful emptiness of the North becomes apparent when you consider that the Yukon is somewhat larger than California, which has a thousand times the population! Around 24,000 inhabitants live in Whitehorse. Dawson City and Watson Lake are roughly similar in size with about 2000 people each. Those few remaining residents are at home in thirteen small communities, all accessible by road except Old Crow in the far north.

WHY VISIT THE YUKON?

Are there any other reasons to visit the Yukon — besides wild scenic wonders and mile upon mile of nature at its best and purest? Of course! First, there is the fascinating culture of the First Nation peoples who have lived here for thousands of years; subdued by this harsh land but not submitting to it.

Second, there is the rather recent influx of fur traders, hunters and seekers of quick riches, almost entirely based on the exploitation of gold. Along with their hopes, they brought their culture to this northern land. The Klondike story has been told and retold many times: three partners and friends out for a hunt hiked up Rabbit Creek, dipping their gold pans into the frigid waters as they fought their way upstream through dense underbrush. It was August 16, 1896, when they made one of the largest gold discoveries of all time. It would not only change their lives, but the course of history.

The Gold Rush began slowly. At first, nearby mining camps emptied themselves of their gold-thirsty inhabitants. One year later, world headlines were made when a few gold-laden miners unloaded their ton of precious metal in the ports of Seattle and San Francisco. It soon became a flood. Everybody who dared, headed north - the great Klondike Gold Rush was on.

The following years shaped the Yukon as nothing else could have. Tens of thousands of hopeful men and women poured into this virgin land, leaving behind not only their footsteps but their relics and their culture. Their impact on the face of the territory is for us to witness, to explore and to follow. The Chilkoot Trail, for example, is 53 km/33 miles of pure history. All that is needed to experience the trail is four to six days, good health and the right hiking equipment. The Yukon River, between Whitehorse and Dawson City, also is pure history for those with a couple of weeks to spare and not afraid to get their feet wet paddling a canoe, a kayak or a raft. Raw nature is thrown in for free!

Dawson City, where it all began, is as alive today as it was a century ago. The difference is that once there were 30,000 gold-seekers milling about, and now there may be 4000 to 5000 in the summer, a number which includes locals and visitors. Gold is still being found. It remains the largest local industry after tourism. Dawson City would be a much poorer place if it were not for the gum-shoed gold miners doing their grocery shopping next to the visitor from "down South". Remember: August 17, is an annual holiday in the Yukon. Try to be in Dawson City for the special celebrations.

The Yukon was part of the Athabasca Territory until 1870, when the British turned over all unallocated lands to the Dominion of Canada as part of the newly created country's crown lands. The boundaries of the Yukon were first drawn in 1895, when it became a district of the Northwest Territories. The sudden increase in population during the Klondike Gold Rush of 1897-98 prompted the Canadian Government to show a stronger presence. The district became a separate territory in 1898, a distinction it retains.

A SHORT HISTORY OF THE YUKON'S FIRST PEOPLE

There seems to be enough evidence to indicate that the first people to cross onto the new continent did so around 30,000 years ago. These first people must have travelled in small groups following game or awaiting the arrival of salmon, and over many generations, moved further south. Over the centuries more and more Asiatic migrant groups moved from Siberia to Alaska, either via a land bridge or with their own boats. The latest group appears to be the Inuit, arriving about 5000 years ago. The Inuit have previously been known as "Eskimos", a term that is not preferred any more. Inuit means "real people". Few Inuit live in the Yukon except when roaming for game in the far North.

Most aboriginal people of the Yukon can be divided into 8 major groups: the GWITCHIN in Old Crow; the HAN living from Dawson City to Eagle in Alaska; the NORTHERN and SOUTHERN TUTCHONE that inhabit the large central parts of the Yukon from Burwash Landing and Whitehorse to Pelly Crossing; the KASKA from around Watson Lake and Ross River; the UPPER TANANA from the area around Beaver Creek; and the TLINGIT living in the Carcross and Teslin area. Except for the Tlingit, all groups speak variations of the Athabaskan language - a language that is very similar to languages being spoken by other native groups in the Central and Southern United States. Today, only a few of the native people of the Yukon speak their respective tongues, but recently interest has grown considerably to preserve the languages. Many schools are now teaching these languages to children and adults, and Native language radio stations, books, and newspapers are being established.

Only 100 years ago, the native people of the North were facing terrible threats to their survival from the onslaught of hordes of trappers, traders, gold miners and road builders. Thousands died from imported diseases, or were culturally crippled by government or church-run boarding schools that prohibited the use of their own language, their music, and their traditional ways. The last few years have seen changes for the better, but the road still has many miles to travel before the First Nations peoples of the North can feel secure in their culture again.

TERRITORIAL SYMBOLS

Flower: Fireweed is a pale purple, long-stemmed flower, growing all over the territory. Look for it at roadsides, in gravel pits, in mountain meadows and areas where there has been a forest fire. It blooms between June and August and most parts of the plant are edible.

Bird: The common raven - you cannot pass a day without noticing this most common of northern birds. If you can't see it, you definitely will hear its loud and varied gaggle of sounds. The raven is a hardy soul, a survivor that lives in the Yukon all year.

Gemstone: Lazulite is found in remote corners of the northeastern Yukon; this semi-precious gemstone is quite rare. "Laza" is an Arabic word meaning heaven - its colour is azure blue.

The Yukon Flag: The green panel to the left symbolizes the green taiga and the forest. The white panel in the centre represents the winter snow. The blue, to the right, reflects the deep blue of the northern Arctic Ocean. In the centre panel are two fireweed embracing the Yukon coat of arms and a white malamute dog standing on a mound of snow. The flag was designed in 1967 by Lynn Lambert, a student from Haines Junction.

Political System: In 1898, the Yukon Act provided for a Commissioner and an appointed legislative council answering directly to Ottawa, the capital of Canada. Subsequently, elected officials were included on the council and, in later years more and more responsibilities were given to a Yukon-elected Council. Since 1979, the Ottawa-appointed Commissioner no longer participates in the running of the Yukon Territory, but an elected government leader and his or her Executive Council deal with the Yukon's affairs, similar to their Provincial counterparts in the rest of Canada. Responsibilities over the Yukon's minerals, forests, timber, animals and of all bodies of water and fish, are still under Ottawa's jurisdiction. The Provinces control these areas of legal jurisdiction. In future years, Ottawa will relinquish control gradually over some (but not all) powers mentioned above and, in the far future, there may be a Province of the Yukon - no longer a ward of the Federal Government.

ANIMALS

Although Yukon's human population would fit within a few city blocks in a metropolis, the numbers of creatures in the Territory are much more impressive. Across the Territory there are approximately 10,000 black bears, up to 7000 grizzly bears, and a handful of polar bears in the far north. Fifty-thousand moose, take or leave a few, roam the forest and wetlands, and 150,000 caribou migrate over huge distances. Two-thousand mountain goats and 22,000 mountain sheep call the mountains to the south their home, and roughly 5000 wolves would like nothing better than to find one of them. Forty-five hundred musk oxen live along the northern coast and about 100 newly reintroduced wood bison keep drivers alert near Kluane National Park. Coyote, squirrel, hares, foxes, and numerous other furry-legged animals are well represented. There are roughly 35 trillion mosquitoes, black flies, and other insects providing not only meals for birds but also keeps us humans entertained by slapping our exposed arms around camp fires.

For those who wish to observe northern wildlife, the numbers and opportunities are mind-boggling. Over two hundred species of migratory birds call the Yukon their summer home, some of them travelling from the most southerly tip of South America. The most fascinating is the endangered Peregrine Falcon, one of the fastest creatures on earth, with an estimated top speed of 200 km (125 miles) an hour. Thirty-four species of ducks, geese and swans use the Yukon as a fly-over or as a breeding ground. 10,000 types of insects and eighty different species of butterfly feed on a whole range of beautiful wild flowers and plants. One of the most visible is the fireweed - found almost everywhere from roadsides to mountain meadows. More than 1300 plant species thrive in this northern land; the summers may be short but days are long, giving plants a furious rate of growth. Mushrooms and berries are readily available for visitors who wish to supplement their freshly grilled grayling, but do exercise caution as many may be either unhealthy or quite deadly. Before eating wild plants or mushrooms, inform yourself about them.

FISHING AND HUNTING

For those who fish, there are three types of salmon and 17 freshwater fish, from trout to grayling to northern pike. Do not forget to purchase the appropriate sport fishing licence. For hunters, there is a cornucopia of fur-bearing animals available to be killed in the prime of life and this writer does not want to hide that he prefers the weapon to be a camera, a "kill" to occur with the "shot" of film. Hunting regulations have been tightened recently, and a thorough study of current hunting laws should be mandatory. Note that Canada has more weapons restrictions than does the USA, if you plan to bring any firearm into the country please check the regulations (including those of your airline) before you leave home to avoid having an unpleasant experience with Canada Customs officers.

Yukon River salmon fishers.

Fishing: Fishing regulations have been tightened since 1996 and any angler is advised to obtain the up-to-date <u>Sport Fishing Regulations</u> from Yukon Renewable Resources, Box 2703, Whitehorse, Yukon, Y1A 2C6. It's quite an entertaining guide with all the do's and don'ts one needs to know - and free. It is available anywhere that licences are sold and at any Visitor Centre. For a non-Yukoner the fees are $35 for the season, $20 for six days, and $5 for one day. They are valid from April to March 31 of the following year. Other permits are necessary if fishing in lakes such as Tatimain or Wellesley, or for dipnetting or setlines to catch burbot. Many lakes, called High Quality Lakes, are subject to special regulations such as using barbless hooks or a lower daily limit than in other waters. Some of these lakes are Quit Lake, Dezadeash Lake, Ethal Lake, Aishihik Lake, Teslin Lake, and Big Salmon River, as well as 27 other lakes. All fish under 20 cm (8 inches) must be returned unharmed to the water. Yukon fish species include Chinook, coho, chum and sockeye salmon, as well as the land-locked sockeye salmon called kokanee. Other fish include rainbow and lake trout, dolly varden, Arctic char, Arctic grayling, whitefish, inconnu, pike, and burbot. Always have your licence handy; a $100 fee is assessed for fishing without a licence.

Hunting: The free booklet, <u>Hunting Regulations</u>, has a total of 87 pages of information ranging from what, when and whether to shoot, to how to field dress your "kill". The booklet and hunting licences are available from the same office as given under "fishing", as well as most sporting goods stores, RV parks, and the front desk of the YTG building in Whitehorse. There were a couple of major changes for 1997. Now visitors other than Canadian citizens importing hunting guns into the country need to pay a $50 fee per weapon at the border or airport. Visitors borrowing hunting guns from a Canadian citizen need to register this transaction and pay a $30 fee. This latter permit is valid for 60 days only. In all cases, guns must meet Canadian legal standards or they will be confiscated, so please leave your Uzi, Magnum, or Colt 45 at home.

Hunting fees:

Big and small game   - Yukon residents, $10 - Non resident Canadian, $75 - Non Canadian, $150

Small game only - Yukon residents, $5 - Non Yukon residents, $20

Snowshoe hare, Arctic ground squirrel, porcupine and grouse are considered small game. For each big game animal to be hunted a "seal" has to be bought, ranging from $25 for a grizzly to $5 for a moose, black bear or caribou. ALL non-residents of the Yukon need to employ the services of a local Yukon holder of a guiding licence. Trophy fees for big game add to the overall costs; a further $750 for a female grizzly, $250 for a mountain sheep, $150 for a moose and $50 for a coyote. An export permit is needed for all wildlife parts, even if it is only a sun-bleached moose antler found in a highway ditch. Animal parts of grizzly, black bear, wolf, otter and lynx need a special CITES (Convention on International Trade in Endangered Species) export permit which are still issued free of charge but require 24 hours notice. Special regulations exist for baiting, poisoning and bow hunting. The use of crossbows, pistols or revolvers, and silencing devices is illegal. Please read the booklet Hunting Regulations carefully to avoid violations of the Wildlife Act. Violations include fines of up to $25,000 and / or imprisonment for up to 24 months are possible. For a list of registered hunting outfitters write to the Yukon Outfitters Association, Box 4548, Whitehorse, YT, Y1A 2R8. Tel. 668-4118, Fax 667-7390.

Trapping: Non-Canadians may not trap in the Yukon and special requirements apply for Yukon residents. There are about 750 licensed trappers in the Yukon of which 60% are of native ancestry. Fourteen animal species are commercially trapped for their fur in the Yukon. In most cases, the meat of trapped animals is utilized.

Bears

The creatures most likely to send the visitor's blood pressure sky-high include the 35 trillion mosquitoes and black flies, followed closely by the 10,000 black bears and 7000, or so, grizzly bears that roam the forest, mountain valleys and wetlands. Most wilderness travellers will encounter mosquitoes and black flies, but not bears; this might be disappointing to some hikers or paddlers, but it means simple bear safety precautions were followed. Keep the campsite clean, do not cook within 50 m (150 feet) of the tent, and don't keep clothing in the tent that was worn while cooking. Do not store food of any type, salt, soaps or similar goods in the tent. It is not a good idea to pitch the tent on a wilderness trail - those trails were not built by people for people but by bears for use by bears. You can understand that a bear might not feel too kindly, finding a "structure" on HIS trail! Do not camp too close to noisy running streams, inhibiting the bears ability to hear humans ahead. Bears usually prefer to keep out of a human's way if given the chance. If you don't want foxes in the hen-house, don't leave the hen-house door open. Those who do not want bears in the tent should keep cookies and anything else with a strong smell out of it. If climbing into your tent after having wiped your fish-knife on your jeans (let's hope not onto your sleeping bag!) is your way of doing things, do not blame the bear for - let us say - having a bit of a look.

Bear cub (3 months old) visits a cabin.

The wilderness is the home of bears, moose and all the other animals of the North. It is humans who are the visitors, and the natural rules are written by nature, not us. It is our responsibility to learn, to understand and to follow the rules. In recent summers, some motorists along northern highways have been badly injured when they fed bears from their cars. One driver had his child on his lap while feeding a black bear by pushing pieces of bread through a partially opened window. When the food did not come fast enough the bear reached through the window with his paw, seriously injuring the driver and the child. Another black bear pushed a car window in when the occupants stopped feeding him. In all these, and many other cases, two things have been achieved - first, the car occupants put themselves in great danger and, second, a normally wild animal shy of humans has been spoiled and made into a "garbage bear". A spoiled bear is a bear that no longer has fear of humans and now relates the scent of humans to easily accessible food.

No wilderness traveller would knowingly feed a bear. For one thing, tents don't offer much protection! An untidy camp destroys the relationship between humans and animals. Do not leave any food scraps behind, empty cookie boxes, meat cans that have not been burned out, discarded banana peels or carelessly left candy wrappers. Every year approximately 100 black bears and 15 to 20 grizzly bears pay the highest price. Through no fault of their own, they are exposed to garbage created by us - and are destroyed as "nuisance bears".

Generally a river traveller will see black bears. Hikers, since they tend to do their trekking mostly above tree level, might see either black bears or grizzlies. Black bears are at home almost everywhere in the territory, except the extreme north. They certainly feel more comfortable in the lower forest, along the rivers and lake shores where they find juicy fresh grass, roots and fruit. Black bears kill for meat as the opportunity arises, but try to stay clear of grizzlies - they are food for grizzlies! Black bears, especially the young ones, are a curious lot, which is why they are often found near human settlements. Although black bears seem to be named for their colour, they come in a variety of shades -from extreme black to every possible shade of brown up to light blond and even a slight blue. The weight of a black bear reaches about 120 kg (260 lb.). Although they are very strong and can move over short distances at 45 km / h (28 m.p.h.), they can be driven away by stick or rock throwing, or loud aggressive noises; sounds that a grizzly would find rather amusing.

Grizzly bears are at home everywhere in the territory, but they prefer to stay on higher and treeless ground, except in early spring when drawn to lower elevations in search of animals that have died during the winter, and in autumn when salmon, in their spawning creeks, are on the menu. Grizzlies also come in all colours from black and shades of brown to blond. Their average weight is around 200 kg or 440 lb. and over short distances they can reach a speed of 60 km/h or 37 m.p.h.. The quickest way to differentiate between these two kinds of bears is to notice the emphasized hump the grizzly carries on his shoulders. Both type of bears are good swimmers and setting up camp on an island does not mean the happy camper can become careless! Both bears can be as harmless or as harmful as can be; but surprising a bear, especially a mother with her young, can turn a picturesque situation quickly into a dangerous one. The main point is to not surprise a bear - place stones in tin cans, hang pot lids together from a backpack or use a shrill whistle; but these will not leave you with many friends in that peaceful, pristine valley either! If only mosquitoes could be kept away with banging pots! For a lone traveller, it is enough to occasionally talk loudly, sing or whistle. Even banging two stones together or breaking a twig every few seconds should be sufficient. A group of people is definitely capable of maintaining a constant noise level. Cyclists should be especially careful because of their quiet, rather fast approach.

Bears hear, smell and see quite well and almost every bear will get out of a human's way if given the chance. If a hiker is moving into the wind a bear will find it difficult to smell an approach and it is up to the hiker to move in such a way as to ensure the bear finds easy escape routes. A surprised bear, especially if it has been sleeping, feeding, or is with its young, can very quickly get into an attack position, which does not mean it will attack. The initial reaction of a surprised bear will usually be to recognize the danger and when possible to go around it. It is up to the person to leave an escape route open for the bear. Don't run away, but be calm and make a slow retreat, which is easier said than done! Even though we feel we should be running our dear little hearts out, we also know it makes no sense, as any bear is faster than us AND can climb a tree. Our behaviour opposite an aggressive, angry bear should be the same as our behaviour opposite an aggressive, angry dog - talk in a calm reassuring way promising the bear a version of a pie-in-the-sky, and all the time retreating in a slow and measured fashion.

Should it be a black bear that confronts you, aggressive movements or making yourself as large as possible by climbing on your backpack or on a rock might help to convince the bear that he has taken on too large an opponent. If you are in a group stand close together to show the black bear or young grizzly that you are BIG and if it comes to the unthinkable - the bear attacks - fight back with all you have got. (Authors note - I know of local Yukoners who go nowhere without their personal walking stick - a baseball bat!) Do not think about fighting back if it is an adult grizzly who is facing you down. Grizzlies use baseball bats for toothpicks! Older and larger grizzly bears do not like climbing too much, and sweet talking yourself to a tree that won't snap should the bear lean against it is the first line of defence - climb at least 4 m (13 feet) off the ground! If there are no trees at your disposal then there is only one thing left to do: play dead. Pull your knees into your stomach, fold your hands together protectively behind your neck and move as little as possible. In this position the most important body organs are protected, and when the grizzly lets go of the motionless victim the person should survive this "adventure" in more or less good shape. Although this might sound truly terrifying, one must not forget that only a minute percentage of human-bear encounters turn out badly for the human. The biggest loser is still the bear.

If hiking in the northern wilderness, be it for one hour or one week, do not carry sweets or other pleasant smelling foods in your shirt pocket or anywhere else on your body. Do not carry food loosely thrown into your backpack or, heaven forbid, rolled into your sleeping bag. Carry food in containers such as super strong freezer bags that are fairly air-tight. Be ready to throw food away from you at a moment's notice, should you encounter an aggressive bear. Consider if you really need to take along aftershave lotion, those sweet smelling lipsticks, or that can of fish. When cooking or grilling, get as far away as possible from your tent and be sure that the smoke from your cooking fire does not blow onto or into your tent. Be absolutely certain to leave anything that smells like food; looks like food; even remotely resembles food - or has come in contact with food OUT OF YOUR TENT. Toothpaste and similar items count as food!

Bear proof food containers are the ultimate to have along on a wilderness trip. Back country hikers into Kluane National Park are issued a type of food container which is unbreakable by even the most desperate of bears. Bears still will be able to smell any type of food, but not being able to get at it, they will learn to disassociate food smell from people. Hougens Sportshop on Main Street in Whitehorse will sell these containers beginning in 1997. They come in two backpacker sizes: 12 inch or 18 inch long, with a diameter of 8 inches. To order direct, contact Garcia Machine, 14097 Ave. 272, Visalia, California, 93292. USA. Tel. 1-209-732-3785.

A few words about bear spray: Cans of various sizes are sold in most camping stores mentioned in this book, and also at the Integraphic Copy Store on 411 Strickland in Whitehorse. Prices range from $60 to $80 per can. Some canoe rental companies rent them to their customers. Bear spray can give important protection against inquisitive bears - if used properly. Take care when aiming and do not shoot into the wind!!! Any bear would choke up with laughter watching teary eyed humans trying to escape from a cloud of pepper. Carrying bear spray - or any other type of weapon - is no substitute for exercising the utmost of care at all times.

The moose is another animal that deserves respect. With a shoulder-height of up to 2 m (over 6 feet) and approximately 650 kg (1400 lb.) of flesh, bones and antlers, a moose not only is majestic in stature, but also lightning quick in reaction. A cow-moose with her calves can react very aggressively if she gets the feeling of danger - and not only from humans. Even grizzly bears, to their regret, have to learn that a mother moose is not to be toyed with.

If there is a beast in the Yukon to really fear and respect, it should first be the **mosquito**, followed closely by **squirrels**. Against the first there are tinctures, creams and long-sleeved shirts, but against those sweet and lovable cheeky and quick thieves, nothing but metal food containers will do. Without any remorse, these little nimble-footed buggers will eat or gnaw holes in anything remotely edible.

Squirrels are cute thieves.

To feed these cute little animals can mean with considerable certainty that by the next morning a once watertight food bag will no longer hold any water.

BUILDING A CABIN:

The building of cabins anywhere in the Yukon without the proper permits is illegal. Special considerations exist for holders of legal trap line permits, as well as mining claim holders. Look for "how to stake a claim" later in this book.

NO TRACE CAMPING

No Trace Camping is based on a very simple concept: do not do what you would not wish to be done to yourself. In other words - leave a clean camp. Better still - leave your wilderness campsite as if you have not been there at all; with "no trace" of a tent site, no fire ring, no food scraps and no floating streams of toilet paper gracing nearby shrubs, to interfere with a true wilderness experience for the next person who comes along. One step further still - always carry a few extra garbage bags to clean up after those who believe leaving their garbage behind is a sign of attained manhood. For example, a fire ring in an often frequented tenting spot can be a good idea if just this one fire ring is being used, but in an out-of-the-way alpine valley with little or no human traffic it can scream as loudly as a fast-food billboard; "have been here and have gone again...!" So would leftover and partially burned wood, your dental floss wrapped around a strand of flowers, and lumps of burned pop cans in the wood ash. Please burn out tin cans (do you need to take them along in the first place?) to remove the odours of food and take them out with you, and wash your dishes away from streams and lake shores. Try to leave a tent site as clean as you found it - and maybe a little bit cleaner.

HYPOTHERMIA - THE SILENT KILLER

A certain number of deaths in the northern regions can be attributed to hypothermia; and one need not be a steely mountain climber, an extreme wilderness hiker or an adventurous river runner to suffer the effects of hypothermia. In news reports, the word 'exposure' is often used - it means the same thing, hypothermia! If you have ever shivered because of the cold, or if you have ever had goosebumps because of having been underdressed or wrongly dressed, then you have gone through the first stages of hypothermia. In most cases, you will be near a source of warmth. For example, if you are working in the yard, you can get a sweater from your house. The problem arises if there is no 'home' nearby or no sweater to put on. You are out on a trail, or in a canoe, and you and your friends figure that a little shiver won't get a real guy down: 'Hey! - it's only two more hours to the next campsite, no problem!' It may not be a problem if the next campsite consists of a heated cabin and a hospital three blocks away, but it is a big problem if you are in the wilderness.

So, what is hypothermia? Hypothermia is a lowering of the body's inner temperature, and a loss of heat. Shivering, a sensation most of us have experienced, is the first sign of hypothermia. If a persons clothing is wet and the person is extremely tired from physical activity, the shivering may become intense and uncontrollable. Symptoms of the first signs of hypothermia may appear 5 to 6 hours after the threshold of tiredness has been passed. It may only take an hour from the first symptoms to collapse and possible death. Violent shivering, speaking difficulties, and the inability to think straight and make decisions will appear if the body's temperature falls below 35°C to 32.5°C. By 30°C the body will grow rigid, walking is sluggish and jerky, and the person generally is unable to comprehend the situation. If a single hiker has come to this point, that person will die unless help arrives as soon as possible. The person will become irrational, drifting slowly into a stupor. By 25°C the person becomes unconscious and the heartbeat becomes erratic. Death is then minutes away.

A single hiker or river traveller has to be able to read those first signs. If they appear, stop for a rest and start a campfire, drink something hot (no alcohol or caffeine) and eat sweets, proteins or fats. This should take care of the problem. In a group of people, when anyone shows the signs of hypothermia, at least one person in that group needs to be a leader and make sure that the group puts up camp and builds that all-important fire to prevent further heat loss. Have you ever witnessed groups of hikers, all listlessly sitting around on a dripping-wet forest floor, with no one being able to make a decision on what to do next? That is hypothermia.

So, what to do? Heat loss is the enemy, and heat loss must be prevented at all costs. The first secret is proper clothing. Layers of clothes with windproof and rainproof outer protection; waterproof shoes, warm headgear, and warm, dry clothing available in waterproof bags, in case of a capsized canoe, is the best prevention.

In cold and windy-rainy weather, nibble food almost continuously - nuts, raisins, sweets and fruits. These high energy foods warm your body from the inside out. Carry a tent, sleeping bag and extra clothing in waterproof bags, and put up camp before shivering will make it difficult to erect your tent or strike the match to start a fire. If hypothermia is too far advanced and you are alone, you might die. It does not matter if your sleeping bag is the best one in the world - a cold body rolling itself into a cold sleeping bag will remain cold. Applying external heat is important, and the most readily available heat source is a dressed down 'warm' body who either pre-heats a sleeping bag, or joins the hypothermia sufferer if the bag is large enough. If the victim is conscious, warm fluids should be given (no alcohol or caffeine) - if unconscious, the person needs to be kept in a prone position with only external heat being applied.

A river traveller faces an entirely different type of hypothermia - the almost instant type!!! Waters of northern rivers and lakes barely reach a temperature of 5°C - often less. This cold water cools a body much more rapidly than the air or wind.

DRIVING ON GRAVEL

First and foremost - always drive with your headlights on. In fact, it is the law in the Yukon! Driving on gravel means dust and dust means reduced visibility and that means that, without your lights on, you are invisible to oncoming cars. Imagine an oncoming car passing another one just ahead of you - the passing car is in your lane, he can not see you! Not a pleasant thought - turn on your lights! Dust can be quite bad on gravel roads, but paved highways are not a lot better since most of them have unpaved shoulders where dust can become thick just as quickly.

Be especially careful around curves where loose gravel can have the effect of marbles on a teak floor. If being passed by a vehicle, slow down. If necessary slow to a crawl. Passing cars, or worse - trucks, throw the type of rocks, and plenty of them, against which no windshield is immune. If you are passing another car stay on the left lane as long as is safe - it might save the windshield of the car you have passed. You know why there are so many cracked windshields in the North? Read the previous sentence again! Minimize the dust inside your car by keeping the windows closed, by opening all vents, and by turning the fan to "defrost". Recycling the air and building pressure inside your car helps keep the dust down. Try it. It does not work in my car, but it might in yours.

If you need to stop your vehicle, perhaps because of a flat tire, remember that you are being trailed by a cloud of dust that might make it difficult for a car behind to see you. Slow down gradually, turn on the emergency flashers and come to a stop as far to the right as possible.

If it is raining, the situation is entirely different. Some stretches of northern roads are surfaced with a clay-sand type substance that makes for good driving when dry, but when wet becomes extremely slippery. Slow down, really slow down and if it gets too bad, like on some sections of the Dempster Highway, find a gravel pit, make a cup of coffee, dig out a book and wait. Always carry extra gas, a second spare tire, extra water and food, flares, a fire extinguisher, a first aid kit and a few good books. Travelling during the off-season, always carry a warm sleeping bag and spare warm clothes, gloves, candles and wind proof matches or lighters, a shovel, a tarp and / or blanket, a bag of kitty litter for traction, a small axe, a thermos with something nice and hot inside and - well - a few more good books.

MORE DRIVING TIPS

You may notice a 40 km/25 mile difference in distance measurements between BC and the Yukon sections of the Alaska Highway. The highway, year by year, is straightened, levelled and re-routed, shortening the road by quite a few miles since construction. A few years ago the BC highway department finally went to work re-measuring their part of the Alaska Highway and kilometre posts were realigned to reflect new realities. In the Yukon, kilometre posts still reflect distances as measured by historical mile posts. As odd as that may seem - just keep driving and you will eventually arrive at your destination!

You <u>MUST drive with your headlights on</u> at all times. It's the law.

The speed limit on Yukon roads is 90 km/h (55 m.p.h.).

If caught speeding in excess of the limit the fines are as follows:

1 - 15 km/h = $ 25   16 - 29 km/h = $ 40   30 - 49 km/h = $ 75   50 & up km/h = $150

Plus there is a 15% surcharge for a "victim of violence" fund.

HOW TO GET TO THE YUKON

For simplicity sake, let us assume that Vancouver, in Canada's most westerly province of British Columbia, is the starting point for your journey north to the Yukon Territory. This beautifully situated city should not be bypassed by northbound travellers. Another approach to the Yukon is from the southeast via Calgary, Edmonton or the Rocky Mountain communities of Banff and Jasper. For those taking the ferries of the Alaska Marine Highway, Bellingham, 86 km/53 miles south of Vancouver, in the state of Washington, will be the starting point to the **Alaskan** ports of either **Haines** or **Skagway** -just south of the Yukon Territory. The ferry ride through the Inside Passage is a magnificent three to five day mini-cruise, passing by one of the most beautiful coastlines of the world.

Those visiting Seattle may wish to stop at the Interpretive Center of the **Klondike Gold Rush National Historical Park** at 117 South Main Street. The Center is open daily from 9 a.m. to 5 p.m. and provides information about Skagway and the Chilkoot Trail. If you have not seen the 1925 Charlie Chaplin movie classic "The Gold Rush", the Center shows it every first Sunday of each month at 3 p.m. The Center's phone information line is 206-553-7220. For those heading north through California, Oakland has **Jack London Square** on its waterfront. There you will find the "other" rustic looking log cabin Jack London called home during the winter of 1897-98. You will read all about it in the Dawson City section of this book. Do not fail to visit the **Jack London Museum** and book shop. Don't miss the **"First and Last Chance Saloon"** next to the log cabin; truly an original place. It used to be London's hang-out when he was still a kid. After he returned from the Yukon, he sat in the saloon hatching stories that brought him fame and fortune. Another place to prime yourself for your Yukon trip is the **Jack London State Park**, near Glen Ellen, just north of San Francisco in the wine country. He had his home built here after leaving the Yukon and lived in it until he died at age 41, on November 22, 1916. For information about this park, see ITM's guidebook to Northern California.

> "I am the sailor on horseback! Watch my dust! Oh, I shall make mistakes a-many; But watch my dream come true. Try to dream with me my dream of fruitful acres. Do not be a slave to an old conception. Try to realize what I am after." (by Jack London)

BY PLANE

From Seattle, the traveller can fly directly to Juneau, the capital of Alaska, and from there take another direct flight to Whitehorse, capital of the Yukon. Other possibilities are flying from Seattle to Anchorage, then to Fairbanks, and from there to Dawson City.

From Vancouver there are daily direct flights to Whitehorse, more frequently in summer than winter. **Canadian Airlines** (CP) depart Vancouver daily at 07:45 arriving in Whitehorse (YXY) at 10:10; also daily except Saturday at 13:20, arriving at 15:40. Flight schedules change frequently, so be sure to check with your travel agent or call Canadian Airlines: within Canada   1-800-665-1177. In French 1-800-363-7530, from the US 1-800-426-7000 and TTD in Canada call 1-800-465-3611. Several non-stop flights a day connect Vancouver with Prince George, and still further north in BC, with Fort St. John, the largest regional airport along the Alaska Highway.

Other airlines serving northern British Columbia are **Air Canada** (AC): 1-800-661-3936, **Air BC** 1-250-360-9074 out of Dawson Creek, northern BC, **Canadian Regional Airlines**: 1-800-663-1661 and **Central Mountain Air** (9M): 1-800-663-3905.

New Air Services:

In 1996 **Royal Airlines** (QN), commenced summer service from Toronto to Whitehorse via Calgary, Edmonton and Yellowknife. Call Fiesta West 1-800-663-9757 for information. Flights leave Toronto Tues. at 11:00, arrive Whitehorse at 19:50 (now there are Friday flights too). Leave Whitehorse Wed. at 10:05, arrive Toronto at 23:15. Fares $479 one-way; Edmonton-Whitehorse $229.

NWT Air (NV): call 1-800-661-0789 or Air Canada for more information, operates from Vancouver to Whitehorse leaving at 12:30 arriving 14:45, daily except Sat., which leaves 19:35 and arrives 22:10. Whitehorse to Vancouver leaves daily 08:40, arrives 11:00, daily except Sat., which leaves 15:20 and arrives 17:40. Edmonton to Whitehorse, Sat. only, leave 21:45 arrive 23:20. Whitehorse to Edmonton, Sat. only, leave 15:45 arrive 19:10. Fares are about $380 one-way.

First Air: This airline connects Yellowknife, capital of the western part of the North West Territories, with Whitehorse every Mon., Wed. and Friday. Leave Yellowknife at 9:30. Arrive Whitehorse at 11:35. Return to Yellowknife at 12:05, arriving at 16:05. One-way costs $526, and special weekend returns are available. All flights stop-over in Fort Simpson along the Mackenzie River. For reservations from across North America call 1-800-267-1247. First Air also connects Ottawa and Montreal with Yellowknife, with stopovers at northern communities with names like Igloolik, Iqaluit and Umingmaktok.

If you do not have too much luggage, flight-hopping will also get you to Whitehorse taking the coastal route. For example, Canadian Airlines serves Prince Rupert, the only Canadian port serving both the Alaska Marine Highway and BC Ferry terminal twice a day. Scheduled passenger float planes connect Prince Rupert with Ketchikan almost daily. From Ketchikan, the first Alaska Panhandle port served by the north-bound Alaska Ferry, numerous float plane companies connect all other towns and communities in Southwestern Alaska - including Juneau, with a direct flight to Whitehorse via Air North.

BY BUS:

During the summer, **Greyhound** buses bound for Whitehorse leave daily from the Vancouver bus depot (next to the VIA station at Main and Station St.). This is a 2800 km / 1740 miles, 50 hour, trip requiring several changeovers. For those who love sleeping while sitting up, this is the trip of a lifetime. The one-way fare from Vancouver to Whitehorse is $290. Between Vancouver and Prince George, there is normally one day-time and one night-time bus, the journey lasting 12 hours. After a stop-over and change of bus, it is another 8 hours to Dawson Creek, at the beginning of the Alaska Highway. Then you are in for the long haul to Whitehorse - a 20 hour rumble with the worst part being the arrival time in Whitehorse, at 4:30 in the morning.

There are at least three buses a day from Edmonton to Fort St. John via Dawson Creek (10 hours), connecting with the buses from Vancouver. Another possibility from Edmonton is by way of Jasper to Prince Rupert (19 hours) which allows for a good night's sleep on the Alaska Ferry. Call Greyhound Bus at 1-800-661-8747 or 1-800-661-1145 for more information.

Alaska Overland Tour Bus runs from Prince Rupert to Whitehorse, 342 3rd Ave. West, Besner Heritage Building, Prince Rupert, BC, V8J 1L5. Telephone 1-250 624-6124, Fax 1-250-624-6429.

Consider an Alaska Pass - discounted prices allowing unlimited travel on participating ferries, buses and trains throughout Alaska and the Yukon. For more information call 1-800-248-7598 from either the USA or Canada or from the UK Tel./TDD 0800-89-8285. Tollfree fax numbers are : from the USA and Canada 800-488-0303, from Germany 0130-82-0550, and from Switzerland 155-6511. The Alaska Pass covers just about every transportation company between Bellingham and the Yukon and Alaska for trips ranging from 8 to 45 days with prices from $499 to $949.

TAXIS:

In **Watson Lake** call Bud's Taxi at 536-2777. In **Faro** and **Ross River** call 994-2433, and in **Mayo** call 996-2240. If, for example, you want to go to any of the three above mentioned communities, call them from Whitehorse. One of their taxis might be in town offering a good rate, so that they don't go back empty. All taxi companies in the Yukon will drive you to anywhere in the Territory - for a price!

BY TRAIN:

It might be a bit more fun by train - for at least part of the way. **Amtrak** connects Seattle to Vancouver with a daily trip each way. Call 1-800-872-7245 for reservations and information.

BC Rail from North Vancouver to Prince George departs every Wed., Fri. and Sun. at 07:00, arriving in Prince George at 20:30 the same day. Continue by bus or by VIA Rail. Call BC Rail at 604-984-5246 for information and reservations.

As of the summer of 1996, the schedule of the **VIA** train service from Edmonton to Prince Rupert has been changed. It now requires two overnight stops, one in Jasper and one in Prince George - which has turned this route into an excursion trip with no night time travelling. Leave Edmonton Wednesday, Friday, or Sunday at 08:55; arrive in Jasper at 14:20 the same day. (This train continues to Vancouver.) The following day a train departs from Jasper at 13:00; arriving in Prince George at 19:15 the same day. The next day it leaves at 07:45 and arrives in Prince Rupert at 20:00. Economy class costs $123 one-way and touring class, which includes meals served at your seat, costs $239. Overnight accommodation in Jasper and Prince George is the responsibility of the traveller. This train ride requires advance reservations. **In Western Canada call toll free 1-800-561-8630** or contact a travel agent.

Another way to get to **Prince Rupert** is to take the train from **Victoria** on Vancouver Island to **Courtenay**; it leaves daily from Mon. to Thu. at 08:15; Fri. and Sat. at 07:45 and 18:00 and Sun. at noon. The journey takes four and a half hours. From Courtenay continue on by bus (or bicycle!) to **Port Hardy**. In summer a BC ferry leaves **Port Hardy** every second day for **Prince Rupert**. Departure time from both ports is the same: 07:30 arriving 15 hours later at 22:30. During the winter season there is only one departure a week in either direction: Sat. at 18:00 from Port Hardy and 11:00 from Prince Rupert on Fridays. Rates vary depending on the season. The summer rate for a walk-on passenger is $90, in the off-season it is $54. If travelling by car, reservations need to be made far in advance. **Call BC Ferries** from 7 a.m. to 10 p.m. daily: In B.C. tel. 1-888-223-3779; outside B.C. tel 1-250-386-3431, Fax 1-250-381-5452. Internet: http // bc ferries.bc.ca / ferries.

Note that after October 19, 1996 the area code for BC, except for the Lower Mainland, Fraser Valley, Sunshine Coast & Whistler/Howe Sound changed to (250).

BY RENTAL CAR:
Every car rental company under the sun (and then some) can be found in either Seattle or Vancouver or any other city on the continent. Remember, though, that renting a car or motorhome / RV "down South", in Vancouver for example, means you not only will have to drive 3000 km to Whitehorse but also drive back - and that is more than a week of hard driving! So, unless you have the time or are willing to pay a steep drop-off charge, it might be better to rent one's vehicle in either Whitehorse, Anchorage or Fairbanks. (Check with rental companies given in the Whitehorse section of this book).

There is a low-cost option for passenger cars out of Vancouver: **Norcan Leasing,** a car rental company working out of Whitehorse. Their Vancouver - Whitehorse one-way rate will cost you between $100-$200 depending on the car rented. This offer is usually good only in early summer. Call them at 1-800-661-0445 (in Whitehorse) for more information and arrangements.. Their rental rates for going south, from Whitehorse to Vancouver are around $1000. Look under Whitehorse for their address and one other rental company with low-cost rentals going south in late summer.

BY FERRY:

The most peaceful and relaxing way to reach the Yukon is by the Alaska Marine Highway Ferry. Reservations are required for cabin space or if taking a vehicle on board. For those with sleeping bags and who love hard surfaces, there is plenty of open deck space, with a limited number of outside lounge chairs available. There are recliner chairs and carpeted space inside. Showers are available for those without cabins, as are a cafeteria, restaurant, lounge, TV room, book and gift shop, and children's corner. In summer, most of the eight vessels of the ferry system offer nature lectures and films about interesting aspects of ports of call.

The southern terminus is Bellingham, 1 1/2 hours north of Seattle and one hour south of Vancouver. From May to July, northbound sailings are booked heavily, as are the southbound sailings from the end of July to August. Reversing your travel route is worth considering. Between May and September one ferry leaves Bellingham every Friday at 18:30 (6:30 p.m.) - which works out to 4-5 runs each month. Winter sailings are slightly less frequent. Reservations for Bellingham - Skagway should be made well in advance, especially if taking a car or motorhome on board. Arrival time in Skagway is on Mondays between 13:00 and 18:30 depending on the route that is taken. Southbound ferries always leave on Monday, but departure times vary. Arrival day in Bellingham is early Friday morning. Going north, the first port of call is Ketchikan, thirty-seven hours later. These ferries do not call at Prince Rupert.

A few prices (1997) between Bellingham and Skagway, in US dollars:

Deck space (no cabin or food) - $246. A child between ages 2 and 11 - $124. Bicycle - $40. Motorcycle - $181. Vehicle up to 10 feet (3.3 m) - $270, and up to 15 feet (5 m) - $581. The price increases with the length of your vehicle. Household pets (horses don't count) cost $40. Cabin space is extra; prices vary between $263 for an outside cabin for two, and $311 for an inside cabin for four.

There are many more services between **Prince Rupert and Haines/Skagway**. During the summer there are almost daily departures, but some vessels only go to Juneau; in some cases this requires an overnight stay before one can continue to either Haines or Skagway.

Prince Rupert Information:
Both ferry terminals of the B.C. Ferry and the Alaska Marine Highway Ferry are located side by side at the port of Prince Rupert. There are no services on site, but a very good seafood restaurant can be found near the gate to the commercial harbour entrance, within walking distance from both ferry terminals. The distance to the centre of Prince Rupert is about 3 km and along the way are at least three motels/hotels and one RV/campground. **Park Avenue Campground** is located less than 1 km from the ferries. Toll-free 1-800-667-1994 or tel. 1-250-624-5861, fax 1-250-627-8009; serviced and unserviced RV sites and tenting. **Pioneer Rooms**, on 3rd Ave. East in the downtown area, offers budget and hostel type accommodation ranging from $15 to $20 per person. Tel. 624-2334 on 167. There are plenty of other hotels in all price ranges. The **Travel Infocentre** is at 100 - 1st Ave. East. Tel. 1-250-624-5637. Fax 1-250-627-8009. Toll-free from the USA and Canada 1-800-667-1994.

Departure and arrival times in Prince Rupert vary depending on routing - some vessels stop at Sitka, a pleasant detour, and some do not.

A few prices (1997) between Prince Rupert and Skagway, in US dollars:

Deck space (no cabin or food) - $124. Child between 2 and 11 - $ 62. Bicycle - $ 23. Motorcycle - $ 90. Vehicle up to 10 feet (3.3 m) - $134. Vehicle up to 15 feet (5 m) - $286. Pet - $ 10.

Travel time between the various ports:

Prince Rupert to Ketchikan - 6 hours. Ketchikan to Wrangell - 6 hours. Wrangell to Petersburg - 3 hours. Petersburg to Juneau - 8 hours. Petersburg to Sitka - 10 hours. Sitka to Juneau - 7.75 hours. Juneau to Haines - 4.5 hours. Haines to Skagway - 1 hour.

For reservations and more information write, phone or fax to the Alaska Marine Highway P.O. Box 25535, Alaska, 99802-5535. Within the USA call toll-free 1-800-642-0066. Fax 1- 907-277-4829, from Canada call 1-800-665-6414. Hearing or speech impaired call TDD 1-800-764-3779.

Call the ferry terminal direct if the above numbers are busy: Bellingham 1-360-676-8445, Prince Rupert 1-604-627-1744, Haines 1-907-766-2111, Skagway 1-907-983-2941, or Anchorage 1-907-272-4482, Fax 1-907-277-4829, or ask your travel agent.

The winter rates for the ferry runs are lower than in the summer. Unfortunately, the winters in the Yukon are not what the average northern visitor has in mind. If you miss a ferry, or just feel like looking at the magnificent coastline from the sky, remember that all ports between Prince Rupert and Skagway are connected by scheduled float plane - the "lumbering truck of the North".

OTHER LOGISTICS

AREA CODE

Please note: The area code 403 for the Yukon will change to 867 starting October 1997.

TAX REFUND FOR VISITORS TO CANADA (GST)

If you are not a resident of Canada, spend at least $100 (CDN) or more on goods or accommodation, and if you take these goods out of Canada within 60 days of purchase, you qualify for a refund of the 7% GST. It is important to save the original receipts of goods purchased - credit card slips only are not accepted.

Only goods purchased to be taken home qualify (except alcohol and tobacco products), and your stay in an individual lodging establishment may not have been longer than one month. Of course, you can stay in as many places as you like.

No refunds will be paid for meals and any type of beverages; any type of transportation, including fuel for your rental car; camping fees; boat, bike or other rentals; any service like repairs or entertainment; or goods which were left behind in Canada.

Apply for a refund at any Canadian Duty Free Shop at airports or at border crossings for a maximum refund of $500, or by mailing a completed application form with all original receipts to Revenue Canada, Customs and Excise, Visitor Rebate Program, Ottawa, Canada K1A 1J5. Refunds have to be applied for within one year after purchase of goods or use of accommodation.

RECYCLING

Most communities in the Yukon have some sort of a recycling program for the collection of clean glass containers, rinsed-out metal cans, pop cans, most types of plastic containers, and paper products, as well as household type batteries. Raven Recycling at 138 Industrial Road, Whitehorse, tel. 667-7269, collects recylables from surrounding communities and you can drop off your items at their location, 24 hours a day. Liquor and/or beer containers can be taken to any of the liquor stores Yukon-wide for refunds.

ALCOHOL

There is a deposit payable on each beer or liquor bottle and can. Deposits can be returned at liquor stores Yukon-wide. Most saloons sell take-out beer and wine. All communities in the Yukon prohibit public consumption of alcohol. The minimum age to buy alcohol and to enter bars and saloons is 19.

BANKING

The **Canadian Imperial Bank of Commerce** (CIBC) maintains a cash machine in Porter Creek, along the Alaska Highway; in the D.J. Grocery Store; in Dawson City; and in Watson Lake. *All other Yukon based banks in th Whitehorse area maintain cash machines. Look in the Whitehorse chapter for more information.*

Other bank locations: CIBC in Dawson City, with regular hours. Tel. 993-5447 / 6915; **CIBC in Watson Lake**, with regular hours. Tel. 536-7495; **CIBC in Teslin** at the Native Band Office. Tel. 390-2033; **CIBC in Ross River** at the Service Centre. Tel. 969-2212; **CIBC in Carmacks**, Northern Tutchone Trading post. Tel. 863-5015; **CIBC in Haines Junction**, Madley General Store. Tel. 636-2820; **CIBC in Mayo** at the Government Building. Tel. 996-2039; **CIBC in Pelly Crossing** at the Band Office. Telephone 537-3515. **TD in Faro**. Tel. 994-2629; **TD in Beaver Creek**. Tel. 862-7409 and **TD in Old Crow**. Tel. 966-3819.

Western Union has three Money Transfer offices in the Yukon. In Whitehorse, at Cashplan Financial, 201 Hanson Street, Whitehorse, YT, Y1A 1Y3, Telephone 667-2274, Fax 667-2509. In Watson Lake, at the Gateway to Yukon RV park; and at the Morley River Lodge at Mile 777, Alaska Highway.

Frequent visitors from outside Canada might find it convenient to open an account in any bank. Normally a **Bank Convenience Card** (not a credit card) is issued right away. It gives access to your account at all their branches, but also to all cash machines of other banks across the continent. Only the banks in Whitehorse will exchange overseas currency, and rather unwillingly. The Royal Bank seems to be the least reluctant! One more thing - do not cash your traveller cheques at banks, as they will charge $1 to $2 for each cheque - any business does it for free!

MAPS

For road maps and topographical maps covering the Yukon, Alaska and northern B.C., visit or contact **World Wide Books & Maps** in Vancouver, 736A Granville Street, Vancouver, B.C. V6Z 1G3. Tel. 1-604-687-3320. Fax 1-604-687-5925. Available are road maps of the Yukon (#373), Alaska (#873), and various maps covering British Columbia. Also in stock are all 1:250,000 topographical maps covering Western Canada and Alaska. The store carries one of the largest collections of travel books and maps on the continent, open 9 a.m. to 6 p.m. from Mon. to Sat. **International Travel Maps** (ITM), at their new store on 345 West Broadway, Vancouver, V5Y 1P8, tel. (604) 879-3621, fax (604) 879-4521, sells excellent tourist maps of the Yukon, Alaska and British Columbia, as well as other parts of the world.

Yukon Topographical Maps: Six 1:250 000 topographic (topo) map sheets are required to cover the Yukon River from Whitehorse to Dawson City. They are: Carmacks 115I, Dawson 116B(+C), Lake Laberge 105E, Stevenson Ridge 115J(+K), Stewart River 115O(+N), Whitehorse 105D. 1:50,000 are also available, but they tend to be dated, and numerous maps would be needed to cover the river between Whitehorse and Dawson City. If you can read German, look for a Yukon River guide book, 'Yukon', by this author, and published by Conrad Stein, Germany, with maps covering the river between Whitehorse and Dawson City. It is for sale in many Whitehorse and Dawson City stores, at the two Vancouver Hostels, the Victoria Hostel, some BC ferries, and Wanderlust Books in Vancouver, 1929 W. 4th Ave., tel. 604-739-2182 or Manhattan Books in Vancouver, 1089 Robson St., tel. 604-681-9074.

Maps are available from the **Canada Map Office** - National Air Photo Library. 615 Booth St., Ottawa, Ont., Canada K1A 0E9. Tel. 1-613-952-7000. Fax 1-613-957-8861.

MEDICAL CARE

Only the hospitals in Whitehorse, Dawson City and Watson Lake are staffed 24 hours a day, and only the Whitehorse General Hospital is equipped to handle most major medical emergencies. All other communities in the Yukon are either staffed by nurses or medical doctors on a 24 hour stand-by basis. The Whitehorse General Hospital is located on the east side of the Yukon River opposite the Rotary Peace Park. Their non-emergency telephone number is 667-8700. **In**

A red fox.

emergencies dial 911 or 668-4444. All Yukon health facilities charge a user fee for non-resident foreign visitors amounting to $93 per out-patient visit to any of the hospitals or nurse stations. The in-patient fee comes to $220 per day, except in Whitehorse where the fee climbs to $1177.50 per day. Cash or credit cards are okay, but no personal cheques are accepted. CARRY INTERNATIONAL HEALTH INSURANCE! Canadian residents of other provinces might be asked to pay, but they will be reimbursed by their provincial health plan.

ateway to the Yukon

Railroad bridge acrosss Lake Bennett near Carcross.

THE PORT OF HAINES

Haines is the first port with road access to the Yukon. The ferry will take one more hour to Skagway. Note that Haines offers more direct road access to those bound for Alaska or Kluane National Park. Haines offers a lot of nature and history, in addition to the facilities one would expect of a town of 2300. "DTEHSHUH" (Day-shoo) is the original First Nations name for Haines. The town is located on the Upper Lynn Canal, framed by the Coastal Mountain Range. Both the Chilkoot and the Chilkat clans of the Tlingit Nation used this area as a trading post for the region now known as the Yukon. The first white traders arrived in 1878, and the town became an important port for pre-Klondike Gold Rush fur traders, miners, hunters and missionaries. Very few gold seekers used Haines as a starting point to Dawson City. In 1903, Alaska's first army post was established at Haines. It was named Fort William H. Seward after the Secretary of State who had negotiated the purchase of Alaska from Russia in 1867.

Buses out of Haines

Alaskon Express Bus leaves Haines for Haines Junction in the Yukon, every Sun., Tues. and Thu. at 08:15, arriving at 13:15. US$71 one-way. Tickets are available at **Wings of Alaska** on 2nd Ave. across from the Information Center. Tel. 1-907-766-2030 / 2000. They run scheduled services onward to Alaska and Whitehorse. The bus to Haines Junction connects with their bus to Whitehorse arriving there at 16:30; it costs US$82.

Alaska Denali Transit is located at 701 W. 58th Ave., Box 4557, Anchorage, AK, 99510. Tel. 1-907-561-1078, 24 hour recorded message: tel. 1-907-273-3234. This bus line has services to Tok and the Denali National Park via Fairbanks.

Alaska Direct Busline, Tel. 1-800-770-6652, serves most points in Alaska, Whitehorse and Skagway. It only runs pre-booked charters out of Haines, but might start a scheduled service by 1997.

By Air and Water Taxi: Three scheduled airlines connect Haines with Skagway and Juneau. A water taxi leaves Haines for Skagway daily in summer at 08:30 and 15:00 - one-way US$18, return US$29, bicycle US$5. Call 766-3395 for updates.

More information about Haines is available from the **Haines Visitor Bureau**, P.O. Box 530, Haines, Alaska, 99827-0530. Tel. 1-907-766-2234. Fax 1-907-766-3155. Call toll-free from anywhere in North America: 1-800-458-3579. The office is open 7 days a week from 8 a.m. to 9 p.m., May to Sept. Winter hours are Mon. to Fri. 8 a.m. to 5 p.m.

Other important telephone numbers:

Call 911 for POLICE, FIRE or AMBULANCE. Their non-emergency numbers are: **Police** 766-2121, **Health Center** 766-2521, **Fire** 766- 2115, **State Troopers** 766-2552, **US Customs** 767- 5511 and **US Immigration** 767-5580. **Alaska Marine Highway Terminal** call 766-2111, schedule only 766-2113, reservations 1-800-642-0066. **Weather Information** 766-2727. **Bank**: National Bank of Anchorage on Main St., open 10 to 4 p.m. An **ATM bank machine** is located inside Howsers Supermarket, also on Main Street. For the **Chamber of Commerce**, call toll-free 1-800-246-6268.

Accommodation Guide to Haines: All prices quoted in the Haines and Skagway sections are in US$. Nine hotels and motels, seven B&Bs, and ten RV and/or campgrounds cater to the visitor, as well as one summertime hostel.

Bear Creek Hostel Small Tract Road, Box 908, Haines, AK, 99827. Tel. 1-907-766-2259. The hostel is located 1.2 miles from the town center, and will pick up guests from the ferry. Rates start at US$6 for tenting, to US$15 per bed and US$37 for a cabin. Bike rental is available.

Captains Choice Motel. Tel. 1-907-766-3111. Toll-free from the lower USA 1-800-247-7153, or from Alaska, B.C. and the Yukon 1-800-478-2345. Fax 907-766-3332. Room rates are from $88 to $103. Car rental in house and wheelchair accessible.

Eagle Nest Motel. Tel. 1-907-766-2891 or 1-800-354-6009 from the lower USA. Fax 1-907-766-2848. Prices range between $70 and $95. Car rental in house and wheelchair accessible.

Ft. Seward Lodge. Tel. 1-907-766-2009 or 1-800-478-7772. Fax 907-766-2006. Rates from $50 to $85.

Ft. Seward Condos. Furnished apartments for $85 a day for two day minimum. Tel. 1-907-766-2425.

Hotel Halsingland. Tel. 1-907-766-2000 or 1-800-542-6363 from the USA and 1-800-478-2525 from Alaska, B.C. and the Yukon. Fax 1-907-766-2445 or toll-free 1-800-478-5556. E-Mail: halsinglan @ aol.com. Room rates from $39 to $ $93. Avis car rental in house and wheelchair accessible.

Mountain View Motel. Tel. 1-907-766-2900 or toll-free 1-800-478-2902. Rates from $59 to $ $64.

Porcupine Pete's Hotel. Tel. 1-907-766-2909 or 766-9999. Only four rooms from $70 to $90.

Thunderbird Motel. Tel. 1-907-766-2131 or 1-800-327-2556 from the USA only. Fax 907-766-2045. Room rates are from $62 to $82. Motel is wheelchair accessible.

Bear's Den. Tel. 1-907-766-2117. Furnished apartments for $90 per day. Two day minimum rental.

Bed and Breakfasts in Haines:

A Sheltered Harbor. Tel. 1-907-766-2741. From $70 single to $115 for one suite.

Chilkat Eagle B&B. Tel. 1-907-766-2763. From $65 single to $90 triple.

Chilkat Valley B&B. Tel. 1-907-766-3331 or 1-800-747-5528. Close to the Eagle Preserve. $70-$80.

Ft. Seward B&B. Tel. 1-907-766-2856 or 1-800-615 NORM. Single $72 to $85 double and one suite for $105.

Officers Inn B&B. Tel. 1-907-766 2003 or use same numbers as Hotel Halsingland. Rates from $50 to $94.

The Riverhouse B&B. Tel. 1-907-766-2060. 1 mile from town. Large rooms (for families) for $115.

Summer Inn B&B. Tel. 1-907-766 2970 From $60 single to $90 triple.

RV Parks and campgrounds in Haines:

Eagle Camper Park. Tel. and fax 1-907-766-2335. Full service RV park with Good Sam discounts.

Haines Hitch-Up RV Park. Tel. and fax 1-907-766-2882. Full hook ups and laundromat.

Oceanside RV Park. Tel. 1-907-766-2444. Fax 1-907-766 3589. Full hook ups, laundromat and showers.

Port Chilkoot Camper Park. Tel. 1-907-766-2000 or toll-free 1-800-542-6363 from the lower USA and 1-800-478-2525 from Alaska, B.C. and the Yukon. Fax 1-907-766-2445 or toll-free 1-800-478-5556.

Salmon Run RV Park. Tel. 1-907-766-3240, 32 wilderness sites with firepits and showers.

Swan's Rest RV Park. Tel. 1-907-767-5662, 27 miles from Haines with 12 full hook ups and boat rental.

PORTAGE COVE. Less than one mile (1 km) out of town. Camping for backpackers and cyclists only.

Forest Service Cabins. Can be rented around Haines and elsewhere in Alaska. Contact the US Forest Service Information Centre in Juneau at tel. 1-907-586-8751.

What to do in Haines:

For those who fish, Haines is a dream come true. The list of businesses catering to anglers is a very long one and the Visitor Center, the Chamber of Commerce or your hotel/motel/RV park can help you with further information. Contact the **Alaska Department of Fish and Game** at Box 330, Haines, Alaska 99827, tel. 1-907-766-2625. For those who like to eat fish, there are plenty of restaurants to keep you happy.

Worth a visit is the **Sheldon Museum and Cultural Center** in the town's center. Open daily in summer from 1 to 5 p.m. with limited hours during the months of winter, tel. 1-907-766-2366. Their bookshop has a large selection of books on Alaska. Do not miss the **Chilkat Dancers** who give daily performances during summer. Their tel. is 907-766-2160. Learn more about eagles at the **American Bald Eagle Foundation** (tel. 1-907-766-3094). The **Natural History Museum** is open daily in summer from 10 a.m. to 6 p.m., and in winter on Sun., Mon., and Wed. from 1 p.m. to 4 p.m. There is no admission charge. There are many wilderness tours offered out of Haines. **Glacier Bay National Park** near Haines can be reached via tour boats or flightseeing tours.

Festivals in Haines include the annual **Alaska Mardi Gras** at the beginning of June (tel. 907-766-2000); the **Summer Solstice Celebration** on June 22 (call 907-766-2476); the **Independence Day Celebrations** on the fourth of July (call toll-free for info. at 1-800-246-6268); and the **Southeast Alaska State Fair** which is held the first half of August, also featuring the **Bald Eagle Music Festival.** Call 907-766-2476 for more information. The **Bald Eagle Festival** is held in the middle of November, with guided tours to the Eagle Reserve and educational seminars, as well as plenty of family events and entertainment. Call above toll-free number for more information. The only road connecting Haines with the outside world travels through traditional Tlingit territory, passing the **Alaska Chilkat Bald Eagle Reserve** where eagles can be observed year-round.

EAGLE RESERVE

The reserve stretches for 5 miles / 8 km along the Chilkat River and is home to about 200 resident Bald Eagles. Since some areas of the river remain ice-free during winter, late runs of spawning chum salmon attract thousands of eagles from as far away as southern British Columbia and throughout the North. From late October to February, carcasses of salmon provide ready food for eagles and many other animals, including bears. In this period of time, nearly 4000 eagles gather in a relatively small area and observing 20 or more eagles in a single tree is quite a possibility.

EAGLES

An adult eagle sports a 'bald' white head and white tail feathers usually developed by age 4 or 5. Immature eagles are a motley brown. A female eagle is slightly larger than a male, with a wing span of between 6-8 feet or 2 - 2.5 metres, and an average weight of about 13 lb. or 6 kg. Eagles can fly at speeds of 30 miles / 50 km an hour and are able to dive at speeds of 100 miles / 160 km an hour. Bald eagles mate for life and can reach the age of 40. Until 1953, there was a bounty on eagles of $1 to $2 a bird; over 128,000 of these proud birds were killed before the bounty was removed.

The **US / Canada** border is 42 miles (67 km) from Haines, and the distance to Haines Junction, in the Yukon, is 160 miles (257 km). Once past the international border, the road (Highway #3) travels for a short stretch through British Columbia, skirting the newly created **Tatshenshini - Alsek Wilderness Provincial Park**. The park is known for its spectacular rafting and kayaking trips down the Alsek and Tatshenshini rivers, ending in the glacier-filled waters of the Pacific Ocean at Glacier Bay. Further information about the provincial park is available from BC Parks, Bag 5000, 3790 Alfred Ave., Smithers, BC, V0J 2N0. Tel 1-250-847-7320 or Fax 1-250-847-7659.

Advice to aviators into the above area - the private airstrip at Windy Craggy exploration site is no longer serviceable as indicated by two X markings on either end of the runway.

For information about **Glacier Bay National Park** contact the US Park Service, Box 140, Gustavus, Alaska, 99826. Tel. 1-907-697-2230; fax 1-907-697-2410. Permits for rafting trips ending in the Glacier Bay NP are issued from the National Parks headquarters in Gustavus. For trips remaining in Canada, and within the Provincial Park, permits are issued in Haines Junction at the **Kluane National Park**, Canadian Parks Service, Box 5495, Haines Junction, Yukon, Y0B 1L0. Telephone 1-403-634-2251; fax 1-403-634-2686. Only one boating party may leave per day. Half the permits are reserved for commercial rafting companies with the remainder going to private parties. The waiting list for private permits can be up to three years. For guided rafting trips check with **Tourism Yukon**, Box 2703, Whitehorse, Yukon, Y1A 2C6. Or call them at 1-403-667-5340 and Fax 1-403-667-2634. *Note that the area code for the Yukon will change to 867 starting October 1997.*

The **Tatshenshini-Alsek** was created in October 1993 and has been declared a World Heritage Site by the United Nations. Combined with all adjacent parks in Alaska, BC and the Yukon, this area forms the largest protected park system in the world with approximately 8.5 million hectares in a public domain.

Haines Junction is a beautifully located little town at the fringes of the Kluane National Park. From there it is 158 km (98 miles) to Whitehorse and 299 km (186 miles) to the Yukon / Alaska border at Beaver Creek. More about these places later. First, let us go back to Skagway, the last stop of the Alaska Marine Highway.

SKAGWAY

The name of Skagway seems to have gone through more spelling changes than the flight pattern of a mosquito. SKAGUAY or SKAGUO seem to be the favoured ones, with SCHKAGUA, SHKAGWAY, SKAGUA, SCHKAWAI and even CQUQUE for seconds. The meaning of the word seems even less agreed upon. From "Windy Place" to "Home of the North wind" or "Spirit of a cruel wind" to even (can this be serious?) "Lady relieving herself on a rock" to (and let's get adventurous now) "Gull peeing in flight wetting his mate flying below".

The years 1997 and 1998 will be great ones for Skagway. One hundred years ago, many thousands of gold-seekers filtered through this narrow inlet, covering the wet tidewater beaches with tents, luggage and cargo. Skagway grew out of nothing into a lawless bustling town with a population of up to 20,000. It is framed by steep coastal mountains and one rough little river called Taija. Today, the population hovers around 700 permanent residents with about another 400 seasonal summer workers to service the 350,000 guests who visit each year. Over 300 cruise ships call at Skagway each summer, with up to four ships a day, raising the Skagway population to over 3000 for a few hours.

The Centennial projects promise to be a magnet for lovers of history and historical re-enactments, such as the "Ton of Gold" voyage planned for 1997. One hundred years earlier, on July 17, the SS Portland, with its ton of Klondike Gold, steamed into Seattle Harbor and started the avalanche of gold-seekers. Only six days later, another steamer, the Queen, loaded with the first fortune hunters, landed at the beach now called Skagway. There will be re-enactment races, with packs and all, along the famed Chilkoot trail toward the gold fields of the Klondike at Dawson City. Contact the Skagway Centennial Committee. Box 415, Skagway, Alaska, 99840. See the appendices for a listing of centennial happenings in 1997/1998 and beyond.

Skagway has escaped the fate of so many other historical towns in the North - fire. The center of town is largely intact, with buildings straight out of the Gold Rush era, complete with false fronts and creaky floors, and the core of town is only a few steps from the ferry terminal. Broadway is the heartstring of town, slicing through Skagway in its entire length, and the street that funnels all traffic off the ferry and toward the Yukon.

The first building one comes to is the old White Pass and Yukon Railroad Depot, built in 1898. It is now the **National Park Service Visitor Center** and an important place for all those who want to tackle the Chilkoot Trail. (see below). The train used to leave from here, chugging down the middle of Broadway toward Whitehorse, 180 km (112 miles) away. Now it leaves from a newly-built station, one building further over, and only goes as far as Canadian Customs, at Fraser, 13 km (eight miles) beyond the US/Canada border. There are also some special steam train trips to Lake Bennett at the end of the famed Gold Rush Chilkoot Trail.

The **Red Onion Saloon**, kitty-corner from the depot, was also built in 1898. It still is a Wild-West watering hole, complete with original furniture and sawdust on the floor. The **Golden North Hotel**, a bit further down the street, may be the oldest hotel still operating in Alaska. Next door must be the most original of all buildings in the North - the 1899 **Arctic Brotherhood Hall**. It can easily be classified as late Victorian "rustic" architecture, with 10,000 plus driftwood sticks nailed to the exterior of the building. A labor of love if there ever was one! The Arctic Brotherhood Hall also houses the Skagway Historical Museum & Archives, open daily in summer from 9:00 to 5:00.

The **Visitor Center** is also inside the Arctic Brotherhood Hall. During the off-season visitor information can be found at city hall - east on 7th off Broadway. Both above-mentioned places are currently under renovation and a temporary location for the visitor center is at 5th Ave. between Broadway and State. For further information write to them: P.O. Box 415 Skagway, Alaska 99840. Tel. 1-907-983 2854. Fax 1-907-983-3854 or internet: http://www.skagway.org. The office is open daily in summer, and Mon. to Fri. with regular hours in winter.

Some additional important information:

Call 911 for either POLICE, FIRE or MEDICAL EMERGENCIES. Their non-emergency numbers are: **Police** 983-2232; **Hospital** 983 -2255; **Fire / Ambulance** 983-2300. **Klondike Highway Road Report** 983-2333. **United States Customs** call 983-2325 and **US Immigration** at the border call 983-3144. **Ferry Terminal** 983-2941.

Bank: **National Bank of Alaska** on Broadway. Open Mon. to Fri. 10 to 5 p.m. Tel. 983 2264, 24 hour ATM. **Thomas Cook** Foreign Exchange Booth: (a little red rail car) on 2nd Ave. across from the train station. **Post office**: Broadway between 6th and 7th, open Monday to Friday from 8:30 to 5 p.m. **Public Telephone**: Broadway and 5th. Its a small Alascom booth - make a direct call and pay afterwards. Bookstore and newspapers: **Skagway News Depot** on Broadway between 2nd and 3rd.

For those needing **supplies** to hike the Chilkoot Trail, Skagway offers one-medium sized supermarket and a limited number of stores selling hiking and camping gear. Whitehorse offers plenty of department stores with all that might be needed, as does Juneau. The hostel in town will store luggage for their guests, and so will most hotels and B&Bs. The luggage lockers within the ferry terminal are only accessible for three hours before arrival of a ferry and while it is in port.

Showers and / or **washing machines** are available at all RV parks and campgrounds for a fee. A coin laundry on 2nd. is open 7 a.m. to 11 p.m., daily.

Skagway offers **accommodation** in seven hotels, five bed and breakfasts, one private hostel, and four RV parks and campgrounds. Reservations are highly recommended, especially since at least one night has to be spent in town for late ferry arrivals. Those arriving in the early morning might find it possible to continue their trip north by either bus or train. Those wanting to hike the Chilkoot may need more supplies and must register with the parks office. All hotels, bed and breakfasts and the hostel are downtown, except the Wind Valley Lodge, which is 21 blocks from the ferry landing.

Hotel information:

Golden North Hotel. Tel. 1-907-983-2294 or 983-2451, Fax 1-907-983-2755. Single $60; twin $75; triple $85; quad. $95. Restaurant and lounge in house and courtesy van pick-up to and from the ferry. The hotel is being renovated to its former glory, and will include the historic Skagway Brewing Co., which operated from 1897-1919. Rumors have it that a ghost named Mary roams the rooms of the hotel. The friendly ghost is the spirit of a woman whose husband never returned from the Klondike.

Gold Rush Lodge. Tel. 1-907-983-2831, Fax 1-907-983-2742. From single $65 to triple $95. Located next to Skagway's airport. Offers non-smoking rooms and a courtesy van.

Portland House. Tel. 1-907-983-2493. Single, $50 with shared bath.

Sgt. Preston Lodge. Tel. 1-907-983-2521. Single $55 to $60, double $65 to $75, triple $70 to $90.

HOW TO GET TO THE YUKON

Legend

- –·– International Border
- —— Alaska / Cassier Hwy.
- —— Other Highway
- ·········· Ferry
- ▬▬ Railway

0   100   200 km
0   50   100 mi

YUKON

Beaufort Sea

Herschel Island
Territorial Park

Davidson Mts.

British Mountains

Ivvavik
National
Park

Herschel I.

Mackenzie
Bay

Tuktoyaktuk

Vuntut
National
Park

Mackenzie
River Delta

**ALASKA
(U.S.A.)**

Old Crow

Aklavik **Inuvik**

Fort
McPherson

Porcupine River

Chalkyitsik

Richardson Mountains

5

Arctic Red
River

Peel R.

Arctic Circle

Circle

Yukon Charley
National
Reserve

Mt. Burgess
1600m

Oglivie Mts.

Eagle Plains

Peel River

Arctic Red River

Fort Good Hope
Norman
Wells

Fort Franklin

Arctic Circle

*Great Bear
Lake*

Mt. Klotz
1799m

YUKON

Dempster Hwy.

Bonnet Plume River

Mackenzie Mountains

Fort Norman

Eagle Mt. Harper
1874m

Wernecke Mts.

Selwyn

N O R T H W E S T

Top of the World Hwy.

9

**Dawson
City**

Klondike Hwy.

Silver Trail

Elsa

Mt. Joy
2235m

Tok

Mayo
Stewart
Crossing

MacMillan R.

Carol Road

T E R R I T O R I E S

Tetlin

Yukon R.

2

Pelly Crossing

Minto

Klondike Hwy.

Pelly R.

Faro

6

Tungsten

Nahanni
N.P.

Beaver Creek

Alaska Hwy.

T E R R I T O R Y

Carmacks

Aishihk
Rd.

Ross River

Robert Campbell Hwy.

10

Nahanni
Butte

Mt. Bona
5005m

Wrangell

St. Elias
N.P.

Destruction Bay

Kluane

Haines
Junction

Teslin Hwy.

Pelly Mountains

Logan Mts.

Tuchitua

Nahanni
Range Rd.

4

Coal River Springs
Territorial Park

Fort Liard

Mt. Logan
6050m

National

1

6

Mt. Logan
6050m

National

Haines Rd.

Whitehorse

Johnson's Cr.

Alaska Hwy.

1

Watson Lake

Carcross

1

Teslin

Alaska Hwy.

Liard R.

Yakutat

Park

3

Skagway

Atlin

Atlin
Prov. Park

37

Alaska Hwy.

97

*Gulf
of
Alaska*

Road

Haines

Glacier Bay
National Park

B R I T I S H   C O L U M B I A

0   100   200km

Inset map

*Beaufort
Sea*

*Grønland
(Denmark)*

Whitehorse

C A N A D A

*Labrador
Sea*

Edmonton

Vancouver   Winnipeg

Montréal

Toronto

Ottawa

*Atlantic
Ocean*

U. S. A.

Westmark Inn. Tel. 1-907-983-6000, Toll-free 1-800-544-0970. Single and double $99, triple $114. This is a full service hotel with three restaurants, a lounge, Avis car rental and wheelchair accessible.

Wind Valley Lodge. Tel. 1-907-983-2236, FAX 1-907-983-2957. Single $65, double $75, triple $85, quad $95. Restaurant next door and courtesy car to and from the ferry and airstrip.

Miner's Cache Hotel. Tel. 1-907-983-3303. Fax 1-907-983-3304. Historic Hotel built in 1899. No children, pets, drinking or smoking allowed. There is a 11 p.m. curfew. Single $45 and double $60.

Gramma's B&B. Tel. 1-907-983-2312. Charges single $55, double. $65 and triple $75

Mile '0' B&B. Tel. 1-907-983-3045. Single $70, each additional person $20.

Skagway Inn B&B. Tel. 1-907-983-2289. FAX. 1-907-983-2713. From $60 single, to double $75, and five in one room for $120.

Cindy's Place. Tel. 1-907-983-2674. Out of town on the Dyea Road. Two night minimum. Single from $74; double $79 and triple $ 85.

The Whitehorse B&B. Tel. 1-907-983-9000. In an historic building.

The Skagway Home Hostel is THE place for the budget traveller who does not mind sharing. Tel. 1-907-983-2131, $13 a night. An amazingly friendly place. First come first serve, but nobody gets turned away.

Many of the above places are non-smoking or offer non-smoking rooms. Ask when making reservations.

For those with RVs, the most convenient place is the **Pullen Creek RV Park** right next to the small boat harbor, just off the ferry terminal. Tel. 1-907-983-2768, 42 sites with water and power, $18 per site and $10 dry.

Other RV and campgrounds:

Back Track Camper Park. Tel. 1-907-983-3333. Dry sites $8 and with power $16.

Garden City RV Park. Tel. 1-907-983-2378. Nightly charge $18.

Hanousek Park (no hook ups). Tel. 1-907-983-3333. Tents and small campers $8.

All above RV parks and campgrounds offer showers, laundromat (except Hanousek Park) and dump station.

The National Park Campground is located 9 miles (14.5 km) from Skagway at the Chilkoot trailhead near Dyea. First come, first served, with no charge and a two week limit. **The road to Dyea is too narrow for larger RV'S or motorhomes to navigate.**

What to do in Skagway:

Skagway offers plenty of entertainment, be it strolling down Broadway or sipping your favourite beverage in historic surroundings. You may spend time in four splendid little museums filled with fascinating objects from a rich past. Or consider the **Days of 98 Show** with the town "Bad man of the past", Soapy Smith, in a daily shoot-out with the town's hero Frank Reid. You could listen to **"Buckwheat"** recite **Robert Service ballads**, including 'The Cremation of Sam McGee'. How about a rousing 26 km (16 mile) summit to sea downhill bike trip organized by Sockeye Cycle? They drive you up

- you cycle down! You could hike miles of nature trails (no better way to get in shape for the Chilkoot trail) including a strenuous four hour, 5 mile (8 km) hike up to AB Mountain (5000 feet/1524 m) with mind boggling views over Skagway and Taija Inlet.

Air and water taxi services out of Skagway:

Three Air Taxi operations run scheduled flights to Haines, Gustavus, Juneau and other regional communities. Skagway Air Service alone runs six flights a day (fewer in winter) from Skagway to Juneau, $120 round trip. Views of the coastline are spectacular. There is a water taxi service between Skagway and Haines, with two departures a day during the summer. Leave Skagway at 9:45 and 18:00; leave Haines at 08:30 and 15:00. One-way $18, round trip $29 and a bicycle $5. Space is restricted! For more information call 907- 766-3395 in Haines. It's a great day trip renting a bike in Skagway (or Haines) to visit the other town by water taxi. The M/V Sea Venture II can accept up to 80 passengers for this 15 mile one way trip.

One further passenger ship might ply the waters between Skagway and Haines. The M/V Fairweather, a 250 passenger ship purchased from the Holland America Line is said to run passenger only services between these two ports, but no schedule or prices were finalized by the beginning of 1997. For info call 1-907-983-2257.

Of course, fishing charters are possible, as is going on a guided gold-panning hike - check with the Skagway Convention and Visitor Bureau.

Restaurants in Skagway:

There are 24 eating establishments in town - some are good, some are better and some can be forgotten. And all are easy enough to find. Only five of those are open year-round. For better eating, go to any of the restaurants attached to a hotel. For a good cup of coffee and a perfectly brewed espresso, direct your steps to **Mabel G. Smith Cafe**, a gift shop / mothers living room and cafe all in one, and there's no smoking. It is on 5th Ave. just off Broadway and open year-round.

How To Leave Skagway: In short: either leave with your own car, by renting one, by bus and train, or on your own two feet - over the Chilkoot trail.

Car Rental: There are three car rental companies in town.

Avis Rent A Car on 3rd and Spring. Toll-free 1-800-331-1212 or 907-983-2247.

Sourdough Car And Van Rental. 1-800-478-2529 or 907-983-2523, Fax 907-983-2553.

ABC Motorhomes (also rent Mopeds). Toll-free 1-800-421-7456 or 907-983-3222.

By Bus:

Alaskon Express departs Skagway daily in summer at 07:30. Arrive and depart Logcabin, B.C., at 09:30. Arrive and depart Carcross, Yukon at 10:30. Arrive in Whitehorse at 11:30. One-way US$54 from May to September. The bus leaves from the Westmark Inn Hotel on 3rd and Spring. Call for information, tel. 907-983-2241.

Alaska Direct. Departs from the ferry terminal at 15:30 and arrives in Whitehorse at 17:30. Summer only. US$35 one-way. Call for more information, tel. 1-800-770-6652, in Anchorage 907-277-6652. In Whitehorse 403-668-4833. Their winter bus from Whitehorse-Skagway-Whitehorse leaves every Monday, and the time depends on the ferry's arrival. Check with the company for more details.

Combination Train & Bus: Depart Skagway by train at 12:40 Alaska time. Depart Fraser (border) by bus at 14:40 Alaska Time. Arrive at Whitehorse by bus at 18:00 Yukon Time. Depart Whitehorse by bus at 08:00 Yukon Time. Arrive at Fraser by bus at 10:20 Alaska Time. Arrive at Skagway by train at 12 noon Alaska Time. One-way US$95, children half price.

White Pass Summit Round Trip to the international border: leave at 08:30 and arrive back in Skagway at 11:35. Leave at 13:00 and arrive back in Skagway at 16:05. This 65 km (40 mile) round trip goes from sea level to 850 m (2800 feet). Round trip US$75, children US$37.50, Infants are free.

All times are local - Alaska time is one hour earlier than Yukon time.

ROUTES FROM SKAGWAY

Lake Bennett Train

Latest news for 1997 - A steam train will connect Skagway with Lake Bennett, at the end of the Chilkoot Trail in Canada. You need to rush out to reserve your seat because only seven trips are scheduled for the 1997 season. Those departure days are all on Saturday's; June 14 & 28, July 12 & 26, August 9 & 23 as well as September 1 - a Monday. Departure time is 8:10 arriving in Lake Bennett at 11:15 and leaving again at 1:15. Chilkoot Trail hikers can be accommodated if space is available. Round trip fare is US $150, and $75 for a child. Lunch is included. There might be more departures for 1998 - or none! Rates for hikers from Lake Bennett are as follows - US $75 back to Skagway, reservation is required and US $49 back to Fraser - first come, first serve. The steam train offers about 150 seats.

> All trains are wheelchair accessible. Independent travellers (not cruise ship passengers) should reserve tickets at least thirty days in advance or have time to wait for available stand-by tickets. Bicycles can be taken to the border by train - for US $25 and a dog will cost you US $20.
>
> For more information call, write or fax to White Pass and Yukon Route, P.O. Box 435 Dept. B, Skagway, Alaska 99840. Tel. from the U.S. Toll-free 1-800-343-7373. From northwestern Canada Toll-free 1-800-478-7373, locally 1-907-983-2217, Fax 1-907-983-2734.

The railbed was dynamited out of almost impossibly steep terrain. The WP&YR connected Skagway with Whitehorse for passengers and freight, from 1900 to 1982. Construction of the narrow gauge (3 feet / 914 mm) railway began in 1898 at the height of the Gold Rush. It was completed in 1900 by over 3500 workers. The 110 mile (176 km) long engineering marvel opened again in 1988, but only for summer round-trips as far as Lake Bennett. The original steam engine is used for these excursions - with the help of a modern diesel on steeper stretches. On September 10, 1994, the railroad was declared an "International Historic Civil Engineering Landmark", putting it at par with 19 other engineering landmarks world-wide, including the Panama Canal and the Eiffel Tower. Many people dream the train will one day again connect the coast with Whitehorse.

> **A Train Guide:**
>
> If possible, sit facing the direction of train travel: on the left side going up hill, and on the right side going down hill.

Mile 0 The old steam engine No. 73 might be used to pull the train to the end of town, from where a more modern and stronger diesel engine will take over for the steep haul to the summit.

Mile 0.3 The new White Pass Depot. The old one next door is used by the National Park Service.**Mile 2 The White Pass Shops**. All repairs to engines and rolling stock are done here.

Mile 2.5 The Gold Rush Cemetery. Outlaw Soapy Smith and local hero Frank Reid are buried here.

Mile 5.8 (5A) Located here is a bridge and the head of the **Denver Glacier Trail**. The railway crosses East Fork of the Skagway River.

Mile 6.9 Rocky Point offers a great view back down the valley toward Skagway. Watch for Mt. Harding and the Harding Glacier. A wagon road built in 1898 crosses the railroad at mile 7.

Mile 8.6 At Clifton railway work gangs lived here for many years. The Klondike Highway skirts the canyon above.

Mile 9 (9A) Bridge and Pitchfork Falls.

Mile 10.4 Black Cross Rock. Two railroad workers were killed here during blasting on August 3, 1898. A total of 35 workers died during construction.

Mile 11.5 Bridal Veil Falls. Several cataracts tumbling off Mt. Cleveland Glacier can be seen across the valley. Below are the remains of a Gold Rush tent town called White City.

Mile 14.1 Glacier Station. Tickets can be purchased to this point by those who want to hike up to the Laughton Glacier. There is a Forest Service Cabin there but space must be reserved in advance.

Mile 16 Listen for the train whistle alerting passengers to one of the **highest points of the trip.**

Mile 17 On a clear day there is a **beautiful view back over Skagway**.

Mile 18.6 Steel bridge. In 1901, it was the tallest steel cantilever bridge in the world.

Mile 18.8 The bridge and tunnel were built in 1969. Past the tunnel, be ready for the view down to **Dead Horse Gulch**. During the Gold Rush, about 3000 packhorses were worked to death on this trail. Their bleached bones still can be seen.

Mile 20.4 The White Pass Summit and US/Canada Border is at an elevation of 2865 ft or 873 m. The Summit Excursion will turn back from here, but the train to Fraser continues. It would be 90 more miles (145 km) by train to Whitehorse.

Mile 28 Fraser. Canadian Customs and, for those going on to Whitehorse, time to change to the bus. If you have a ticket to Lake Bennett stay on the train - if there is a service!

Mile 32 Log Cabin was a tent city in 1898. The tracks cross the Klondike Highway. The Mounted Police used to have a customs station here. This is the highest point along the railroad, at 2916 feet/889 m.

Mile 36.5 Watch for beaver ponds next to tracks as well as the occasional moose, black bear or lone hiker. Watch them interact!

Mile 39 Lake Lindeman, is where, during the Gold Rush, 10,000 Klondike-bound gold-seekers camped over the winter of 1897-98, building boats and waiting for spring.

Mile 40.6 Lake Bennett. That winter over 30,000 stampeders camped here waiting for the ice to break. The ice finally did break on May 26, 1898, and 7000 boats of all shapes, sizes and quality rushed off toward Dawson City. The construction of the railway gave Lake Bennett a new lease on life until the highway was built. Only the church and the train station still stand. This is the end of the line - for now!

KLONDIKE HIGHWAY NO. 2 TO WHITEHORSE

A short description of the Klondike Highway for those travelling with their own car, by bus or bicycle follows. Construction of the highway started in the 1950s but didn't open for traffic until 1978. Before 1986, the road was not open from October to May, and Skagway was a very sad town indeed. There always seems to be a danger that government funds will run dry for the winter upkeep of the highway. If lack of money does not close the road, the winter snow sometimes does for a day or two.

Driving distances from Skagway are: Whitehorse 110 miles (177 km), Atlin 150 miles (241 km), Dawson City 435 miles (700 km), Haines 360 miles (580 km), Fairbanks 710 miles (1143 km), Anchorage 830 miles (1336 km).

Mile 0 / km 0 Ferry terminal. Take historic Broadway straight out of town. Don't forget to gas up - the next service station is at Carcross 65 miles (104 km) away.

Mile 1.4 / km 2.3 Skagway river bridge. White Pass & Yukon Rail are to your right. Turn off for the Gold Rush cemetery just before the bridge.

Mile 2.1 / km 3.4 Turn off to Dyea and the Chilkoot Trail Head. It is 8 miles or 12.9 km over a very narrow and twisty gravel road, which is not meant for large RVs or motorhomes. For a time, the town of Dyea rivaled Skagway, with a population of over 10,000, but the railroad drained all life out of Dyea. See the Chilkoot Trail section later in this chapter.

Mile 2.5 / km 4 Liarsville is a campground and picnic area next to Skagway River. During the Gold Rush years reporters and journalists from all over the world camped at this spot to gather stories from returning miners or would-be miners. Hence Liarsville.

Mile 5.2 / km 8.4 The turnout with an historic display includes a view of the railroad and the old Bracket Wagon Road. Bracket, a past mayor of Minneapolis, built this former toll road between Skagway and the White Pass, before selling out to the railroad.

Mile 7 / km 11.3 US Customs. This new border station was built in 1994. It is open 24 hours a day year-round. Just past customs are the Pitchfork Falls, tumbling down from Goat Lake in the mountains above. US Customs telephone 907-983-2325.

Mile 8.8 / km 14.2 A view of the railroad and the Gold Rush tent city of White Pass below.

Mile 10 / km 16.1 A view of Bridal Veil Falls flowing off Mt. Cleveland.

Mile 10.8 / km 17.4 Capt. Moore Bridge is named after the founder of Skagway. When built in 1977, this bridge was the only one of its kind in North America. It was rebuilt in 1992-93.

Mile 11.3 / km 18.2 Large turnout with beautiful view of Capt. Moore Bridge, Mt. Cleveland Glacier and the Sawtooth Range.

Mile 14 / km 22.5 Summit at 3290 feet/1003 m. Congratulation cyclists - you've done it!

The international border and waterfalls are half a mile (800 m) further. **You are changing from Alaska time to Yukon time.** The next 35 miles / 56 km are in British Columbia.

km 26 / mile 16.3 Plenty of turn-outs allow great views over **pothole lakes**. Some might even be warm enough for a swim.

km 35.6 / mile 22.1 Fraser and Canada Customs. Open 24 hours a day in summer. Call 1-403-821-4111. For winter hours call 1-403-667-3943 / 3944. The turn-out just past customs allows for great views over Fraser Lake.

REMEMBER: The Yukon Area Code 403 will change to 867 after October 1997. Correct dialing sequence for long distance calls within the Yukon are: 1-403 (867)-000-0000.

km 42.6 / mile 26.5 Turn-out and view over **Teepee Valley**, from where the Fantail Trail led to the 1899 Gold Rush town of Atlin. Almost every railroad worker "fled" his job, many taking railway tools with them. Most returned soon after, when they found that most claims had been staked.

km 44.3 / mile 27.5 Log cabin. The road crosses the railroad. Those who want to hike the Chilkoot Trail in reverse can start from here. It is 13 km/8 miles to Lake Bennett following the railroad tracks. Signs proclaim "no trespassing", but ... an official park trail is under construction.

km 48-55 / mile 30-35 The Tutshi (Too-shy) River follows the road until the river empties into Tutshi Lake. It is a beautiful stretch of highway.

km 72.4 / mile 45 The highway rises to a high point between **Tutshi and Tagish Lakes**. The ore crushing mill at the lakeshore was built in 1980 but has never operated.

The old train station at Carcross is now a visitor centre.

km 78 / mile 48.5 The very long and windy body of water to the east is part of Tagish Lake. It stretches for 80 km/50 miles around the mountains to the east. There is good fishing for lake trout.

km 81.1 / mile 49.8 The BC and Yukon Border.

km 83.8 / mile 52   The Venus Mine. The ore crushing mill operated for only six months in 1910. Hardrock gold was mined between 1900 and 1910 out of mountain shafts still visible above the road. Evidence of more recent but also unsuccessful gold mining can be seen for the next two miles (3 km).

km 90.1 / mile 56 Just before the highway swings uphill, the dirt road to the right leads to the remains of an old town-site called **Conrad City**, along "Big Thing Creek". About 300 people lived here and worked for the mining sites nearby.

km 94.5 / mile 58.7 The island visible at the north-end of **Windy Arm** is called **Bove Island**. It was named by Lt. Sckatka after a fellow lieutenant.

km 106 / mile 65.9 Village of Carcross.

CARCROSS

After crossing the bridge that spans the narrows between Lake Nares and Lake Bennett the road to the left leads to the village. Carcross was formerly known as Caribou Crossing because caribou used to ford the narrows. It was a thriving town during the Gold Rush, and on July 29, 1900, the golden spike was hammered into the ground here. The population now stands at around 400. The **Carcross Visitor Centre** is located in the old train depot and is open daily in summer from mid-May to mid-September. Telephone 1-403-821-4431. Fax 1-403-821-3006. The Visitor Radio CKYM - Yukon Gold 96.1 on the FM dial is broadcast from the centre. **Skookum Jim Dancers** perform native Tlingit dances near the Centre at various times during the day. The old **sternwheeler** 'Tutshi' was destroyed by fire in July 1990 and the burned out remains serve as a reminder to be careful with the burning end of a cigarette. The 'Tutshi' used to serve communities between Carcross and Ben-my-Chree on the far eastern end of Takish Lake. **Duchess,** the tiny locomotive next to the train depot, used to carry passengers and freight via a narrow land bridge between Takish and Atlin Lakes.

Where to stay in Carcross:

The Caribou Hotel and restaurant opposite the train depot is the oldest business in the Yukon. Tel 1-403-821-4501. The rooms are rustic with no TV, no phone, with showers on the floor, and cost $35 a room.

Montana Services. Service station and RV park. Tel. 1-403-821-3708.

Yukon Government Campground includes 12 RV's and campsites. First come, first served and $8 per site. All YTG Campgrounds in the Yukon provide firewood, water (needs to be treated or boiled in most cases), individual sites with a firepit, and at least one shelter.

Don't miss the historic **Royal Canadian Mounted Police Barracks**, with their jail cells and life-sized characters of the Gold Rush. The **Matthew Watson General Store** next to the hotel is the oldest store still in operation in the Yukon. It is more a museum than a store, but it sells everything from ice-cream to aspirin.

Transportation to or out of Carcross::

Atlin Express Busline connects Whitehorse with Atlin, year-round. It passes through Carcross at 08:15 for Whitehorse and 13:30 for Atlin, every Monday, Wednesday and Friday. Call 668-4545 in Whitehorse for more information.

Alaskon Express Busline passes through Carcross at about 10:30 for Whitehorse and 17:30 for Skagway. They run only during summer.

Alaska Direct Busline leaves about 17:00 for Whitehorse and 08:45 for Skagway, with reduced services in winter.

Flag stops only, which means buses have to be flagged down on the highway. They stop if space is available. Check the Visitor Centre for updates.

km 106.4 / mile 66.1 The Tagish Road (Highway #8) turn-off leads to the village of **Tagish** (31 km / 19.3 miles). It is 55 km / 33 miles to the **Alaska Highway** and 149 km / 89 miles to **Atlin, BC.**

km 107.6 / mile 66.9 Carcross Desert. The Yukon is known for many things, but not for a desert. But there it is - the world's smallest desert at 260 ha. (642 acres). This area was once covered by a large glacial lake. The sandy lake bottom was left behind as the glacier retreated. Some people question if this area should be turned into a protected park, or if it should remain a playground for four-wheelers and sand buggies. Mt. Caribou looms behind the sand dunes to the east.

km 109.5 / miles 68 Frontier Heritage Park includes RV parking and a Theme and Wildlife Park. Call 667-1055.

km 115.5 / mile 71.5 The Cinnamon Cache Cafe and Bakery is open daily during the summer only. Tel. 821-4331.

km 117 / mile 73 Emerald Lake. Stop at the large turn-out to view one of the prettiest lakes in the Yukon.

km 139.5 /mile 86.5 Turn-off to Robinson and Annie Lakes. The road leads to the abandoned gold mining town of Robinson, and continues to the 18 hole Annie Lake Golf Course. It is open from May to September. No bookings are required, and green fees are $2. A further 16 km / 10 miles brings you to Annie Lake and the Wheaton River. Canoe trips back to Lake Bennett are possible by way of the Wheaton River.

km 152.3 / mile 94.6 Territorial Kookatsoon Lake Recreation Site offers six picnic sites and nice swimming, but no overnighters.

km 157 / mile 97.5 The Yukon Rock Shop is a great place to get to know your minerals and learn about mining. It is open daily, year-round. Telephone 668-2772.

km 157.7 / mile 98 Junction with Alaska Highway. There is a service station with a cafe. Whitehorse is 19.5 km / 12 miles away and offers all services. Before heading to the capital of the Yukon, let us return to Skagway for one last look. So far we have left Skagway by train and by road - now let's hike the Chilkoot Trail, as done by tens of thousands during the Gold Rush.

Bennett City with church at the of the Chilkoot trail.

CHILKOOT TRAIL

The Chilkoot Trail has not just been used during the Gold Rush years. For thousands of years there has been a trail across the mountain pass protected and used by the coastal Chilkoot native tribe of the Tlingit Nation. Dyea was a small permanent Tlingit village protecting access to the trail as an important trading route for fish oil, shells and dried fish. Annual trading trips for animal hides, skins and copper were made to their Southern Tutchone neighbours, whose traditional home is near present day Whitehorse, Haines Junction, Burwash Landing and Champagne. The Tagish Tribe of the Tutchone Nation used the land around the Lindeman and Bennett Lakes as their traditional hunting and berry picking ground. Some of the great names in Yukon history were natives of the Tagish Tribe: Skookum Jim, Kate Carmack and Dawson Charlie, to name a few.

Early Russian explorers had apparently heard of the trail but did not use it. Only in the late 1870s did a miner named George Holt sneak through the pass unnoticed. By 1883, explorer Frederick Schwatka used the trail with the aid of native packers. The first two Canadian officers of the North West Mounted Police (after 1904, the RCMP or Royal Canadian Mounted Police - the "Mounties") crossed the pass in July, 1894, with the aid of Tlingit packers and a guide. They made it to Lake Lindeman in three days. The natives were paid $125 each. Superintendent Charles Constantine and Sergeant Charles Brown had orders to "establish Canadian sovereignty and determine law enforcement requirements in view of the approaching gold rush". They constructed a boat and surveyed the Yukon River that summer. They established themselves at the bustling gold mining town of Fortymile, downstream from present day Dawson City, enforcing Canadian law and collecting taxes on goods imported into Canada. Fortymile was only one of many busy mining towns near where the Klondike River meets the Yukon - where the big strike was made in August, 1896. The first gold in the Fortymile District was found in 1886, and from then to 1896 over one thousand gold-seekers had crossed the trail. With the avalanche of would-be miners swamping Skagway and Dyea in the years 1897 and 1898, the Tlingit had to make way, exchanging their role as guardians of the pass to being paid packers and guides for the stampeders.

The Chilkoot Trail is one of only three trails across the coastal mountains into the interior between Juneau to the south and Yakutat to the west. The others are the White Pass at Skagway and the Chilkat Pass at Haines. The Chilkoot Pass still has what none of the other two offered - a string of lakes at the end of the trail, with a watery access to the Yukon River, making a direct float to the Klondike Gold Fields possible.

All late summer of 1897, thousands of fortune hunters crowded into Dyea and Skagway, creating instant tent cities. A few still managed to cross the trail that summer, building their boats to reach Dawson City before the river froze for the season, or getting caught between Lake Lindeman and the Klondike by ice and snow. One of them was a young, would-be writer and adventurer, who later gained fame and fortune with stories told about the North. His name was Jack London. The majority of gold-seekers though, had to settle for a winter crossing of the Chilkoot Trail. It is the grainy black and white photographs of those thousands, creating human chains of darkly dressed men and women on the white background of snow, working their way up the steep and treacherous slope, which captures the imagination of anyone who has hiked or dreamt of hiking the Chilkoot Trail.

Of course, few hike the trail during the winter months, but over 3500 modern adventurers "do" the Chilkoot each summer between June and September. In October and May / June winter conditions may exist and special precautions have to be taken. Those who hike the Chilkoot Trail in winter must have extensive experience in Arctic outdoor winter travelling. Temperatures might fall to -45°C/-50°F and white-outs and snow-driven winds up to 80 km/50 miles an hour can occur at any time. Designated summer campgrounds may be unsafe due to avalanche danger. Those who wish to visit in winter should contact Canadian or American park officials for an off-season permit. Don't forget that the Chilkoot is a wilderness hike requiring strength, stamina and the proper gear. It is not the type of wilderness hike where you will be all on your own. July and August are the busiest months, and it can get quite crowded during the high season.

Chilkoot Trail hiking updates:

The National Park Services have implemented some changes, starting with the 1997 hiking season. One change would be to impose a hiking fee of CDN $35 and to restrict the numbers of hikers to 50 per day. This hiking fee will only be charged by Parks Canada for the Canadian portion of the trail. The US side of the trail will still be 'free' but that might change for the 1998 season. The way this will work is as follows - those wanting to hike the trail can call ahead to reserve a hiking permit. The non-refundable reservation fee is $10 per person. The permit fee is $35 per adult, $17.50 per child (6-15 years), 5 and under are free. A Parks Canada official will work out of the Skagway Park Service Visitor Centre where above-mentioned permits also can be purchased. First come, first served will apply then. For the 1997 hiking season, those permits will be checked at the border on the very top of the Chilkoot Trail. Those who leave Dyea without a permit will be turned back at the border. For the 1998 season, permits might be checked directly at the trail head in Dyea. For the latest regulations, maps, permits and information, all hikers should visit **Skagway Park Service Visitor Center on 2nd and Broadway.** It is open daily from 8 a.m. to 6 p.m., May and September, and 8 a.m. to 8 p.m. in June, July and August. The upstairs offices are open year-round. Watch the documentary, "Days of Adventure - Dreams of Gold", which is shown on the hour daily except 11 a.m. and 3 p.m., when a ranger talks about the Chilkoot Trail. Write or

CHILKOOT TRAIL

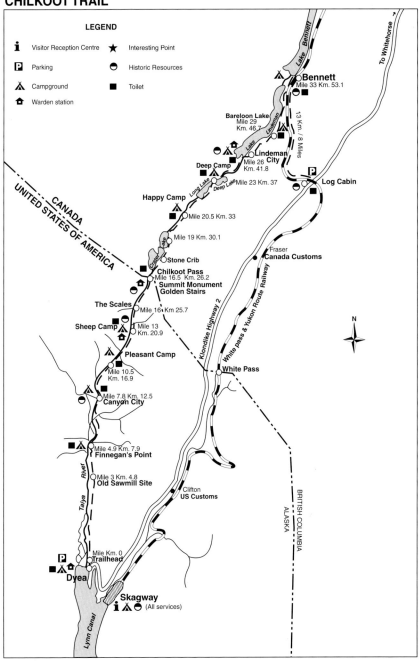

LEGEND

- **i** Visitor Reception Centre
- **P** Parking
- **⋏** Campground
- **⌂** Warden station
- **★** Interesting Point
- **⊖** Historic Resources
- **■** Toilet

Bennett
Mile 33 Km. 53.1

13 Km. / 8 Miles

Bareloon Lake
Mile 29
Km. 46.7

Lindeman City
Mile 26
Km. 41.8

Deep Camp

Mile 23 Km. 37

Log Cabin

Happy Camp
Mile 20.5 Km. 33

Mile 19 Km. 30.1

Stone Crib

Fraser
Canada Customs

Chilkoot Pass
Mile 16.5 Km. 26.2
**Summit Monument
Golden Stairs**

The Scales
Mile 16 Km. 25.7

Sheep Camp
Mile 13
Km. 20.9

Pleasant Camp

Mile 10.5
Km. 16.9

White Pass

Mile 7.8 Km. 12.5
Canyon City

Mile 4.9 Km. 7.9
Finnegan's Point

Mile 3 Km. 4.8
Old Sawmill Site

Clifton
US Customs

Mile Km. 0
Trailhead

Dyea

Skagway
i ⋏ ⊖ (All services)

Lake Bennett

To Whitehorse

Lindeman Lake

Long Lake

Deep Lake

Crater Lake

Klondike Highway 2

White pass & Yukon Route Railway

UNITED STATES OF AMERICA

CANADA

Taiya River

Lynn Canal

BRITISH COLUMBIA

ALASKA

N

phone to the Superintendent, Klondike Gold Rush National Historical Park, P.O. Box 517, Skagway, Alaska, 99840. Telephone 907-983-2921. **In Canada** write to Chilkoot Trail Yukon National Historic Sites, Canadian Heritage - Parks Canada, 205-300 Main Street, Whitehorse, Yukon, Y1A 2B5.

The numbers to call for more information and to make reservation are as follows: Tel. 1-403-667-3910. Fax 1-403 393-6701. From Canada and the mainland US call toll-free 1-800-661-0486. From Alaska call toll-free 1-800-987-6442. Reservations can be paid with Visa / Mastercard and always for the season from Feb. 1st the same year.

A few more thoughts about the trail: Hiking north to south is just as historical as going south to north. Trekking south, you can get to Lake Bennett either by walking along the railroad tracks, by taking the train if it is running, or by chartered boat from Carcross. In any case, inform US Customs in Skagway by calling 983-2325, or call the border at 983-3144. Taking the more common northern route, hikers must check in with Canada Customs (before the hike) by calling the border at 821-4111 or in Whitehorse at 667-6471.

No weapons of any type are permitted on the trail.

<u>ALL</u> artifacts along the trail are protected by law and may neither be disturbed, moved nor removed. The path is littered with everything from rusty pots and pans to old rotten shoes, from turn-of-the-century machinery to piles of broken bottles. The only things you may pick up along the trail are cigarette butts, candy wrappers and similar modern trash left behind by those ahead of you. <u>PLEASE DO</u>!

The Chilkoot Trail is as much a living museum as a wilderness hike. The maximum size for groups is 12 hikers, and all groups have to check in with rangers before departure. No open fires are allowed on the trail except in Dyea. Please, no camping outside designated camping areas. Take out your own garbage, including your cigarette butts, and use the outhouses provided. Purify all water found in the park by either boiling it, or by using iodine or bleach.

One last thing! Early in the hiking season (up to mid-July), a very real avalanche danger exists between Sheep Camp and Crater Lake. If possible, hike only in the mornings, and follow the advice of park officials.

How to get to Dyea: Pioneer Taxi runs a shuttle between Skagway and the trailhead and will pick up hikers from hotels, campgrounds and the ferry terminal. Price depends on the number of passengers. To hike to Dyea, take the foot bridge across the Skagway River at the western end of 1st Ave. and from there it is 13 km / 8 miles to the trail head. It is quite a pleasant hike too! Do get a **Skagway Trail Map** from the Visitor Center. There is plenty of parking near the trailhead.

Dyea: Dyea is a Tlingit word that could mean anything from: "to pack up", "place to look down to", to maybe, "Crazy White men with nothing better to do than hunt for gold". The Park Service Ranger Station is next to the campground. Register there if you have not already done so in Skagway - this now only applies for the American section of the Chilkoot Trail. Read the previous section of this book concerning the Canadian part of the trail.

Dyea Campground: There are 22 sites with picnic tables, fire rings and outhouses. There is no charge and a two week limit.

The old town site of Dyea is 2.5 km / 1.5 miles from the steel bridge across the Taija River. There is not much there except a lot of rotten lumber and old piling stumps. There used to be over 150 businesses here - even a few breweries. Visit the slide cemetery, where an estimated 60 people died on April 3, 1898, when an avalanche near

Sheep Camp buried them alive. As recently as July 2, 1987, a 200 m (650 foot) wide avalanche buried the trail near Crater Lake to a depth of 10 m (33 feet) - fortunately nobody was on the trail. There are a couple of interesting two to four hour hikes nearby that should warm up leg muscles for the big hike. One is the **Lost Lake Hike**, the other is the **West Creek Hike**. Both have tenting spots at the end; check with the rangers.

The Chilkoot Trail: Everything has been said and written - you are now on the trail. You should have all that is needed for at least a five day hike even though it may be possible to hike it in three days if nothing goes wrong. Take your time. You are walking through a museum that is 53 km / 33 miles long. Every bend has a surprise, and every mile something new. Observe and learn; if you must touch, do not take or remove the artifacts along the trail. The next few miles you will be hiking from 0 to 1122 m (3680 feet), and you will be traversing dripping wet rainforest with dramatic changes in terrain, climate and vegetation. Almost every alder, cottonwood, aspen, hemlock or spruce along the densely wooded trail is second growth - during the Gold Rush this valley was denuded of almost everything that spelled wood. Reaching the 3000 foot level (914 m) near the summit, you enter almost treeless alpine tundra with mosses, lichens, dwarfish shrubs and low growing willows. As you descend from the pass into Canada, you enter sub-alpine boreal forest with dense growth of alpine fir, lodgepole pine, willows and alder. The animal world is just as varied; from toads to salmon; fishing eagles and river otters on the lower slopes; and mountain goats, wolves and moose at higher elevations. Black bear may be seen at all elevations, and so may mosquitoes. Study the section about bears in the introduction chapter.

km 7.9 / mile 4.9 Finnegan's Point is the first official campsite with outhouses. Here a fellow called Finnegan and his two sons built a toll bridge across the river, charging $2 per person to cross. Once the masses started arriving, everybody simply ignored them.

km 12.5 / mile 7.8 Canyon City is the next official campsite with outhouses and a small stuffy cabin with a few bunk beds. The original site of Canyon City is across the river via a suspension bridge. By May, 1898, Canyon City was a busy and prosperous town of almost 2000 permanent residents. Collapsed cabins, rusty machinery, and abandoned pots and pans litter the ground.

km 16.9 / mile 10.5 Pleasant Camp has always has been pleasant. There was a restaurant here and a toll bridge to the west bank of the river. In 1897, both banks of the river were covered with tents from here to Sheep camp 5 km / 3 miles away.

km 20.9 / mile 13 Sheep Camp is the last campsite before your legs have to do some serious work - over the Scales, up the Golden Stairs and across the Chilkoot Pass. Sheep Camp, as the name suggests, used to be a base camp for mountain sheep hunters, but during the Gold Rush it quickly grew into a "City of Tents". There were 16 hotels, 14 restaurants, 5 doctors, 3 saloons, 2 dance halls, a post office, and a bath house. By May, 1898, most stampeders had moved on and Sheep Camp turned back into what it always had been - a sheep camp. There is a Park Ranger Station here, and permits might be inspected at this campsite. Shelter and outhouses are at this site. Watch for the remains of telegraph poles and the tramway that was built to ease the burden of stampeders who otherwise needed to make dozens of bone-breaking trips to transport their ton of goods into Canadian territory. The North West Mounted Police stipulated that no one would be allowed into the Yukon without bringing in one year's provisions - a ton of food and clothing. Leaving Sheep Camp the trail climbs steadily to the mountain pass. Five kilometres (three miles) later the hiker will reach the "**Scales**".

During the Gold Rush, the Scales were known as one of the most wretched spots on the trail. This was where loads of cargo and luggage were stored, re-packed and re-weighed for the final climb to the summit. Here, many facing the steep climb ahead gave up either by selling their equipment at a loss or by discarding it, to return to the coast and home. Looking up to the Scales, the Summit can be seen slightly to the left. The opening to the right is the Peterson Trail; which is not recommended because of unstable rocks. In summer it's a hands and feet type of climb that, should it be raining, foggy-wet or blowing snow (even in July), will give today's hiker a quite realistic perspective of yesterday's hardships. Yesterday's "hiker" had one ton of supplies to carry up the pass, with each climb taking up to six hours to the summit and back - and doing the same trip about 30 times! Those with money to spare could hire packers whose rates were the highest over this final section. Alternatively one could trust one's belongings to one of three transportation companies which ran tramways powered by either horses, steam or gasoline. The charge was about seven cents per pound from Dyea to Lake Lindeman.

During the winter of 1897-98 the Scales was home to two hotels, plenty of restaurants, coffee houses and a saloon. Two entrepreneurs carved steps into the snow and charged a fee for using the "Golden Stairs". It is only half a mile (800 m) from the Scales to the Summit, but scrambling over huge boulders and across rock ledges, the 45 degree climb is no breakfast. After having unloaded, the Stampeders came down the Peterson Trail on their rear-ends - in winter, of course!

km 26.2 / mile 16.5 The Summit is only a narrow gap in the stone face of the mountain, but for those thousands who have passed through, it must have been heaven. There is a monument dedicated to all those who came, and to all those who died trying - it also marks the international boundary between Canada and the USA. Canadian permits will be checked here. **Those who leave Dyea without a Canadian permit might face three possible choices at the border, at the top of the trail.**

(A). They may be turned back, but that will also depend on the weather.

(B). One may continue but will be invoiced the fee.

(C). The permit-less hiker will be fined.

Make sure your passport ID is in order.

It was here where countless piles of goods were jealously guarded by scores of exhausted men and women. Try to imagine the shouting and arguing, perhaps overpowered by the squealing of tramlines and the howling of an icy wind. It must have been incredible, but it also must have been a happy crowd because it was downhill from now on; the worst was over.

Having crossed the rain barrier of the coastal range, the SUN might even be shining! Crater Lake, the first of a string of lakes, is only half a mile (800 m) from the Summit. The lake can carry ice into August, and snow fields persist throughout the summer. In winter wooden sleds were used to skid across the lakes to at least Lake Lindeman, and in summer horses or mules could be utilized to transfer cargo to Lake Bennett. Today, the next few miles are a hiker's dream.

km 33 / mile 20.5 Happy Camp is the first campsite after Sheep Camp and the name Happy Camp seems appropriate. The site offers outhouses.

km 37 / 23 miles Deep Lake Campsite includes outhouses. This is a beautiful stretch, as the trail zigzags past tiny ponds and stunted alpine fir passing high above Long Lake. At the north-end of Long Lake the trail works itself down to Deep Lake, which has beautifully located tent spots on its shoreline. From Deep Lake, it is downhill all the way to Lindeman City on Lake Lindeman.

km 41.8 / mile 26 Lake Lindeman Campsite includes outhouses, cabin shelters, a tent museum, and a Canada Park Warden's cabin. Lindeman City is a pleasant place to stay for a couple of days. Relics from the past litter the area and there are a few nice hikes into the country beyond. During the Gold Rush, over 4000 people lived here, denuding every site of trees to make boats, rafts, or cabins, or for firewood. By autumn, 1899, Lindeman was deserted. Lake Lindeman is roughly 10 km or 6 miles long, and is connected with Lake Bennett via a narrow fast-running creek. This creek caused much grief to many stampeders who dared to run it with their fully loaded boats or rafts. Between lakes Lindeman and Bennett is one more campsite.

km 46.7 / mile 29 Bare Loon Lake Campsite includes outhouses and plenty of bugs. There is a trail short-cut to the highway. The trail to Bennett passes numerous abandoned cabins, rusty wood stoves, and piles of tin cans. Do not add your modern can, it will get you a ticket for littering! The proud steeple of the St. Andrew's Presbyterian Church is your first sign of Bennett City; the only Gold Rush structure still standing, it was built by volunteer labour in 1898. In the winter of 1897-98, over 20,000 people collected here, waiting impatiently for the ice to break. It must have been one of the great sights of all time as the lake ice broke on May 29, 1898. Within a few days over 7000 boats of all shapes and condition left for the Klondike. The town of Bennett survived for only a few more years.

km 53.1 / mile 33 Lake Bennett Campsite and the end of the trail - almost.

The modern hiker has various ways and means to continue from here.

(A) If you brought an inflatable or similar craft with you across the trail, then off you go toward Dawson City. There are two dams between here and Whitehorse but they are easy to manage.

(B) You can arrange pick-up by boat or float plane from Carcross. Check with Skookum Jim Trade out of Carcross, telephone 821-3131 or fax 821-3505. Chilkoot Water Charters makes daily boat trips from Bennett to Carcross, and costs $50 per adult, and a return trip costs $75. Children are half price. The first trip leaves from Bennett at 10 a.m., for up to 5 trips during the day. Departure times will be posted at the docks in Carcross and Bennett from June to mid. Sept. only. To transport a canoe to Bennett costs $20. Leave a message at 821-3209.

(C) Continue your hike to Carcross by following the railroad tracks along Bennett Lake. It's about 50 km or 30 miles, and it should take two days. Enjoy the fishing and spectacular views!

(D) Take the steam train leaving the old train depot at Bennett at 1:15 on only seven days during the 97 season (see Skagway). There might be more services in 1998 and beyond.

(E) Most Chilkoot trail hikers walk out to the Klondike Highway along the railroad tracks to Log Cabin. It is a 13 km or 8 mile hike that will teach you to hop and skip from trestle to trestle. From Log Cabin it is 136 km/85 miles to Whitehorse and 44.3 km/27.5 miles to Skagway.

Alaskon Bus passes Log Cabin for Skagway at about 18:30 and to Whitehorse at about 09:30. **Alaska Direct Bus** will pass at about 10:00 for Skagway (US $21) and for Whitehorse at 17:30. All times are Yukon Time and all trips are daily (summer only), but there are no promises that the buses will have seats available, or that the driver will stop.

CASSIAR HIGHWAY -# 37 GOING NORTH

Known as the "alternative" Alaska Highway, the Cassiar stretches over 725 km / 450 miles from Kitwanga, BC, to join the Alaska Highway just west of Watson Lake, YT. The Cassiar was completed in 1972, but for many years it remained a tortuous road of mud, dust, flying rocks and broken windshields. Since then, it has matured into a spectacular drive with only about 200 km (125 miles) left unpaved. The gap is closing fast as every summer more of the highway is being hard-topped. Distances between communities are great; keep the gas tank topped up - better yet carry extra gas and at least two spare tires. Watch out for wildlife, especially bears and moose, as well as those multi-legged monsters called "speeding logging trucks".

For highway conditions call 1-900-451-4997 (charges apply) or 1-250-771-4511.

Camping in BC's Provincial Parks: Since the summer of 1996, reservations can be made for 41 out of 164 parks by calling 1-800-689-9025 from anywhere in North America. The extra fee is $6 per night, payable by credit card. In northern B.C. only **Liard Hotsprings Provincial Park** can be reserved, and a good idea it is!

There are many interesting sights along the highway until Meziadin Lake Junction at km 160 / mile 99. The service station at the Junction has been out of service for many years, and only the squirrels know when it will open again. Fuel up at the Elsworth **Logging Camp 17 km / 10.5 miles** before the Junction. From the Junction it is 62 km / 38.5 miles to Stewart and the Alaskan town of Hyder, and 576 km / 358 miles to the Alaska Highway. Distances are counted from Meziadin Junction.

km 31 / mile 19 The Bell-Irving Bridge stop includes outhouses and picnic tables.

km 90 / mile 56 Hodder Lake Provincial Rest Area offers a boat launch, fishing, outhouses and picnic tables.

km 93 / mile 58 There is a service station with minor repairs, restaurant, rooms and propane.

km 106 / mile 66 The highway doubles as a plane landing strip.

km 120 / mile 74.5 This rest stop is a good place to see beavers and moose in ponds off the road.

km 121 / mile 75 Ningunsaw Pass is 466 m/1530 feet in height.

km 132.5 / mile 82.3 Here is an info. panel about the **Yukon Telegraph Line** that linked Vancouver with Dawson City during the gold rush.

km 133 / mile 82.6 Echo Lake.

km 139 / mile 86.4 Little Bob Quinn Lake offers good fishing.

km 142 / mile 88 Bob Quinn Highway Maintenance Camp will provide emergency assistance. There is an airstrip nearby and access to the lake.

km 190 / mile 118 Eastman Creek Rest Area is a good place to take pictures with your Agfa camera. Yes, the creek is named after G. Eastman of Kodak fame who used to hunt in this area years ago.

Black bear (above).

Fireweed.

Milepost "0" in Dawson Creek (below).

Wildflowers (left) Moss (above).

Along the southern Klondike Highway.

B.C. Ferry between Port Hardy and Prince Rupert.

Carcross Desert in late summer.

km 199 / mile 123.7   Willow Ridge Resort includes a RV park and camping, a store, showers and coin laundry. Radiophone: JJ3-7280 Bob Quinn Channel.

km 203.7 / mile 126.6   Natadesleen Lake Trailhead is a 1 km hike.

km 211 / mile 131   Kinaskan Campground includes 50 RV and tent sites, a boat launch, hiking trails, swimming, fishing and day use. It is the trailhead for hiking into Mount Edziza Provincial Park.

km 236 / mile 146.6   Tatogga Lake Resort includes a service station, RV park and camping, a store and restaurant. Tel. 1-250-234-3526.

km 238 / mile 147.9   Here is access to Ealue Lake Forest Service Recreation Area. 12 km/7.5 miles off highway.

km 242 / mile 150.4   Eddontenajon Lake rest stop offers good fishing.

km 246 / mile 152.9   Iskutine Lodge. Wilderness Tour Operator. Tel. 1-250-234-3456.

km 248 / mile 154   Red Goat Lodge is a wilderness resort that has it all: RV parking, camping, B&B and a Canadian Hostel with 10 beds, canoe rental, and fishing trips. It is open May to Sept. Tel. and Fax 1-250-234-3261. **Black Sheep Motel** and Cafe. Tel. 1-250-234-3141.

km 251.5 / mile 156.3   The village of Iskut includes a post office, grocery store, service station, motel and restaurant, health clinic (call 234-3511), and public telephone. There is an airstrip with a 914 m/ 3000 foot gravel runway. The elevation is 945 m/3100 feet. For the police, call the same number as under Dease Lake.

km 254.4 / mile 158   Mountain Shadow Guest Ranch offers a RV park, camping and cabins. Tel. 250-234-3333.

km 260 / mile 161.6   Bear Paw Wilderness Resort Alpine Hotel with a restaurant. Guided tours are offered into the Mt. Edziza and Spatsizi area. Radio telephone: 2M3 858 Meehaus Channel.

km 261 / mile 162   Trapper's Souvenirs, and store. Cabins for rent for $38. Radio 2M3 520.

km 264 / mile 164   Forty Mile Flats includes a service station, lodging, restaurant and RV parking. Mobile radio YJ 36205 Iskut Channel.

km 269 / mile 167   This rest stop includes a view towards the dormant volcano **Mt. Edziza.** The elevation is at 2787 m/9143 feet. The Provincial Park, to the southwest, is only accessible on foot or by air.

km 271 / mile 168   Here is the access road to Morchuea Lake Forest Service Campsite.

km 274 / mile 170   Stikini River Recreation Area.

km 283 / mile 176   This rest stop includes outhouses and information panels. Stikini River Bridge.

km 308 / mile 191   Upper Gnat Lake rest stop includes outhouses and picnic tables.

km 315 / mile 196   Gnat Pass Summit.

km 326 / mile 202   Tanzilla River Bridge rest stop offers outhouses and picnic tables.

km 335 / mile 208   Village of Dease Lake and Junction to Telegraph Creek. The village offers a hotel, motel, restaurant and cafe, and a lounge. There is a service station with car and tire repairs. Lodging is available at the **Northway Motor Inn**, call 771-5341; and the **Arctic Divide Inn**, call 771-3119. **RCMP detachment** (call 1-771-4111) and **health nurse** (call 771-4444). The elevation is 792 m / 2600 feet. For more information about the area write to Dease Lake and Tahltan District Chamber of Commerce, Box 338, Dease Lake, BC, V0C 1L0. Tel. 1-250-771-3900.

km 356 / mile 221   Dease Lake (the lake, not the village) is to the west.

km 365 / mile 227   Rabid Grizzly Rest Area includes outhouses, picnic tables, and info. panels, as well as pleasant views.

km 377 / mile 234   Access to Dease Lake (the lake - not the village!) for very good fishing.

km 389 / mile 242   Rest stop next to Dease River.

km 403 / mile 250   Nice rest stop next to Pyramid Creek.

km 410 / mile 255   Pine Tree Lake rest stop offers good fishing.

km 420 / mile 261   Mighty Moe's Place includes RV parking, camping, canoe rental, a small store, and good fishing.

km 429 / mile 266   Cottonwood River Bridge is a rest area with good fishing.

km 438 / mile 272   Simmons Lake rest stop offers outhouses, shelter, and a beach with fishing.

km 450.5 / mile 280   Jade City includes 40 unserviced RV spots and campsites, and a large store with an extensive display of local jade from one of the largest jade mines in the world.

km 452 / mile 281   The junction with Cassiar Mine Road leads to the Cassiar asbestos mine which closed in 1992. There are no services here.

km 467 / mile 290   Centreville is an almost abandoned former gold mining town. In its glory days, 3000 people lived here. The biggest gold nugget ever found in BC was dug out of the ground here - it weighed 72 troy ounces (2.24 kg). The area still is actively mined for gold.

km 474 / mile 295   The village of Good Hope Lake offers a service station and a small grocery store.

km 487 / mile 303   Boya Lake Provincial Park includes 44 RV camps and campsites, with a picnic area on the lake shore, and fishing, swimming and boating. The park is located 2.5 km off the highway.

km 516 / mile 321   The French Creek Forest Service Campsite is 1 km off the highway.

km 546 / mile 339   Blue Lakes rest stop is a good place to try fishing for grayling.

km 570 / mile 354   The BC and Yukon border is at the 60th parallel. From here on you will need a Yukon fishing licence.

km 573 / mile 356   The junction with Alaska Highway includes a service station with car and tire repairs, and propane. A RV park, camping, motel and restaurant are available. Tel. 1-403-536-7391. (*Area code will change to -867- in October 1997*).

From the junction it is 432 km or 269 miles to Whitehorse, and it is 22 km or 13.6 miles to Watson Lake.

THE ATLIN ROAD HWY #7 - FROM JAKE'S CORNER

It is 92 km / 57 miles on a well-maintained gravel road to Atlin. The highway was built in 1949 by the Canadian Armed Forces to connect the Alaska Highway with the small community of Atlin. A rich gold mining district since August 1898, it was second in importance to the gold fields at Dawson City. Fifteen-thousand Klondike bound gold-seekers changed direction when gold was discovered near present-day Atlin. The White Pass & Yukon Railway lost over 80% of its work force and many tools - all heading for Atlin. Atlin Lake is about 145 km / 90 miles long and the Tlingit call it "Ahklen" or "Aht'lah", meaning "Big Water". It must be one of the most beautifully located lakes in all of North America, and is known as the "little Switzerland of Canada". The lake offers very good fishing for grayling, Dolly Warden and white fish. A valid B.C. angling licence is needed. The lake is known for quickly developing high winds, and across-lake travelling by canoe is not recommended.

km 0 / mile 0 Jake's Corner on the Alaska Highway.

km 3 / mile 1.8 A narrow gravel road leads down to the shores of **Little Atlin Lake** about 12 km/7.5 miles away.

km 4 / mile 2.4 Rest stop with a non-maintained camping area and a boat launch on Little Atlin Lake.

km 12.3 / mile 7.6 "Pride of the Yukon" Campground includes 40 unserviced RV and campsites. Cabins and boats are for rent and a roadside stand sells fresh vegetables in season. Telephone 403-668-3596.

km 22.2 / mile 13.8 A narrow gravel road leads to **Lubbock River**, which connects Little Atlin Lake with Atlin Lake and offers good fishing.

km 26 / mile 16.2 Snafu Lake Government Campground includes 4 RV sites and campsites with a boat launch. Snafu is an army acronym standing for "situation normal - all 'fouled' up".

km 32.2 / mile 20 The Tarfu Lake Government Campground offers 4 RV sites and campsites with a boat launch. Tarfu is supposed to stand for, "things are really 'fouled' up".

km 35 / mile 21.8 This rest stop includes a great view over Atlin Lake - with its 798 square km / 307 square miles, the largest natural lake in BC.

km 38 / mile 23.6 The Hitching Post includes RV and tent sites, as well as cabins, and boats for rent; horseback riding and fishing trips can be arranged. Call Tagish village at 399-4424.

km 41.2 / mile 25.6 The Yukon / British Columbia Border is located here; the road follows the lake shore from now on.

km 43.1 / mile 26.8 Shelter.

km 52.6 / mile 32.7 Hitchcock Creek shelter with good fishing. A B.C. campground is a bit further, with six sites and a boat launch.

km 64.7 / mile 40.2 A guest ranch and cabins of a big game outfitter are here.

km 72.7 / mile 45.2 Shelter.

km 80.1 / mile 49.8 The paved road begins here.

km 83 / mile 51.6 The turn-off for the Ruffner Mine Road leads to **McDonald Lake**, three kilometres away.

km 88.8 / mile 55.2 Here is the turn-off for **Como Lake**, a designated float plane landing.

km 92 / mile 57 Community of Atlin.

RCM Police 1-250-651-7511. **Fire** 1-250-651-7666. **Clinic** 1-250-651-7677. **Ambulance** 1-250-651-7700. **Atlin Visitor Association.** Tel. 1-250-651-7522. Fax 1-250-651-7721. Write to them at Box 365 M, Atlin, BC, V0W 1A0, Canada. The **Bank of Montreal** is open on weekdays from 10 a.m. to noon, and 1 p.m. to 3 p.m.

Sidha Tours rents canoes and kayaks. Tel. and Fax 250-651-7691. Box 368 V, Atlin, BC, V0W 1A0.

Norseman Adventure rents canoes and houseboats. Tel. 250-651-7535, Fax 250-826-2559. Box 184, Atlin, BC, V0W 1A0.

The population of Atlin hovers between 400 and 500 people, with more in summer and a lot less in winter. For the bus schedules between Atlin and Whitehorse look under "Transportation" in the Whitehorse section. Atlin maintains a scheduled charter air service to Juneau across the mountains on the coast. Peterson Airfield has a 1204 m / 3950 foot long landing strip at an elevation of 683 m / 2240 feet.

Where to stay:

Atlin Inn. Restaurant and Kirkwood Cottages. Full facility hotel, lounge. Tel. 1-250-651-7546, Fax 1-250-651-7500.

Comfortable Pew B&B. Tel. and Fax 1-250-651-7660.

Fireweed Inn B&B. Tel. 1-250-651-7729, Fax 1-250-651-7719. No smoking nor pets. From $55.

The Noland House B&B. Tel. 1-250-651-7585, Fax 1-250-651-7739. From $75 a night, summer only.

The Northern Place. Tel. 1-250-651-7503, Fax 1-250-651-7536.

Northern Adventure RV Park. Tel. 1-250-651-7535.

Quilts & Comfort B&B. Pillman Rd. Tel. 1-250-651-7476

Pine Creek Community Campground. 14 sites for $5 per unserviced site 1.5 km / 1 mile from Atlin. Please pay at any business in town or at the museum.

There are more campgrounds at the end of **Discovery Road** 19 km / 12 miles from Atlin at **Surprise Lake**, and at the end of **Warm Bay Road**. In Atlin you will find three restaurants, a grocery store, a government liquor store, one coin laundry with public showers, service stations, several stores and a museum.

Atlin Historical Museum is open from June to September and offers walking tours of town. Please call 1-250-651-7522.

MV Tarahne (Tah-ron) is a former lake passenger boat that connected Atlin with Scotia Bay on the other side of the lake. There used to be a 3.2 km / 2 mile long railroad which brought passengers and freight to Takish Lake, and from there other lake boats would continue service to Carcross. The Tarahne was built in Atlin during 1917, and retired in 1937. Tour's through the Tarahne are held in summer, and more information can be obtained by calling the Atlin Historical Society at tel. 1-250-651-7522. There is talk about re-floating it for use as a tour boat.

Atlin Centre of the Arts is used as a summer school and retreat for artists who want to get away from it all. For more information contact the Atlin Centre of the Arts. 19 Elm Grove Ave., Toronto, ON, M6K 2H9. Atlin is home for many creative people, from potters to writers.

Mineral Springs. Help yourself and fill up your containers with the crystal-clear waters of this spring at the northern end of town.

Atlin Provincial Park, south of Atlin, is the third largest in BC with 271,134 ha. or 669,977 acres. There is no road access, and only a few walk-in wilderness campsites exist. Most areas of the park can only be reached by float plane or by boat. About one third of the park is covered by glaciers; the

A typical gravel road in the Yukon.

Llewellyn Glacier being the largest. A valid park-use permit can be issued at B.C. Parks in Smithers, B.C. Call them at 1-250-847-7320 or Fax 1-250-847-7659. During the Gold Rush, one all-Canadian route to the Klondike passed through where the park is now located. About 5000 gold seekers were persuaded by the Canadian government to use this inland route, following the Stikine River and Telegraph Creek to Atlin Lake. It was supposed to be an easy and patriotic route to the gold fields, but only a handful made it. Many died starving or froze to death along a non-existent trail.

Two short roads lead out of Atlin.

The Discovery Road: Stop by at the Pioneer Cemetery just outside town. The road passes the airport and the recreational gold panning area on Spruce Creek Road. Gold is still being mined in this area, and visitors are reminded not to trespass on working gold claims. Taking photos is okay - from a distance. At 9 km / 5.6 miles from Atlin you will come to the ghost town of **Discovery**, where the 1898 Gold Rush got its start. Surprise Lake Campground is at the end of the road, 20 km / 12 miles from Atlin.

Warm Bay Road continues to follow the shoreline of the lake for 26 km / 16.5 miles. At McKee Creek, 15.3 km / 9.5 miles from Atlin, the famous "Atlin Nugget" was found in July, 1981. It was the size of a potato, weighing 33.88 troy ounces (1.05 kg). At km 23.3 or mile 14.4, a natural warm spring awaits the traveller. **Atlin Spring** can be found about 1 km south of Warm Bay. There is only a small bathing pool with a water temperature of about 30° C or 85° F. There are many cozy campsites on the lakeshore in this area. At the end of the road is the **Grotto Recreation Site** with camping and good drinking water at the "hole in the rock" - an underground stream which surfaces at the "Grotto".

TAGISH ROAD HIGHWAY #8 - FROM JAKE'S CORNER TO CARCROSS.

This 54.7 km / 34 mile long, part gravel, part asphalt road connects the Alaska Highway at Jake's Corner with Carcross on the Klondike Highway. This is also a short-cut to Skagway for those who want to bypass the city of Whitehorse. The highway was built in 1942.

km 0 / mile 0 Jake's Corner (Alaska Highway km 1392.5 / mile 865).

km 21 / mile 13 The village of Tagish has a population of around 100 persons. It is a popular summer recreation spot for Yukoners, with many cabins dotting the shorelines of either Tagish or Marsh Lake. Tagish straddles a narrow strip of land between these two lakes and the Six Mile River (or Tagish River) connecting them is part of the Yukon River System. The mad dash of thousands of boats toward the Klondike Gold Fields filtered through here. A police post required all boats to register. Present-day Tagish sprung up at the bridge head during construction of the bridge across Six Mile River in 1942. The original site of the native village of Tagish had been a few miles away. The word "Tagish" stands for "fish trap" reflecting the original use of this area. Tagish Charlie was one of the three partners who discovered gold at Bonanza Creek on August 16, 1896. He was also the first Yukon Native who, by an Act of Parliament, was given the full rights of a Canadian citizen, allowing him all the rights other male Canadians at the time took for granted. He died on January 26, 1908.

Services in the village of Tagish:

Barney's Fishing and Tours is located at the Tagish Bridge, with a service station, store, marina, post office, pay-phone, water taxi, and boat and houseboat rental. Tel. 399-3474.

Tagish Lake Government Campground includes 28 RV and tent sites with shelter, boat launch and fishing.

Tagish Service includes a service station with car repair and a fast food stand. Tel. 399-3663.

The Government Recreation Site at the west end of the bridge offers 4 picnic sites, but no overnight parking.

km 35.2 / mile 21.9 Ten Mile Ranch is a few kilometres off the highway. Tel. and Fax 667-1009. It is a lakefront resort with RV and tent sites, cabins, boat and canoe rentals, and German is spoken.

km 54.7 / mile 34 Junction with the Klondike Highway. To the left the road will take you south to Carcross, just a short distance away and further to Skagway, while to the right the road leads to Whitehorse.

Buffalo crossing the Alaska Highway north of Whitehorse.

Alaska Highway

Rush hour on the Alaska Highway in early summer.

ALASKA HIGHWAY FROM DAWSON CREEK TO THE ALASKA BORDER

The Alaska Highway was never meant to be more than a wartime military road - and for a short time it was just that. But once the war in the Pacific was over, military vehicles were quickly replaced by the curious, by the seeker of the almost untouched wilderness straddling the 2647 km (1645 mile) asphalt strip, and by anyone who just wanted to get away from it all. It took eight months and twelve days to complete the road from Dawson Creek to Fairbanks. Included in this "North-West Highway System" is the Haines Road from Haines Junction, Yukon, to Haines in Alaska. Construction officially started on March 8, 1942. Some 27,000 workers, including 3,700 Canadians, hacked, shoveled, dynamited and bulldozed this muddy strip out of almost impossible terrain. The road brought a drastic change to the economic history of the North. This sheer, endlessly winding, grey ribbon of mud and gravel, now all but replaced by asphalt, also brought death, diseases and social ills, like alcohol and tobacco, to aboriginal people living along the route of the new road. Countless Native Indians died from introduced diseases, and traditional life-styles were torn to shreds by the influence of a foreign culture and its machines.

By the end of 1942, the Alaska Highway wasn't much more than a narrow, frozen lane cut through bogs, wetland and mountain forests. The writer of a 1943 National Geographic magazine article described the drive as akin to being in a small boat thrown about on wild seas. Only by

Alaska Highway overlooking Teslin Lake.

1948 was the road opened for civilian traffic, then closed for a period in 1949, having been declared "suicidal". Since then, the highway has been upgraded, straightened, leveled, paved and re-paved; costing the Canadian government annually about $40 million for maintenance and repairs. Today the Alaska Highway never sleeps. Trucks of all sizes supply the North with goods of all kinds, and a never-ending stream of summer adventure seekers search for the mystic experience the "Alcan", as the highway is known the world over. In the following section, I will describe the stretch from Dawson Creek to the Alaska/Yukon border and beyond to the first Alaskan town of Tok, a distance of just over 2000 km. Along the British Columbia portion of the highway, kilometre posts are placed every 5 km/3 miles. In the Yukon those posts can be found every 2 km/1.2 miles

Mile '0' Dawson Creek

Look for the downtown intersection of 10th and 102nd Avenue, and you will find the large MILE "0" memorial right in the middle of the cross-roads. Watch out for traffic when photographing the mile post! Dawson Creek is a busy town of about 12,000, serving the huge Peace River agricultural region, with very extensive logging operations nearby. The city offers all services one would expect from a town that size.

A few telephone numbers:

Tourist information booth: 782-9595. **Road reports** for the Alcan and other roads in B.C. 1-900-451-4997 (charges apply), or locally 250-774-7447. **Police**: 782-5264 and **Medical**: 782-2211. While in the Dawson Creek area, listen to CJDC (890 AM) radio for road reports at 6 a.m., 8 a.m., 12:30 p.m. and 5 p.m., plus weather on the hour. Dawson Creek was named after George Mercer Dawson, a geologist who in 1879 surveyed the Peace River area. Dawson City, in the Yukon, is also named after the surveyor. The elevation of the city is 660 m/2165 feet.

km 16 / mile 10   Farmington Fairways Campground. Tel. 843-7774. 28 sites, $10 per site, and a 9-hole par 36 golf course with shop.

km 25 / mile 15.5   Village of Farmington. Small store, gas, cafe and public telephone.

km 28 / mile 17.4   Kiskatinaw Provincial Park. 28 sites on 58 ha. (143 acres) It is 3 km off the Alcan, on a stretch of the old Alaska Highway including the original wooden Kiskatinaw River Bridge. Visiting the bridge provides a lesson in the difficulties and hardships faced by the early construction crews.

km 55 / mile 34   Taylor Landing Provincial Park. Day use only, boat launch. There is also access to the **Regional Peace River Park**, and there are 20 campsites on 17.5 ha., including four group campsites, and a playground.

km 55.4 / mile 34.4   Peace River Bridge was built in 1942-43 by the same firm that constructed Brooklyn Bridge in New York. The original structure lasted until 1957 when it collapsed into the river. By January, 1960, a new bridge was in operation.

km 56 / mile 35   The community of Taylor includes 1000 inhabitants, many of whom are employed at the large petrochemical plant, or at the sawmill. The town is named after a homesteader who settled here in 1906. Look for what may be the world's largest golf ball - originally an old fuel tank with a diameter of 12.8 m. A service station, restaurant, grocery, golf course, RV parking, motel and a swimming pool can be found in the village. Call 789-9015. Ask for the date of Taylor's annual gold panning championships in August.

km 76 / mile 47   Fort St. John. Elevation 693 m / 2274 feet. This large town, with a population of over 14,000, calls itself the "Energy Capital of BC". It is one of the oldest 'White' settlements in northern BC, dating back to 1793 when it was founded as a fur trading post. It is a busy place with all services - even a skyscraper hotel! Listen to CKLN (560 AM) for road reports at 7:30, 8:30 a.m. and 5:15 p.m., and weather on the hour. **Visitor information: 785-3033. RCMPolice: 785-6617. Ambulances: 785-2079.**

Fort St. John was a staging point for one of the more foolish treks in Canadian history, the so-called "all Canadian" Edmonton Trail to the Klondike Gold Fields during the 1897-98 Gold Rush. Promoted by unscrupulous Edmonton merchants and newspaper writers, over 1500 stampeders, including a few women and their babies, were persuaded to try reaching the Klondike over non-existent trails through unexplored terrain, over distances up to 4000 km (2500 miles). Many died in the wilderness, many more gave up, returning to Edmonton or settling along the route. Only a very few reached the Klondike - long after the Gold Rush had spent itself, and most riches had been taken by those who had come via the coastal route.

km 80 / mile 50   Beatton Provincial Park has 37 campsites on 312 ha. It is 8 km/5 miles off the highway on a paved road. There is a sandy beach, playground, swimming, and boating. Tel. 787-3407.

km 81 / mile 50.3 <u>Charlie Lake</u> is a small village with a gas station, cafe, pub, restaurant, store, post office and RV parking. Call 787-1569. The United States military had their Mile Zero Post located in Charlie Lake, and many locals still consider their town the true beginning of the Alaska Highway.

km 86 / mile 53.5 Highway 29 branches off the **Alcan** to go south towards the towns of Chetwynd and Prince George. There is a gas station, cafe, and truck stop here. **Charlie Lake Provincial Park** is just off the junction, and includes 58 campsites on 92 ha. There is good fishing, swimming, boating and hiking trails at Sani station. Tel. 787-3407.

km 115 / mile 72 Shepard's Inn. Motel, RV park, gas station. Tel. 827-3676.

km 162 / mile 101 <u>Town of Wonowon (one-o-one)</u>. This town of 150 people, first took its name from the Blueberry River, but the location of Wonowon at Mile 1-0-1 along the highway must have been enough incentive for local townsfolk to rename their town. It offers all tourist related facilities, such as motels, a gas station, stores, and a campground. During construction of the highway, a military checkpoint was located here. From Wonowon the Alcan finally becomes more of a wilderness road, leaving farmland and clear-cut forests behind. **RCMPolice** tel.: 785-8100, **Medical** tel.: 785-2079 - both are in Fort St. John.

km 226 / mile 141 Pink Mountain Truck Stop. Elevation 1100 m/3600 feet. Gas station, cafe and restaurant, Greyhound bus depot, hot showers, coin laundry, liquor store. Tel. 772-3234.

km 252 / mile 156.6 Sikanni Hill, colloquially known as Suicide Hill, is 4 km from where you will cross from Mountain, to Pacific Standard Time (in effect from October to April).

km 256 / mile 159 Sikanni Chief River Bridge is at the bottom of a steep 5 km descent. This river eventually flows into the Arctic Ocean.

km 256.5 / mile 160 Sikanni Chief Tourist Facilities. Gas station, lodge, RV park and cafe. Tel. 774-1028.

km 278.5 / mile 173 Buckinghorse River Provincial Park offers 30 campsites on 55 ha., and swimming and fishing. Tel. 787-3407. Trutch Mountain, in the Rocky Mountain foothills, is nearby. Trutch was a civil engineer who also served as the first Lieutenant-Governor of BC. At the north end of the bridge is a motel and cafe, as well as free camping.

km 349 / mile 217 Prophet River Provincial Park includes 45 campsites on 115 ha., and fishing and swimming. The park is located high above the Prophet River with a trail leading down to the water. This is bear country - take care!

km 365 / mile 227 Historical milepost 233 is at the **community of Prophet River,** with a population of about 100. The town offers most services, including a gas station, repairs, propane, post office, motel and coffee shop. Tel. 773-6366. By removing curves and flattening hills, six miles have been shaved off the length of the highway by this point.

km 426 / mile 265 Andy Bailey Lake Provincial Recreation Park. 35 campsites on 174 ha. It is 11 km off the highway on a gravel road. There is a picnic area for day use, fishing, and swimming on beautiful sandy beaches at Jackfish Lake. There is a boat launch, but no power boats are allowed.

km 454 / mile 282 City of Fort Nelson.

Tourist information booth: 774-6400. **Alaska Highway Road Report** for highway between km 133 and km 968: 774-7447. **RCMPolice**: 774-2777. **Medical**: 774-6916. **Ambulance**: 774-2344. For road conditions, listen to CFNL (590 AM) at 7:30, 8:30, 9:05 a.m., 5:15 p.m., and weather on the hour. CBC is at 1610 AM. The elevation is at 422 m (1383 feet).

Fort Nelson has a population of about 4000, with all services available. It was named by Alexander Mackenzie, the well known explorer and fur trader, after the famous English Admiral, Lord Nelson. The town started out as a North West Company fur trading post in 1805. The forest around Fort Nelson supports a large disposable chopsticks plant, and BC Rail's freight-only line ends here. For local crafts visit the Fort Nelson-Liard Native Friendship Centre on 49th Avenue, as well as the Historical Museum; or play golf at the Poplar Hills Golf Club. It is 525 km (326 miles) north to the next biggest town on the Alaska Highway; Watson Lake in the Yukon Territory.

km 483 / mile 300 The junction with Highway 77. Highway 77 (or Liard Highway) branches off the Alcan going north for 137 km/85 miles to the BC/NWT border and beyond to the small settlement of Fort Liard. This narrow, lonely gravel road goes on to connect with the Mackenzie Highway, which leads to Yellowknife to the north, or Edmonton to the south.

km 509 / mile 316 Kledo Creek Provincial Park. 23 simple campsites on 6 ha., fishing.

km 532 / mile 330 Historical mile 351. **Steamboat Mountain.** Tel. 774-3388. It is a small year-round settlement with a gas station and RV parking. Watch for rest stops and hiking trails, such as **Indian Head**, and **Teetering Rock** along the highway between **Steamboat Mountain** (1067 m / 3500 feet) and **Tetsa River Provincial Park.**

km 554 / mile 344 Tetsa River Provincial Park. 25 campsites on 115 ha. It is located 2 km off the highway, along the river.

km 571 / mile 355 Tetsa River Services. Tel. 774-1005. There is a gas pump, cafe, RV parking with camping and hot showers. Many of these small communities consist of either a family, or a handful of people running the highway service. Some places are not always open for business from late autumn through early spring.

km 594 / mile 369 You are now entering Stone Mountain Provincial Park (25,691 ha.). Watch out for caribou and bighorn stone sheep on the highway. Please do not feed the animals, and do not park on the highway.

km 597 / mile 371 Summit Lake. Highest point of the Alcan at 1295 m / 4250 feet. There is a motel, RV park, and service station with repairs and propane, as well as a restaurant. The resort is open from May to September. Tel. 232-7531. Mt. St. George, behind Summit Lake, is 2201 m/7419 feet high. The Provincial Campground has 28 sites at the southern end of Summit Lake.

Bighorn stone sheep.

There are hiking trails, a boat launch, and good fishing. For more information about the park call 783-3407, in Fort St. John.

km 606 / mile 376 Rocky Mountain Lodge. Tel. and Fax 232-7000. There is a service station which can do some repairs, a motel, camping, and a cafe.

km 609 / mile 378 Northern end of **Stone Mountain Provincial Park**.

km 615 / mile 382 115 Creek Provincial Campground. 8 sites with tables and water.

km 647 / mile 402 Toad River. Highway Maintenance Camp and Toad River Lodge. Tel. 232-5351. There is a service station, tire repairs, lodging, camping, and a cafe. The Lodge is known for its huge collection of hats - numbering almost 4000 and growing.

Toad River has a few private homes, a school, post office and an ambulance service: Tel. 232-5351. The gravel airstrip is 701 m/2300 feet long, at an elevation of 732 m / 2400 feet.

km 652 / mile 405 The Poplars Campground. Service station, cafe, cabins and RV park. Tel. 232-5465.

km 679 / mile 422 The Village. Gas, cafe and camping.

km 698 / mile 434 Entering Muncho Lake Provincial Park (88,412 ha.). The highway skirts the beautiful jade-green lake for a total distance of 12 km / 7.5 miles. There are plenty of pull-outs for picnics, fishing, and swimming. Watch out for wildlife on the road, and for rock slides, and slow moving "sight-seeing" drivers. Within the park are four lodges with gas pumps, cafes / restaurants and RV camping, plus one Provincial Park with 30 campsites. The lake has a reported depth of 122 m / 400 feet. The mountains around the lake reach up to 2134 m / 7000 feet.

Places to stay in order of appearance going north:

Double "G" Service Lodge. Tel. 776-3411.

Strawberry Flats Provincial Campground. 15 sites.

Highland Glen Lodge. Tel. 776-3481.

MacDonald Provincial Campground. 15 sites.

Muncho Lake Lodge. Tel. 776-3456.

J&H Wilderness Resort. Tel. 776-3453. Open year-round.

All four lodges organize wilderness tours by boat, plane or on horseback.

km 712 / mile 442 Viewpoint over lake, outhouses.

km 737.5 / mile 458 Northern boundary of Muncho Lake Provincial Park.

km 763 / mile 474 Lower Liard River Bridge. The bridge was built in 1943. The Liard, French for cottonwood tree, is a mighty river flowing toward the Arctic Ocean.

km 764 / mile 475 Liard River Lodge. Service station, motel, RV camping, restaurant, Greyhound Bus stop. Tel. 776-7341.

km 765 / mile 475 Liard River Hot Springs Provincial Park is a must stop! The 53 campsites on 668 ha. fill up fast during the early parts of the day. Camping is first come, first serve, or make a reservation by calling 1-800-689-9025. During the 20's, a homesteader named John Smith worked his farm in this area. Word travelled south of a tropical Shangri-La in the northern wilderness, a paradise with unknown animals, and a valley where tropical fruits such as bananas and grapefruit grew the size of soccer balls. A nice thought, but in 1942 highway workers considered the hot springs their personal sanctuary.

A wooden boardwalk leads to two large hot mineral pools - the Alpha and Beta. The water temperature ranges from 38° to 54°C (100° to 129°F), with a volume of over 4000 litres per minute (over 900 gal/min.), and can be called nothing but luxurious after a long drive. The water is clear, and a strong sulphurous smell is quite obvious. Please, no soap or shampoo, and no alcohol or smoking on the boardwalk or in the pool area. The hot springs have created their own micro-climate, with plants otherwise not found anywhere else this far north, and they need to be protected. There are changing rooms and bio-outhouses at the pools. Watch for moose grazing in the warm water wetlands;

The hot springs.

they sometime join bathers in the pools! In the winter, the hot springs are a magic wonderland of snow and steam. There is a public phone at the entrance to the park.

Opposite the entrance to the park is **Trapper Ray's Lodge**. The lodge includes a service station, restaurant and cafe, cabins and RV camping. It is open year-round. Tel. 776-7349. In the lobby, look for the stuffed remains of an almost white Kermode bear, a species known to survive only in the west central parts of BC. This is one of the rarest types of black bear - shot by a brave hunter who needed evidence that this type of bear existed.

km 792 / mile 492 Smith River Bridge. A 2.6 km / 1.6 mile gravel road leads to the river and a pleasant picnic site near the Smith River Falls, which has good fishing.

km 823 / mile 512 Coal River Lodge. Tel. 776-7306. Service station with lodging, camping and cafe. Before the road was asphalted, the surface of the highway consisted of a mixture of gravel and local coal. After it rained, cars used to look like coal trucks.

km 831.5 / mile 517 Whirlpool Canyon Viewpoint is an unofficial campsite, with great views over Liard River and the canyon on the south side of highway.

km 839 / mile 521 Fireside Lodge is a truck stop with a cafe, RV parking and all car services. Tel. 776-7302. It is open in summer only. One of the largest forest fires in BC's history partially destroyed Fireside in 1982.

km 882 / mile 548 Allan Lookout includes a rest stop with outhouses and picnic tables overlooking Liard River and Goat Mountain to the west.

km 909 / mile 565 Contact Creek and Historic Milepost 588. This is where road construction crews, working from the south and north, connected on September 24, 1942. Watch for an information sign and an historical marker.

km 910 / mile 565 You are entering the Yukon Territory, but you will leave it again shortly. Over the next few kilometres the highway bounces back and forth between the Yukon and BC.

km 913 / Mile 567 Contact Creek Lodge. Tel. 536-2262. This is a service station with lodging, RV camping, and a cafe. You can purchase BC and Yukon fishing licences here year round.

km 922 / mile 573 Iron Creek Lodge. Tel. 536-2266. This lakefront motel includes a cafe, RV camping, and car services. During construction, trucks had to put on tire irons (chains) to make it up the hill - hence the name.

km 937 / mile 582 Hyland River Bridge offers good fishing for grayling, trout and dolly varden. Frank Hyland was an early independent trader competing with the huge Hudson Bay Company. He is known to have printed his own currency.

km 957 / mile 595 Access to the village of Lower Post, which is a few kilometres off the Alcan on a gravel road. There is a cafe, store and BC Forest Service office. In historic times, Lower Post was a Hudson Bay Trading Post and a native village. The trading post has disappeared.

km 967.5 / mile 601 Historic mile post 627 marks the BC / Yukon border. Watch for the "Welcome to the Yukon" sign. The highway will continue to dip back into BC a few more times but, rest assured, eventually will stay in the Yukon until leaving for Alaska.

km 1012 / mile 629 Lucky Lake Recreational Day Use Area. Lucky Lake is a rather shallow lake, warming quickly during hot summer days. The lake is stocked with rainbow trout and there is a water slide - the only one north of 60° latitude.

km 1017.5 / mile 632 Campground Services Ltd. Tel. 536-7448. Gas station and RV park with food market. It is open year-round, and is an agent for **Western Union money transfers.**

km 1021 / mile 635 City of Watson Lake.

WATSON LAKE

(Yukon Area Code 403. Changing October 1997 to T-O-P or 867).

The **visitor centre** is located next to the **Sign Post Forest**: call 536-7469. It is open daily from 8am to 8pm, from May to September. For information about the Yukon portion of the Alaska Highway, including the Haines Road, call Whitehorse, tel. 667-8215. Listen to CBOB (990 AM) for road reports at 4:35 p.m., and on weekends at 6:45 a.m. and 8:45 a.m; weather is on the hour. CKYN 96.1 FM Visitor Radio has general information about the Yukon.

RCMPolice: 536-5555. Ambulance and hospital: 536-4444. Fire: 536-2222. Forest Fire: 536-7335. If there is no answer, call toll-free from anywhere in the Yukon, **RCMP**: 1-403-667-5555; **Hospital**: 1-403-667-3333, or call the operator at "0" for instant assistance with the above numbers. **Watson Lake Airport**: 536-2525. **Dental Clinic**: 536-2595. **Women Shelter**: 536-7770.

Bank services: The Canadian Imperial Bank of Commerce (CIBC) is open Mon. - Thurs. 9:30 to 3:30, and Fri. 9:30 to 6 p.m. Tel. 536-7495. It has a 24 hour ATM machine. Winter services are available on Mon., Wed. and Fri. only.

Watson Lake has a population of over 1700, and was named after Frank Watson, a trapper and prospector who settled here in 1898. He had come up the ill-fated Edmonton Trail heading for the Klondike Gold Fields, but decided to stay and build a cabin close to where Watson Lake is located now. Before 1941, Watson Lake was just a sleepy trading post. The construction of the Alcan changed that. Today, the town is a dynamic little place; with businesses lining both sides of the Alaska Highway.

The Visitor Centre is located at the far north end of town, next to the **Sign Post Forest**. The first sign was put up by a very homesick US Army GI named Carl K. Lindley whose home was in Donville, Illinois. He painted the name of his home town on a piece of wood, added the mileage and an arrow and nailed it to a post pointing south. Since then, over 30,000 other signs have sprouted into a very special type of forest - if not a jungle! Before leaving home, ask your city folks for a sign to be put up in Watson Lake. Even though it seems rather crowded, there still is space for plenty more signs.

The Visitor Centre next to the sign post forest is open daily from mid-May to mid-September. It offers all kinds of information, including laser disc views of other attractions in the Yukon.

WATSON LAKE

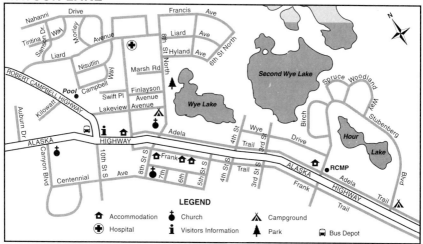

In Watson Lake there are six hotels, two B&B and two RV parks / campgrounds.

Alcan Motel. Tel. 536-7774, Fax 536-7732.

Belvedere Motor Hotel. A full service hotel. Tel. 536-7712, Fax 536-7563.

Big Horn Hotel. New and downtown. Tel. 536-2020, Fax 536-2021.

Cedar Lodge Motel. Free coffee. Tel. 536-7406.

Gateway Motor Inn. CAA-AAA approved. Tel. 536-7744, Fax 536-7740.

Watson Lake Hotel.- non-smoking rooms and sauna. Tel. 536-7781, Fax 536-7536 Prices from $45 to $100.

Heritage B&B. German spoken. Tel. and Fax 536-2400.

Wye Lake B&B. No smoking. Tel. 536-2163. Both charge from $55 to $65 for one or two people.

Camping at:

Downtown RV Park. Centre of town. Tel. 536-2646 summer, 536-2224 winter. All services.

Gateway to Yukon RV Park. Southern end of town, open year-round. Tel. 536-7448. All services.

Yukon Government Campground, with 55 RV and tent sites, 4 km out of town and north at the lake of Watson Lake. Boat launch.

All Yukon Government Campgrounds charge $8 per site or per tent offering fire wood, fire pit, shelters and water.

There are plenty of eateries in town, from restaurants located within hotels and campgrounds, to a place called "Pizza Palace" - serving guess what type of food.

There are various easy hiking trails around Wye Lake in the centre of town. The indoor pool is open only in summer and a 9 hole par 35 golf course is located 10 km out of town. There are downhill skiing facilities, for those passing through in winter. On a rainy day, visit the Public Library, which offers an excellent selection of northern books, and a story hour every Saturday afternoon. They have a free book exchange for pocket books.

Note - The Watson Lake Administration Building burned down in the summer of 1996, also destroying the library and other public service offices. Should you be travelling with too many books, they will gladly relieve you of the extra weight.

Coal River Springs Territorial Park and Ecological Reserve is a very special place. The reserve is located approximately 80 km/50 miles east of Watson Lake and only about 15 km/9.5 miles off the Alcan. The nearest Alaska Highway lodge is Contact Creek, at km 913/mile 570, and information on how to find the Sulpetro Road might be obtained there. The Sulpetro Road is an unmarked and unserviced trail that may be passable by a four-wheel drive. Even then, at least two kilometres have to be bushwhacked through burned deadfall to get to the southwest bank of the Coal River. Before Coal River Springs can be entered, the river must be crossed - and that's no joke. It might be easier to fly in using the services of Frontier Helicopters out of Watson Lake. Call them at 536-7766.

Coal River Springs are a jewel of descending limestone terraces and overflowing dripping pools of dark blue waters. The Thermal Spring is rated one of the top five springs in Canada, and was declared Yukon's second Territorial Park and first Ecological Reserve on September 17, 1990. There are designated trails and tent spots in the park. Please be extremely careful, since the unique limestone pools are very fragile. Ask for more information at the Watson Lake Visitor Centre, or write to the Government of the Yukon, Department of Renewable Resources, Box 2703, Whitehorse, Yukon, Y1A 2C6. Telephone 1-403-667-5648.

Annual Festivals in Watson Lake:

February. Mid-month, Kiki Karnival. For more information call 536-2246.

March. First half of month, Curling Bonspiel. Tel. 536-2104.

May. Open Golf Tournament. For more information call 536-2477.

July. 1st of July, Canada Day Celebrations. For more information call 536-2246.

August. Mid-month. Discovery Weekend. Closest to August 16-17.

Check with the Visitor Centre for other festivals.

Leaving Watson Lake going north, it is 270 km / 168 miles to **Teslin**, the next community. To **Whitehorse** it is 455 km or 283 miles. To **Dawson City** is 995 km or 618 miles, and to **Anchorage** it is 1620 km or 1007 miles. Going south to **Edmonton**, it's 1611 km or 1001 miles, and to **Vancouver** the distance is 2200 km or 1367 miles.

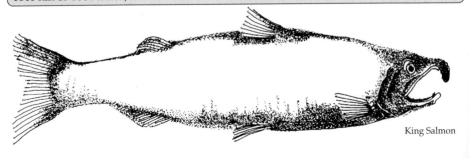

King Salmon

ALASKA HIGHWAY FROM WATSON CREEK TO WHITEHORSE

km 1021 / mile 634.5 Junction with Campbell Highway #4 connecting Watson Lake with Carmacks. This road will take you to Dawson City, if you do not mind bypassing Whitehorse. This mostly gravel highway, and the communities along it, are discussed in the Campbell Hwy chapter.

km 1032 / mile 641.5 Green Valley Trailer Park. Tel. 536-2276. Store with RV and tent sites overlooking Liard River. Free gold panning. Showers and laundromat.

km 1033 / mile 642 Village of Upper Liard. Service station, motel, camping and cafe. Open year-round. Telephone 536-2271 and Fax 536-2280. Greenway Golf course with 9 holes par 35, is open daily in summer, no reservations required.

km 1043 / mile 648 Junction with the Stewart Cassiar Highway #37 (More information about the Cassier highway in the Gateway Chapter) going south toward Prince Rupert and Prince George. There is a service station with a cafe and restaurant, lodging, camping, and a truck stop. Tel. 536-2794 and Fax 536-7391.

km 1044 / mile 650 Northern Beaver Post. Tel. 536-2307. Open May to September. A native craft shop, free RV overnight parking and coffee shop are here.

km 1085 / mile 674 Big Creek rest stop, picnic area, fishing.

km 1144 / mile 711 Rancheria Hotel/Motel. Tel. 851-6456. Gas station with RV parking, camping, propane and cafe. Rancheria got its name in the 1870s, no doubt from a homesick prospector who may have wanted to be somewhere else. Rancheria is Spanish for a ranch, small settlement or walled farm compound.

km 1156.5 / mile 718.5 Rancheria Falls Recreation Site. There are 4 picnic sites and a short trail to the falls, as well as fishing.

km 1162 / mile 722 Walkers Continental Divide Lodge. Tel. 851-6451. Gas station, motel, restaurant with RV parking and lounge.

km 1163 / mile 722.5 Continental Divide. Up to this point, all rivers have flowed into the Arctic Ocean via the Mackenzie River. All rivers between here and Fairbanks flow into the Pacific Ocean via the Yukon River.

km 1181 / mile 734 Swift River Lodge. Tel. 851-6401, Fax 851-6400. Motel with free RV parking, gas and car services, cafe, lounge. Propane, showers and a coin laundry are available.

km 1181.5 / mile 734.2 The highway dips back into BC for the next 68 km/42 miles.

km 1222.5 / mile 759.6 Smart River Bridge was originally called Smarch River, after a native family who used to live and trap here. Picnic, parking and fishing.

km 1249.2 / mile 776.2 The highway re-enters the Yukon from BC for the last time. Really!

km 1250.5 / mile 777 Morley River Recreation Site. Six picnic sites with water, fishing. Day use only.

km 1252.2 / mile 777.7 Morley River Lodge. Tel. and Fax 390-2639. Motel with riverside camping, restaurant, cafe and boat rental. Service station. Open year-round. A Western Union Money Transfer Agent.

km 1282 / mile 796.5 Dawson Peaks Northern Resort. Tel. 390-2310. Fax 390-2244. RV parking, camping and cabins, restaurant. Guided fishing and lake tours and canoe rentals.

km 1292.7 / mile 803.2 Nisutlin River Bridge. The Nisutlin River empties into Teslin Lake just a stone's throw away. The Nisutlin, meaning "Quiet Water" in the Tlingit language, is one of the easy Yukon rivers for canoe travellers. The put-in is at km 68 on the South Canol Road, for a pleasant 140 km float back to Teslin. For those with time, the trip can be extended to the delta of the Yukon River through 3200 km/2000 miles of wilderness, travelling via Teslin Lake, Teslin River and the Yukon River; one of the longest continuous river trips on the continent. **Teslin Lake** is about 138 km / 86 miles long, up to 3.2 km / 2 miles wide with an average depth of 60 m / 194 feet. The Tlingit called the lake "Teslitoo", meaning long and narrow water. The bridge is the longest on the entire length of the Alcan, at 584 m / 1917 feet.

km 1294 / mile 804 Village of Teslin.

VILLAGE OF TESLIN

RCMPolice: 390-5555. If no answer call toll-free 1-403-667-5555. **Medical or Ambulance:** 390-4444. **Fire:** 390-2222. For weather and road reports listen to CBDK (940 AM) at the same times as in Watson Lake. The elevation is 682 m or 2239 feet. **Teslin airstrip** call: 390-2525. **Banking** is by CIBC on Mon., Wed., Thurs. from noon to 3, and Fri. 9 to 3 p.m. In winter, hours are 11 to 2 p.m. Wed. and Thurs.

The population of **Teslin** hovers at around 450, and it has been permanently settled only since 1903. Originally, this area was used as a summer fishing and hunting camp for the Tlingit. Today, Teslin has a large native population whose livelihood depends on hunting, fishing and trapping, as well as highway work and tourism. Native artists are well represented in the community ,with wood carving; canoe, snowshoe, and sled making; traditional sewing crafts; and hair tufting. During construction of the Alcan, in the winter of 1942-43, many of the village people suffered from imported diseases like measles, meningitis, mumps, whooping cough and jaundice. Many died or suffered long term consequences from the diseases.

The George Johnston Museum has the largest Tlingit art collection in the North, and is well worth a visit. The Teslin Historical Museum Society; Box 146, Teslin, Yukon. Y0A 1B0. Tel. 390-2550 and Fax 390-2104; is open daily in summer from 9 a.m. to 7 p.m. The admission charge is $2.50 for adults and $1 for children.

George Johnston, after whom the museum is named, was one of the more fascinating characters in the Yukon. A Tlingit, he was not only known for his skills as a trapper and hunter, but also for his abilities with a camera. His photographs of early Tlingit life are part of the museum exhibition. Before the Alaska Highway had even been thought of, he imported a 1928 Chevy car, building for himself an 8 km/5 mile long "exclusive" road. During winters he would race the car on the frozen Teslin Lake. The car is the proud centre-piece of the museum.

There are two motels in Teslin:

Northland Motel and cafe with lounge and freshly baked bread. Tel. and Fax 390-2571.

Yukon Motel, with RV parking, cafe, lounge, showers and coin laundry. Tel. 390-2575 or call the motel office at 390-2443. Open year-round. Both above businesses also sell gas and car products.

Nisutlin Trading Post. Established in 1928 - the store sells groceries, clothing, hardware, and fishing and hunting licences. Telephone 390-2521, fax 390-2103.

Nisutlin Bay Marina. Guided fishing trips and lake tours. Cabin accommodation on the lake. Mobile radio call collect JR-2M3259, Teslin Channel or fax to 390-2829.

For information about all radio calls, dial the radio phone operator at 1311.

Annual Events in Teslin:

March. Mini Rendezvous with dog sled and snowmobile races. Traditional Games.

July. July 1st Canada Celebrations. Fishing derby with fish-fry, races and a parade.

For more information call **Village of Teslin** at 390-2530 or **Teslin Tlingit Council** at 390-2532.

The distance to Whitehorse is 179 km / 111 miles, and to Watson Lake is 263 km / 163 miles.

km 1297.5 / mile 806.2 Teslin Lake Viewpoint.

km 1298.5 / mile 806.8 Halsteads Lodge. Tel. 390-2608. RV park / camping and motel with non-smoking rooms, restaurant and a service station. Showers and a laundromat are available.

km 1306.2 / mile 811.6 Mukluk Annie's Salmon Bake. Tel. 667-1200. Motel and cafe with free RV parking and camping. Daily all-you-can-eat salmon bake from 11 - 9 p.m.

km 1307.5 / mile 812.5 Teslin Lake Government Campground,19 lake-shore RV and tent sites, boat launch, fishing.

km 1345.5 / mile 836 Junction with Canol Road (#6 Road) to Ross River, Faro and Quiet Lake Government Campground (77 km / 48 miles) which is the starting point for canoe trips down the Big Salmon River toward Dawson City. For more about this road, see the Canol Road (CAN-adian O-i-L) section in the Campbell Hwy Chapter. **Teslin River Bridge** is a short distance from the junction..

km 1346 / mile 836.5 Johnson's Crossing Lodge. Tel. 390-2607, summer only. Service station with RV parking, camping, cafe and store. This is a favourite drop-off point for canoe trips down the Teslin River into the Yukon River and on to Dawson City.

km 1366 / mile 849 Squanga Lake Government Campground has 12 RV and tent sites with shelter, fishing and swimming. Squanga is a native word for a type of whitefish found here.

km 1392.5 / mile 865 Jake's Corner Inc. Crystal Palace Hotel, tel. 668-2727. Service station with motel, cafe and propane.

-**Junction with Highway #7** to beautifully located **Atlin**, BC. It is 92 km / 57 miles on a gravel road, built in 1949, to this "little Switzerland" of northern BC.

- **Junction with Tagish Road #8** to the village of **Tagish** 21 km / 13 miles away. The distance to Carcross is 55 km / 34 miles. It's either a short-cut to Skagway, or a pleasant detour to Whitehorse.

Highway descriptions for the above two highways can be found in the Gateway Chapter.

km 1413.5 / mile 878.5 Lakeview Resort and Marina. Tel. 399-4567, Fax 399-4747. Service station with motel, cabins, RV parking, camping, cafe, and store. Boat, bike and windsurfer rental. Open year-round.

km 1427 / mile 886.5 Marsh Lake. The lake is part of the Yukon River headwaters and about 32 km / 20 miles long, at an elevation of 656 m / 2152 feet. First called Mud Lake, it was re-named by American explorer Frederick Schwatka for Professor O.C.

Marsh, a paleontologist at Yale University. Schwatka was, in 1883, not the first to travel the full length of the Yukon River, but he was the first to map and chart the river, paving the way for fur-traders and gold prospectors.

km 1430 / mile 888.5 Marsh Lake Government Campground is 500 m off the highway on the lake shore, with 37 RV/tent sites and four tent-only sites. Swimming, fishing, playground and hiking trails. There is a day-use only area near the beach.

km 1453.5 / mile 903 Sourdough Country Campsite. Tel. and Fax 668-2961. RV parking and tenting, coin laundry, showers. Good Sam Park; German and French spoken.

km 1455 / mile 904 Junction with Klondike Highway #2. Carcross Corner Cafe. Tel. 668-3287, Fax 668-3196. Service station with propane, store restaurant and cafe. Free overnight parking with fill-up and video rental.

km 1455.3 / mile 904.3 You are entering the Whitehorse City Limits. The city was incorporated on June 1, 1950, and encompasses 421 square kms or 162 square miles.

km 1458.6 / mile 906.3 Wolf Creek Government Campground has 29 RV/tent sites, 11 tent sites, hiking trails and access to the Yukon River, and shelters. As in all Government Campgrounds in the Yukon, water and firewood is provided, and your stay is limited to two weeks. Overnight fee per site is $8.

km 1463 / mile 909 The highway crosses **White Pass & the Yukon Railroad** tracks, now abandoned. See Skagway section.

km 1465.2 / mile 910.5 Pioneer RV Park. Tel. 668-5944, Fax 668-5947. 144 RV and tent sites with showers, coin laundry, propane. RV and car wash with hot water, 8 km / 5 miles from downtown.

A view of the railroad south of Carcross.

km 1466.8 / mile 911.5 Turn-off for scenic **Miles Canyon and Foot Suspension Bridge**. Great views over the still small Yukon River. Before the Whitehorse Hydro Dam was built, Miles Canyon was a major obstacle for most stampeders, and a disaster for many. Now manageable, Miles Canyon was bypassed by tramways in 1897, to make it easier for gold-seekers to avoid the canyon.

Canyon City, now an important archaeological site, was a bustling town in 1897, but was quickly abandoned once the railroad began running in 1900. It is just 2 km / 1.2 miles upstream from the **Robert Lowe Suspension Foot Bridge** (where there is plenty of parking), and can be reached via an easy hiking trail. Canyon City can also be driven to from Whitehorse via the Chadburn Lake Road. There is no admission charge to the site and interpreters are there from 9 a.m. to 4 p.m., Monday - Friday from July to mid-August. You can either drive back to the Alaska Highway or continue on the same road, which will take you past Schwatka Lake and the float plane base to Whitehorse proper.

km 1467.7 / mile 912 Mountain Ridge Motel and RV Park. Tel. 667-4202.

km 1469.8 / mile 913.3 Robert Service Way to Whitehorse. This road will take you to the **Robert Service Campground**, just one kilometre south of downtown Whitehorse and the nearest one to the city centre. The walk-in campground, is $11 per tent, with showers, and is next to the river, and a good place to start your canoe trip to Dawson City. Call the campground at 668-3721, summer only.

km 1470.2 / mile 913.5 Hi Country RV Park. Tel. 667-7445 or 668-4500, Fax 668-7432. RV park and Campground with coin laundry, showers and gold panning. Toll-free 1-800-661-0539 from the Yukon and northern BC, and 1-800-764-7604 from Alaska.

km 1473.1 / mile 915.4   The Yukon Beringia Interpretive Centre, which formerly housed the Yukon Visitor Centre, has been open since the Spring of 1997. The theme of the Beringia Centre is ice age animals, like the mammoth, mastodon, lions, and other equally fascinating animals of a distant past, as well as the First People who hunted the Yukon steppe over 24,000 years ago. Call 667-8855 for more information, open daily in summer.

The last great ice age occurred 70,000 to 10,000 years ago, causing a drop in sea levels by as much as 150 meters. While most of Canada was covered by massive ice sheets up-to 1 km thick, a huge area just north of Whitehorse, extending far into Siberia, remained ice-free. This steppe-like expanse was home to countless huge animals including mammoth, giant beaver, huge bears, horses and camels. Following these animals were hunters travelling in small tight clan and family groups. The First People's mythology tells about a world under water, and Crow who made the land. As the ice-mass quickly melted, and as temperatures once again rose, the Beringia must have flooded quite rapidly, creating the landscape as we know it today, and the hunters moved on south, building cultures throughout the Americas.

Next door to the Beringia Centre is the **Yukon Transportation Museum**, open daily in summer. There are exhibits from dog sledding to bush planes, and about the Alaska Highway and river boats. Tel. 668-4792, Fax 663-5547.

km 1473.4 / mile 915.6   The Whitehorse International Airport has services to Juneau, Anchorage, and Fairbanks in Alaska; points south and to some communities in the Yukon. The elevation is 702.5 m / 2305 feet. There are three paved runways, the longest being 2195 m / 7200 feet. **Airport manager**: call 667-8400. Within the Airport are car rentals, a gift shop and a cafe / restaurant. Opposite the Airport are two hotels / motels with restaurants. **Airline Inn**. Tel. 668-4400, Fax 668-2641 and the **Airport Chalet**. Tel. 668-2166, Fax 668-2173.

km 1475.6 / mile 916.9 Two Mile Hill. Main access to downtown Whitehorse. It's a steep descent to the Yukon River valley flats where most of the city is located.

- Trail of '98 RV Park. Tel. 668-3768. At the bottom of Two Mile Hill to your left at 117 Jasper Street. All services.

- Sourdough City RV Park. 100 gravel sites on 2nd Ave. Tel. 668-4500, toll-free from Alaska 1-800-764-7604 and toll-free from Yukon and northern BC 1-800-661-0539. This RV Park is almost in the downtown area, with fast food outlets nearby.

Before we return to the Alaska Highway, here is a listing of important Whitehorse telephone numbers:

RCMPolice: 911 or 667-5555 on 4100 4th Ave. Medical: 667-8700 - also call this number for poison control. Ambulance: 911 or 667-3333. General Hospital: 668-4444. Fire: 911 or 667-2222.

To turn in poachers: 1-800-661-0525. Environmental emergencies: 667-7244.

Visitor Information: 667-3084 or Fax 393-6351. The Visitor Centre is located on 2nd Ave. and Lambert.

Chamber of Commerce: 667-7545. Parks Canada Info. for Chilkoot Trail: 667-3910.

Information about Territorial Government Campgrounds: 667-5648

Alaska Highway Road Report and info. about other highways in the Yukon: 667-8215.

Dempster Highway Information: 1-800-661-0752.

Yukon Territorial Government Transportation, responsible for the Alaska Highway: 667-3710.

Radio CKRW (610 AM)- Road report at 12:45 p.m. and 4:30 p.m.

CBC Radio (570 AM)- News and weather on the hour. Tel. 668-8400.

Amateur Radio Repeaters: Whitehorse 146.88/146.94, Haines Junction 146.82, Carcross 444.900.

More Information from the Yukon Amateur Radio Association, Ron McFadyen, tel. 668-8400.

For emergency CB Frequency call Channel 9

Ferry Terminals: Haines 1-907-766-2111 and Skagway 1-907-983-2941, Fax 1-907-277-4829 toll-free from the Yukon 1-800-665-6414. Toll-free from Alaska and Northwest 1-800-642-0066. Departure and Arrivals only (recordings) 1-907-766-2113.

BC Ferries 1-250-386-3431 outside B.C., in B.C. 1-888-223-3779, fax 1-604- 381-5452.

White Pass & Yukon Railway Reservations: from the US 1-800-343-7373, northwest Canada 1-800-478-7373, or Whitehorse tel. 668-7245.

Toll-free numbers to call for any type of information, and requesting brochures: Yukon, 1-800-789-8566; Northwest Territories, 1-800-661-0788; British Columbia, 1-800-663-6000; Alberta, 1-800-661-8888; Saskatchewan, 1-800-667-7191; Manitoba, 1-800-665-0040; Ontario, 1-800-068-2040; New Brunswick, 1-800-561-0123; Nova Scotia, 1-800-565-0000; Quebec, 1-800-363-7777; Prince Edward Island, 1-800-463-4734; and Newfoundland, 1-800-563-6353. The above numbers can be called from anywhere in North America.

Look for more information about the city in the Whitehorse chapter of this book.

THE ALASKA HIGHWAY FROM WHITEHORSE TO HAINES JUNCTION

km 1477.5 / mile 918.3 Kopper King Services. Tel. 668-2347. Fax 668-3976. Service station with car wash and a motel (from $45 to $60) with restaurant, tavern and a lounge; open year-round.

km 1482 / mile 920.9 Casa Loma Motel. Tel. 633-2266/67, Fax 668-4853. 24 rooms with restaurant and live entertainment, pub. Rooms from $59 single.

km 1482.4 / mile 921.2 Trails North Car & Truck Stop. Tel. 633-2327, Fax 633-6637. Full service station with store and propane, motel, restaurant, cafe and RV parking.

km 1483 / mile 921.5 MacKenzie's RV Park. Tel. 633-2337, Fax 667-6797. 52 full service sites and 22 dry sites, store and RV wash.

km 1486.7 / mile 923.8 Rest stop with information sign, city map and pay telephone. You are leaving Whitehorse City Limits.

km 1487.2 / mile 924.1 Junction with Klondike Highway #2 to Dawson City. Also to Takhini Hotsprings, 9 km / 5.6 miles from junction. *For more information about this section of the Klondike Highway, see the Klondike Highway Chapter.*

km 1507.5 / mile 936.7 Old Dawson Stage-Coach Trail. The trail was abandoned when the Klondike Highway was put into service during the 1950s.

km 1543.1 / mile 958.9 Junction with Kusawa Lake Road.

- Takhini River Government Campground. 14.5 km/9 miles off the Alaska Highway on Kusawa Lake Road. 8 RV and campsites, fishing, swimming and boating.

- Kusawa Lake Government Campground. 22.5 km/14 miles off the Alaska Highway on Kusawa Lake Road. 39 RV and campsites, boat launch, swimming and fishing.

Access to both campgrounds is via a narrow, curvy, gravel road that can be quite slippery when wet. The road was built by the US Army in 1945, to access timber for highway construction. **Kusawa Lake** is 72 km / 45 miles long and roughly 3.2 km / 2 miles wide. There is good fishing for trout, pike and grayling. This beautifully located lake is named after a Chilkat Chief, "Kho-klux". Coastal natives used the lake and the Takhini River as a trade route to inland tribes living in the Yukon River valley. Chief Kho-klux was the leader of the war party that attacked and destroyed the Fort Selkirk Trading Post on the Yukon River on August 19, 1852. The Takhini is a popular float trip from the lake back to the Yukon River; a one or two day trip with class III rapids during high water; experience is necessary.

km 1565.5 / mile 973 Kwaday Dan Kenji - Indian Way Ventures. A recreated native camp with a craft shop. Open May to Oct. from 9 to 7:30 p.m. daily. $5 per adult. Free overnight RV parking and tenting. Call 667-6375.

km 1568.5 / mile 974.7 Native Village of Champagne. Jack Dalton, anticipating a gold rush, opened a toll-road on which the first livestock reached Dawson City. It crossed the highway at Champagne, which may have been named after celebrating a successful cattle drive. In 1898, he charged $2.50 per horse and $2 per head of cattle to use an improved native trail. The village cemetery, with spirit houses, is off-limits for curious photo takers.

km 1602.2 / mile 995.6 Junction with Aishihik Lake Road and **Otter Falls Gas Station and Store.** Tel. 634-2812. RV and tent sites, playground, fishing, and ice is available. Thirty km / 18.6 miles toward Aishihik Lake you will find **Otter Falls Government Recreation Site**, with six picnic sites, a shelter, a boat launch and fishing. At the southern end of the lake, 41.8 km or 26 miles from the Alaska Highway, is the **Aishihik Lake Government Campground** with 13 RV and tent sites, a boat launch and good fishing.

The gravel road continues to skirt **Aishihik Lake** for a total of 135 km or 84 miles to the now abandoned native village of Aishihik (AYSH-ee-ak), meaning "High Place". The lake is at an elevation of 914 m / 3001 feet, about 56 km / 35 miles long, and is considered to be at the highest elevation of any lake of comparable size in Canada. Ice on the lake can stay as late as the end of June, and water might be too low for boating. There is good fishing for trout and grayling. A 32 MW Northern Canada Power Dam was built in 1976, and the flow of Otter Falls is regulated.

km 1622.7 / mile 1008.3 Rest stop. There are impressive views over the snow capped peaks of the Kluane National Park, Icefield Ranges and the Elias Mountains.

km 1628.8 / mile 1012.1 Pine Lake Government Campground; 33 RV/tent sites, 7 tent sites, shelter, boat launch, fishing/swimming. The Pine Lake Regatta is held in July.

km 1635.3 / mile 1016 Village of Haines Junction.

HAINES JUNCTION

RCMPolice: 634-5555, if no answer 1-403-667-5555. **Medical and Ambulance**: 634-4444, if no answer 1-403-667-3333. **(Area code will change to 867 by Oct. 1997). Visitor Information at Kluane National Park Office.** Call 634-2345 or Fax 634-7208.

For information about Village of Haines Junction and the nearby area, call 634-2291. Radio Road Report: CBDF 103.5 FM at 4:35 p.m. daily. Sat. and Sun. 6:45 a.m. and 8:45 a.m., weather on the hour. CKYN 96.1 FM for visitor info. **Banking** by CIBC from Mon. to Thurs. from noon to 3 p.m., and Fridays from noon to 4 p.m. Tel. 634-2820.

Haines Junction has a population of approximately 800. The town came to life during construction of the Alaska Highway, when the first buildings were army barracks housing engineers. It was named after Haines on the Alaska coast 257 km / 160 miles away. Haines itself was founded by Presbyterian missionaries in 1879. The Haines Road, connecting these two towns, was built in 1943 as an alternative emergency road to the Alaska Highway. Mrs. Francine E. Haines was the first Secretary of the Committee of Home Missions.

Haines Junction offers all basic services, including health care, a post office, library, liquor store, churches, and grocery and gift stores. The Canadian Imperial Bank of Commerce is located inside Madley's General Store, as is the post office. RCMP and Forestry have their offices opposite the General Store. The junction of the Alaska and Haines Highways dominates the village, and most services are within the immediate area of the junction.

Note-the General Store was destroyed by fire during the summer of 1996, but should be rebuild for 1997.

Accommodation in Haines Junction:

Cozy Corner Motel. Tel. 634-2511, Fax 634-2119. Open year-round. The restaurant burned down in late April of 1996, but may be rebuilt for the 1997 season.

Gateway Motel and RV parking. Tel. 634-2371, Fax 634-2833. Public showers and coin laundry; open year-round.

Kluane Park Inn. Tel. 634-2261, Fax 634-2273. Open year-round. Restaurant, cafe, and lounge with off sales liquor, and meeting rooms.

Mountain View Motor Inn. Tel. 634-2646, Fax 634-2802. The Kluane Country Show - Yukon Tales, Ballads, Sketches - is performed Thu., Fri., Sat., and Sun. at 8 p.m.

The Raven "New" Motel. Tel. 634-2500, Fax 634-2517. Restaurant. All rooms and restaurant are non-smoking. Call collect for reservations. The restaurant has received a one-star rating in Anne Hardy's 'Where to eat in Canada'.

Stardust Motel. Tel. 634-2591. Service station, RV parking, cafe. German spoken.

Laughing Moose B&B. Tel. 634-2335. On a side street near a public swimming pool.

Valhalla R&R B&B. Tel. 634-2135.

"The Cabin" B&B. Tel. 634-2626. Central sauna, shower and sanitary facilities; 27 km toward Haines.

Aspen B&B. Tel. 634-2816 and Fax 634-2034. Just outside town, brand new log cabins.

Frosty Freeze B&B. Tel. 634-2674 and Fax 634-2850. Attached is a fast food restaurant.

Kluane RV Park Kampground. Tel. 634-2709, Fax 634-2735. 60 full service sites, 40 campsites, bike rentals, service station with RV wash, Good Sam Park. Glacier flights.

North Country RV Park. Tel. 634-2505. Service station. Year-round, 7 a.m.to 10 p.m.

For a special treat: **The Village Bakery** sells freshly baked bread, and has a cappuccino bar; it is next to the Visitor Centre. Tel. 634-2867. An **indoor swimming pool** at the community centre is open seven days a week, it has showers. Call 634-2650 for hours.

A new **Visitor and Convention Centre** with a 240 seat theatre and cultural centre is under construction and is scheduled to open in late 1997 or early 1998.

Rentals, and Tour and Wilderness Operators:

Junction Cycle. Tel. 634-2453. Rents bicycles and organizes bike tours.

Silton Air. Tel. 634-2916, Fax 634-2034. Fishing trips and flight tours into Kluane Park.

Trans North Helicopters. Tel. 634-2242. Will fly you anywhere inside and outside Kluane Park, year-round.

Kluane Helicopters. Tel. 634-2224, Fax 634-2226. Heli-fishing, heli-hiking, and sightseeing.

Valhalla R&R. Tel. 634-2135. Boat tours and fishing charters.

Kluane Adventures. Fishing trips, tel. 634-2282.

Kluane Park Adventures Centre. Tel. 634-2313, Fax 634-2802. White water rafting and canoe/bike rentals, trail rides.

Krude Che' Wilderness Guiding. Tel and Fax 634-2378. Native guides of the Tutchone and Tlingit culture. Guiding, photography and fishing in and around Kluane Park.

Otter Falls Wilderness Adventures. Tel. 634-2836. Horseback excursions into the Ruby Range north of Kluane Park.

Rainy Hollow Wilderness Adventures. Tel. 634-2554, cellular telephone 667-1346.

For more info. on individual wilderness operators, write to the Wilderness Tourism Association of the Yukon, P.O. Box 3960, Whitehorse, YT, Y1A 3M6. Or write to the Haines Junction Chamber of Commerce, Box 5444, Haines Junction, Yukon, Y0B-1L0.

Annual events in Haines Junction:

January, last week: Alcan International Snowmachine Race. From Haines, Alaska to Dezadeash Lake, Yukon. Call Diane in Haines at 1-907-766-2503.

February, mid. month: Kluane Classic Cross Country Ski Race. Contact Norm Bastian at 634-2539.

May to September: Monday nights, local musicians play at the Village Bakery Coffee House. Tel. 634-2867.

Mid-April: 27 km auto race on Kluane Lake near Burwash. Tel. 841-4441.

May, last week: Trail of '42 road race. Walk, bike or run the original route of the Alcan. 20 km / 12.4 miles. Tel. 634-2561.

June, first week: Alsek Music Festival, "Music under the Mountain', Contact Wolf Riedle at home 634-2526, work 634-2231/2520.

June, third week: Kluane Park Interpretive Program begins. Tel. 634-2251.

June, last week: Kluane to Chilkat International Bike Relay. Cycle from Haines Junction to Haines in Alaska, in teams of 2-4-6 or 8 riders. Contact Neil Salvin at 634-2453.

July 1st: Canada Celebration. Info. at 634-2291.

July, middle of month: Canada Parks Day. Join a park interpreter for a special event to celebrate Canada's Heritage. Tel. 634-2251.

July, Pine Lake Regatta. The "best beach party in the Yukon". For details call 634-2291.

August, first week: Dalton Trail Gymkhana and Jackpot Rodeo. Contact Barb Eikland at 634-2563 home, or 634-2288 work.

Mid-September: Frog Race and Pheasant Hunt. Prizes and dance. Call Burwash Landing at 841-4441.

KLUANE NATIONAL PARK

The name Kluane is a Tlingit term for "a place with big fish". It was first used in 1903 to refer to a small gold mining settlement near Kluane Lake, where Mile Post 1054 is now located. Kluane National Park must be one of the most extraordinary spots on earth. Magnificent enough to be declared, together with Wrangell - St. Elias National Park, a United Nations World Heritage Site. These two parks encompass 55,000 square km or 21,237 square miles. Kluane Park alone covers 22,015 square km or 8500 square miles with 20 peaks taller than 4200 m / 13,780 feet. Mount Logan, at 5959 m / 19,551 feet, is Canada's highest mountain. Mt. Logan was first climbed in 1925 by W.W. Foster, president of the Alpine Club of Canada, and his American partner A.H. MacCarty. In July 1887, Mt. St. Elias was conquered by the Duke of Abruzzi, a famous mountain climber, with the help of many partners and native packers.

Within this huge mountain massif are the world's largest non-polar ice fields, with glaciers up to 112 km / 70 miles long and ice fields over 1 km / 0.62 miles thick. More than 10 of these mammoth glaciers spawn powerful rivers, such as the Donjak and White Rivers, flowing into the Yukon River; and the Alsek and Tatshenshini Rivers, flowing into the Pacific. Periodically these glaciers will form massive ice dams. This most recently occurred about 1850, when the Alsek River was blocked, flooding the entire valley as far as Haines Junction, creating a lake 150 m / 500 feet deep. When the ice dam broke the lake emptied within two days - it must have been quite a sight!

The National Park not only displays tremendous visual beauty, but also is home to over 200 species of plants of Asiatic, coastal, Arctic, northern prairie and western mountain origin; many are unique. Canada's rarest wildlife, such as Dall's sheep, grizzlies and a large subspecies of moose, share this sanctuary with black bear, wolves, caribou, wolverine, mountain goats, red fox, otter and lynx, to name just a few. Golden and bald eagles are some of the 106 bird species which nest in the park, and many more visit at other times of the year.

A birds eye view of the Kluane Park ice fields.

Within Kluane Park are three basic life zones: grasslands; montane forest reaching up the slopes into sub-alpine zones; and alpine tundra, a treeless expanse extending into a world of permanent ice and snow. Kluane is, geologically speaking, very young. Much of the landscape has developed since the end of the Wisconsin glaciation 10,000 years ago, and the first human occupation can be traced back about 8000 years. This marvelous area has been under great ecological pressure since the Gold Rush. But the construction of the Alaska Highway was, to some extent, responsible for the creation of the park and helped manage mining activities, as well as trophy hunting.

The US Secretary of the Interior, Harold Ickes, was largely responsible for giving American government protection to the Wrangell-St. Elias region in July 1942. He and his Canadian counterpart, T.A. Crerer, worked closely together to duplicate this protection in the Canadian Kluane region. In 1943, 25,000 square km in this southwest corner of the Yukon were declared a Game Sanctuary, and on February 22, 1972, 88% of the Game Sanctuary was declared the Kluane National Park Reserve. Full National Park status will depend on future native land claim settlements. The park is largely inaccessible, except for fly-ins or by hardened hikers. Very few "easy" hikes into the park exist. This displeases some, including residents of Kluane country. Lobbying is under way to open up the park with more roads, more paved parking, more "easy" access for those who do not possess hiking boots, more drivable view-points overlooking those spectacular glaciers, and more economic park spin-offs. The park is one of the last great wilderness areas in the world; which it would no-longer be if some of the "developments" came to pass. It would be a permanent loss for us all.

Note: All overnight hikers need to register either at the Visitor Centre in Haines Junction, or at the Sheep Mountain Visitor Centre, 71.5 km / 44.4 miles north of Haines Junction. Topographic maps can be bought in Whitehorse. Fees for the Kathleen Lake area are $8.60 per party. Back country registration cost $10.75 per party.

For those needing more information about Kluane Park visit, write, call or fax: Kluane National Park, Box 5494, Haines Junction, Yukon, Y0B 1L0. Tel. 634-7201 fax 634-7208.

About 18 of the established trails into the park may be considered short to very long day-hikes and a further dozen or so are 2 to 14 day-long hikes. Off trail hikes can go anywhere, but wilderness hiking experience is extremely important. Both Visitor Centres have all the information needed. Cross country skiing trips are permitted anywhere, but mountain biking is only allowed on the Alsek Trail and the Mush Lake Road Trail.

Tatshenshini- Alsek Wilderness Park

Haines Junction is also the headquarters for the **Tatshenshini- Alsek Wilderness Park**, created in 1993. The "Tat" is not only famous for its scenery and wildlife viewing, but especially for its whitewater rafting and kayaking. Permits are required to float the two river systems. Local rafting companies organize trips, but bookings need to be done well in advance. In addition to the National Park Centre in Haines Junction, information about the "Tat" can be obtained from BC Parks in Vancouver or Park Services in Alaska.

The Visitor Reception Centre (Tel. 634-2345) has interesting exhibits, displays and audiovisuals on the National Park. The Reception Centre is open daily only in summer, but the administration offices are open year-round.

New for 1997 is a new fee structure for guided walking tours into the park increasing from $3 to $5. The Canadian Federal Government also is considering incorporating possible rescue costs into the price of National Park admission. For example, all back country hikers might have to pay from $3 to $5 extra to cover the costs for a rescue, or it might be optional to purchase insurance with those few unlucky ones paying the full cost of rescue.

HAINES ROAD

This highway has three numbers: in the Yukon it's Highway #3, in BC it's Highway #4, and in Alaska it is hwy #7 - all these numbers for a mere 246 km / 152 miles! Starting out in Haines Junction it is km / mile "0" at the junction with the Alaska Highway in the centre of the village.

km 1 / mile 0.6 A bridge over the Dezadeash River. The river flows into the Alsek River, and finally into the Pacific near Yakutat, Alaska. The Dezadeash River is a class I paddling river between Dezadeash Lake back to this bridge. The river flows past Champagne, on the Alaska Highway. It is a four to five day trip over a distance of about 150 km / 93 miles. After the bridge, the river becomes wilder as it enters Kluane Park, where river permits are required.

km 4.5 / mile 2.8 Rest stop with commanding view over Haines Junction.

km 7.2 / mile 4.5 Auriol Trailhead into Kluane Park is a 19 km / 12 mile loop trail for either a long day hike or overnight trip. There is good cross country skiing if there is enough snow. The trail was established in 1983, and named after Vincent Auriol, former President of France.

km 13.2 / mile 8.2 Quill Creek Trailhead. A pleasant two to three day round trip hike over 29 km / 18 miles. The trail takes the hiker into the Auriol Range, and is named for the many porcupines here.

km 20 / mile 12.4 Rest stop with view over Kathleen Lake.

km 26.4 / mile 16.4 Kathleen Lake Lodge. Tel. 634-2319. Open summer only. Service station with a six room motel and restaurant / cafe. Fishing supplies and licences. Open 8 a.m. - 10 p.m.

km 27 / mile 16.8 Kathleen Lake National Park Campground and Day Use Area. 41 RV and tent sites with water, washrooms and firewood, campfire programs and boat launch. $8.60 per site.

- Cottonwood Trail. The trail offers over 100 km / 62 miles of constantly changing scenery. Allow for up to a week, and remember that a back country permit is required.

km 27.2 / mile 16.9 The "Cabin" B&B. Tel. 634-2626. Five self-contained cabins with central sanitary facilities.

km 40.8 / mile 25.4 Dalton Trail Lodge. Tel. and Fax 667-1099. Accommodation for 25 guests, cafe, boat rental, guided trips.

km 44.7 / mile 27.7 Rock Glacier Trail. An easy 0.8 km / 0.5 miles each way. A self-guided trail for all ages and abilities, leads to the unique remains of a former glacier.

km 51.3 / mile 31.9 Dezadeash Lake Territorial Government Campground. 20 RV and tent sites, boat launch, fishing. $8 per site. The highway follows the lake-shore for almost 15 km / 9.3 miles. The name could be a Chilkat term for "lake of the big winds"; which is a very accurate description of the often stormy lake. The canoe trip mentioned earlier via the Dezadeash River back to Haines Junction can commence here. Plan for an early start to get away from the often strong afternoon winds. There is 10 km / 6.2 miles of lake paddling on the first day.

km 54.4 / mile 33.8 Dezadeash Lodge. Closed in 1994, and might re-open by 1998.

- Mush Lake Trail. The trail begins behind the lodge on an old mining road. There is good mountain biking and an easy ski trail. The trail continues to Goatherd Mountain - an 8 to 10 day hike; about 60 km / 37 miles one-way. Both Mush Lake and Bates Lake need to be traversed by canoe. Check with wilderness tour operators to arrange transport.

km 60.5 / mile 37.6 St. Elias Lake Trailhead is a very popular and well maintained summer and winter trail. It is 4 km / 2.5 miles one-way to a beautifully situated lake. There are tent spots at the lake for overnighters.

km 64.4 / mile 40 Turn-off for Klukshu village. It is 0.8 km / 0.5 miles on gravel to this traditional native fish camp, where salmon is still being caught with fish traps. No services are available, unless the museum is open. The National Park boundary is here.

km 77.5 / mile 48.2 Alsek Mountain Range Viewpoint.

km 83.8 / mile 52.1 Turn-off to Dalton Post. There are no services at this former way-station. The Dalton Trail connected the coast with the interior. It is a steep, windy road and not recommended for motorhomes.

km 85.8 / mile 53.3 Rest stop with great views over Kluane Range.

km 89.1 / mile 55.4   Million Dollar Falls Government Campground. 27 RV / campsites, 8 tenting sites, shelter, hiking trails, and fishing. The campground is 1.1 km / 6.8 miles off highway.

km 103.1 / mile 64.1   Highway Maintenance Camp. Emergency help only. Border between the Yukon and British Columbia.

km 147.7 / mile 91.8   Chilkat Pass rest stop. At 1065 m / 3493 feet, this is the highest elevation on the Haines Road. The summit is almost constantly wind blown, and drifting snow can quickly close the road in winter. It is great cross-country skiing and snow machine terrain. The Pass was once guarded by the Tlingit, in order to protect their trading routes to the interior.

km 155.5 / mile 96.5   Three Guardsmen Pass. Elevation 980 m / 3215 feet. A mountain by the same name is to the southwest, with an elevation of 1920 m / 6300 feet.

km 178.3 / mile 110.8   Canada Customs. Open year-round daily from 8 a.m. to midnight, Pacific time.

km 179 / mile 111.2   US Customs. Open year-round daily from 7 a.m. to 11 p.m., Alaska time. Restrooms.

km 190.5 / mile 118.4   33 Mile Roadhouse. Closed Tue. Service station, cafe and store. Pay phone.

km 194.2 / mile 120.7   Entering Alaska Chilkat Bald Eagle Reserve. This 194.3 square km / 48,000 acre reserve was established in 1982 to protect the 3000 to 4000 eagles that gather here to feast on chum salmon between October and February. For more information about the Reserve and eagles look in the Gateway Chapter.

km 200 / mile 124.3   Mosquito Lake State Recreation Campground. 10 RV and tent sites, water, tables, toilets. US$6 per site.

km 213.4 / mile 132.6   Bald Eagle Viewing Area. Do not drive and look for eagles at the same time!

km 229.2 / mile 142.4 You are leaving (or entering) the Bald Eagle Reserve.

km 244 / mile 151.6   Haines. For information about Haines, see previous section.

We now return to Haines Junction to continue our road description from there toward the Alaska border and the first Alaskan town of Tok.

ALASKA HIGHWAY FROM HAINES JUNCTIONS TO TOK, ALASKA

Distances from Haines Junction are: **Anchorage** 1007 km or 626 miles. **Fairbanks** 822 km or 511 miles.

km 1635.3 / mile 1016   Junction of Alaska Highway and Haines Road in centre of Haines Junction.

km 1636.5 / mile 1016.9   Alcan Fuels. Tel. 634-2268, open year-round. Service station, propane, towing and repairs. Next door is the **Stardust Motel and RV park.** Telephone 634-2591. German spoken.

km 1639.8 / mile 1018.9   Kluane Park Warden Quarters. No visitor information.

km 1644 / mile 1021.6 Mackintosh Lodge. Tel. 634-2301. Motel and RV parking, tenting, restaurant, cafe. Wilderness trips on horseback, fishing trips and heli-base.

- Alsek Trailhead. A 29 km / 18 mile two - three day hike. Mountain bikes allowed.

km 1660 / mile 1031.5 Bear Creek Summit is the second highest point between Whitehorse and Fairbanks, at an elevation of 1004.3 m / 3291 feet.

- Mt. Decoeli Trailhead. It is a long day hike over 15 km / 9.3 miles return to the summit of Mt. Decoeli, at 2331 m / 7650 feet. This prominent peak was named in 1950 after a member of the 1913 International Boundary Survey Party.

km 1692.5 / mile 1051.7 Rest stop with interpretive signs about the geological history of Kluane Lake, the local native tribes and the history of Silver City.

km 1693 / mile 1052 Access to the ghost town of Silver City via a 5 km / 3 mile gravel road. Between 1904 and 1924, the town was a trading post and a rest stop on the wagon road from Whitehorse to the gold fields of Kluane Lake.

- Kluane B&B. Mobile radio 2M 3924 (call "0" operator) near Silver City on Kluane Lake.

km 1698 / mile 1056 Trans North Helicopters. Tel. 841-5809. Heli-base for flights into Kluane National Park. Kluane Lake Lodge nearby has been closed since 1994.

km 1703.4 / mile 1058.4 Slims River East Trailhead. A four to five day hike over 30 km / 18.6 miles; return to the Kaskawulsh Glacier. A narrow gravel road off the Alcan, on the east side of Slims River, can be driven for about 6.5 km / 4 miles to a small parking lot. The hike itself is easy. There are two more trailheads here.

- Kluane Plateau Trail is a long day hike for experienced hikers, over 14 km / 8.7 miles to a plateau overlooking Kluane Lake.

- Vulkan Creek Trail goes to the headwaters of Vulkan Creek, within beautiful alpine country. It is a long, 20 km / 12.5 mile hike, for experienced hikers only.

km 1705 / mile 1059.4 Slims River Bridge. Slim was a packhorse that drowned here in 1903. The owner named the river in honor of his horse.

km 1706.8 / mile 1060.6 Sheep Mountain National Park Visitor Centre is open daily in May and September from 9 a.m. to 5 p.m., and is open June to August from 9 a.m. to 6:30 p.m. Hiking permits are for sale here; the only other services are parking and toilet facilities. Various hiking trails originate from the Visitor Centre, either keeping you busy for a few hours or a few days, if not weeks. The **Slims River West Trail** goes to Observation Mountain, overlooking Kaskawulsh Glacier. The much shorter **Bullion Creek Trail** leads to old gold mines and a couple of trails which circle Sheep Mountain, with a good chance to observe Dall sheep. Wardens may discourage hiking on Sheep Mountain during lambing season in spring.

km 1708.6 / mile 1061.7 Soldier Summit. The Alcan Highway was officially opened here with a ribbon-cutting ceremony on November 20, 1942, while a blizzard was blasting the summit.

km 1711.8 / mile 1064 The Bayshore Lodge. Tel. and Fax 841-4551. Motel with RV parking and tenting, restaurant and cafe. Helicopter base.

km 1717.5 / mile 1067.3 Cottonwood Park Campground. Tel. 634-2739, Fax 634-2429. 30 hook-ups, 40 lake-shore sites, tenting, store, mini golf, horseshoe pits and hot tub rental. Mobile radio 2M 3972.

km 1724.3 / mile 1071.5 Congdon Creek Government Campground. 78 RV and tent sites, shelters, playground, fishing, hiking.

- Congdon Creek Trailhead. A two or three day hike over about 30 km / 18.6 miles, rounding Sheep Mountain back to the Park Centre.

There are many more excellent hikes for all abilities. Consider being flown into a remote corner of the park, then either walking out or arranging for a heli-pickup at a different location.

km 1743 / mile 1083 The village of Destruction Bay has a population of about 50. The first buildings here were army construction barracks, which were destroyed by strong winds shortly after they were erected; hence the name - nothing more sinister than that! **RCMP:** 634-5555 (Haines Junction) call collect or dial 1-403-667-5555. **Medical and Ambulance:** 841-4444 or dial 1-403-667-3333. **Fire:** 841-2221. Listen to CBDL (105.1 FM) for weather and road conditions, the same hours as in Haines Junction. There are two lodges / RV parks and camping in Destruction Bay. Boat rentals, fishing trips and flights into Kluane are available.

Where to stay:

Sehja Services & RV Park. Tel. and Fax 841-4807. 24 RV pull-through sites, some free dry tenting, showers, coin laundry, service station with store and cafe.

Talbot Arm. Tel. 841-4461, Fax 841-4804. Open year-round motel, RV parking and tenting with store, showers and coin laundry. Service station with car and tire repairs, restaurant, lounge.

km 1753.9 / mile 1089.8 Halfbreed Creek Trailhead. If driving, turn south onto a narrow gravel road that will continue for about 5 km / 3 miles before turning into a hiking trail. This is an overnight return trek of about 30 km / 18 miles, to alpine Cache Lake, with some rough walking.

km 1759 / mile 1093 The village of Burwash Landing was established in 1904, after gold was found in nearby creeks. It was built by two brothers, Louis and Eugene Jacquot. This outpost trading centre was first called Jacquot Post, but it was then renamed Burwash Landing after Lachlin T. Burwash who, in the '40s, was the local mining recorder. All emergency telephone numbers are the same as in Destruction Bay.

Where to stay

Burwash Landing Resort. Tel. 841-4441, Fax 841-4040. Full service station, open 24 hours. 32 unit motel ($25 and up) with restaurant and lounge, RV parking, tenting, boat launch and rentals, and fishing trips. Gold panning and glacier flights can be arranged.

Duke River Trading Co. Tel. and Fax 841-4000. RV parking with car repairs and welding. Coin laundry, showers, post office, general store with fresh produce and meat. Open daily 9 a.m. to 9 p.m. during summer.

Kluane Dalan RV Park and Campground. Tel. 841-4274, Fax 841-5900. 1 km / 0.6 miles off the Alaska Highway on Kluane Lake. 25 private campsites. Owned and operated by the Kluane First Nation.

What to do and not to miss:

The Kluane Museum of Natural History. Tel. 841-5561, Fax 841-5605. There are outstanding exhibits about native aboriginal artifacts and costumes, as well as exhibits on wildlife, minerals and natural history. There is a store selling handicrafts and souvenirs. It is open daily in summer from 9 a.m. to 9 p.m. Adult, $3.50; child, $1.25 and a family, $6.50. See the "world's largest" gold pan, measuring 8 m/28 feet in length.

Our Lady of the Holy Rosary Catholic church and school was built in 1944. Periodically, services are held in the church (please inquire at 841-5411), but the school and the living quarters have been turned into a museum, where there is a video presentation, and a box for voluntary donations.

km 1761 / mile 1094.2 Yukon Government Airstrip. Elevation 806 m / 2643 feet. The length of the gravel runway is 1829 m / 6000 feet.

km 1768.8 / mile 1099 Donjek River Trailhead and Duke River Bridge. The turn-off is at the west side of the bridge onto a barely passable old mining road. This is a strenuous, almost 100 km / 62 mile long hike, which can take up to 14 days. A loop trail skirts the Donjek Glacier for over 10 km / 6 miles.

km 1787 / mile 1110.5 Abandoned nickel mine that was in operation in 1972-73.

km 1795.3 / mile 1115.5 The Alaska Highway interpretive panel honours all who died during construction of the highway, including 1st Lieut. Roland Small of the 18th Engineers Regiment, who died nearby in a jeep accident.

km 1797.2 / mile 1118 Kluane Wilderness Village. Tel. 841-4141, open year-round / 24 hours. Motel, cabins, RV parking, tenting with restaurant, lounge, service station with repairs and welding shop, groceries.

km 1816 / mile 1128.5 Rest stop with panoramic view of the Donjek River valley and the Icefield Range of St. Elias Mountain.

km 1820 / mile 1130.8 Donjek River Bridge. Donjek is a native term for a pea vine. The river is a major tributary of the silt-laden White River. Canoe float trips into the Yukon River, and on to Dawson City, are possible from either Kluane Lake and Kluane River or via the Donjek and White Rivers. The starting point for going down the Kluane River can be anywhere along the lakeshore. It is about 500 km or 310 miles to Dawson City - 90 km on the Kluane, 160 km on the Donjek, 120 km on the White and 120 km on the Yukon. From this bridge it's about 450 km / 280 miles to Dawson City. Class III paddling skills are required, especially when the water runs high. Due to the nature of these rivers- being very wide and braided with countless log jams, and water the colour of milk coffee- they are not very popular for the average river traveller. However, all three river runs have their fascinating aspects, especially when it comes to wildlife viewing, and every year more people get to Dawson City this way.

km 1844.4 / mile 1146 Edith Creek Bridge. Try gold panning here. You won't get rich, but a few "colours" might end up in your gold pan - if you know the techniques of panning!

BUYING A GOLD PAN

Buy your gold pan in a hardware store and not in a souvenir shop. Both the metal and plastic pans will do the job, but the metal pans definitely are more authentic - you need to red-hot burn them out! New metal gold pan's are greased to prevent them from rusting while still on the store shelf. Gold will not 'stick' to an oily surface but will float straight out of the pan again - as a matter of fact - the rustier a gold pan the better! If you are unsuccessful as a miner, those metal pans double up nicely as frying pans or anti-bear noise makers!

Gold

km 1844.8 / mile 1146.4 Pine Valley Motel and cafe. Tel. and Fax 862-7407. Motel units, cabins, RV parking and camping, service station with most repairs.

km 1853 / mile 1151.4 Lake Creek Government Campground. 27 RV and tent sites with shelter, fishing and boating.

km 1865 / mile 1159 Pickhandle Lake.. Very good fishing for pike, grayling, and whitefish.

km 1872.6 / mile 1164 Koidern River Lodge. Tel. 862-7402. Open 24 hours, 11 room lodge, unserviced RV parking, tenting, cafe, service station, groceries, mineral and rock display.

km 1876 / mile 1167 Bear Flats Lodge. Tel. 862-7401. Motel, RV and campsites, cafe, year-round service station with minor repairs and welding.

km 1881 / mile 1169 White River Motor Inn. Tel. and Fax 862-7408. Motel, RV and tent sites, restaurant, cafe. Service station has jet B and aviation fuel; open year-round.

- White River Bridge. It is about 320 km/200 miles to float to Dawson City. Countless log jams and driftwood make this "white" water river somewhat scary. Superior paddling skills are required. The White River was named in 1850, by Robert Campbell, trader for the Hudson Bay Company, who was the first White man to see it. He named it after its colour, which comes from a tremendous amount of ash deposited after a huge volcanic eruption about 900-1100 AD. Over 427 cubic km (165 cubic miles) of ash were dumped into the White River Valley, but silt - sandy run-off from glaciers, contributes to the gritty water. It has been estimated that by the time the White River joins the Yukon River, over 300 tons of silt each day are being washed into the Yukon, turning this formerly clear river into a rather grey one. The Chilkats called this river "Sand River". The Tanana People called it "Copper River" and the natives of the Stick Tribe called it "Yu-kon Hini", which probably means something like "Not-Clear River".

km 1912.8 / mile 1188.8 Snag Junction Government Campground, 15 RV and Campsites, shelter and small boat launch. A non-maintained gravel road leads to a former weather station and emergency air field at Snag. It was built in 1942, in part because of the airlift to Russia supporting their war effort. On February 3, 1947, the coldest temperature ever recorded in Canada was measured here at -63°C / -81°F.

BEAVER CREEK

km 1934 / mile 1202 Beaver Creek. This tiny community of about 100 people is the westernmost settlement in Canada. **RCMP:** 862-5555, if no answer dial 1-403-667-5555. **Ambulance:** 862-3333, if no answer dial 1-403-667-3333. **Medical:** 862-4444. **Road reports & weather:** listen to CBDM (690 AM) or 93.5 FM, at the same time as in Haines Junction.

The area around Beaver Creek, on both sides of the border, has been prospected for gold since 1904. Rich finds were located just across the border in the Chisane Region. The settlement of Beaver Creek was founded in 1955, and a post office was built in 1958. In 1983, Canada Customs was relocated 3.5 km / 2.2 miles closer to the border. Beaver Creek was one of two places, along the entire length of the highway, where two highway construction teams converged. On October 20, 1942, bulldozer operator Refines Sims, working south, met bulldozer operator Alfred Jalufka, who was working his machine north. One was from Philadelphia and the other from Texas.

Services in Beaver Creek:

The Visitor Reception Centre is open daily from 9 a.m. to 9 p.m. between the months of May and September. Tel. 862-7321. Fax 862-7614. The centre has a book full of dried wildflowers from all over the Territory. The Visitor Radio CKYN Yukon Gold on 96.1 FM is broadcast from this centre, with information concerning the Yukon. There is a public swimming pool in town and a Catholic mission church of "Our Lady of Grace", with services held every Sunday in summer. **Banking** with Toronto Dominion is available on Tues. from 10 to 2 p.m. and Thurs. from 1 to 3 p.m.

Where to stay:

Beaver Creek 1202 Motor Inn. Tel. 862-7600, Fax 862-7601. Toll-free from the Yukon 1-800-661-0540 and from Alaska 1-800-764-7601. Motel, restaurant and lounge, service station; open year-round, free RV parking.

Idas Motel. Tel. 862-7223. Fax 862-7221. Newly built motel with free RV parking and free camping. Service station with restaurant and lounge, open year-round.

Westmark Inn Beaver Creek. Tel. 862-7501, Fax 862-7902, toll-free from US 1-800-544-0970, from Canada 1-800-999-2570. 174 room hotel with RV parking, restaurant, cafe and lounge. Dinner theatre with shows daily during the summer season; service station with store and mini golf.

The Yukon Area Code (403) will change to (867) October 1997.

km 1937.5 / mile 1203.5 Beaver Creek Canada Customs and Immigration. Open 24 hours daily, year-round, tel. 862-7230. **Beaver Creek Airstrip,** tel. 862-7282. Elevation 649 m / 2129 feet. Length of gravel runway 1140 m / 3740 feet. No fuel.

km 1966.1 / mile 1221.5 Yukon and Alaska Border. The highway crosses the 141st meridian. Rest stop with an observation deck and information panels. The 6 m / 20 foot wide cut that marks the border was cleared between 1907 and 1912, and sections of it are periodically kept clear by the International Boundary Commission. The swath continues on a straight line for 966 km / 600 miles from the Arctic Ocean, at Demarcation, to Mount St. Elias in the Wrangell Mountains.

km 1966.3 / mile 1221.8 Port Alcan US Customs Border Station. Open 24 hours every day, year-round. The pay phone accepts collect calls and credit cards. Rest rooms and a post office. Tel. 1-907-774-2242. In emergencies call 1-907-774-2252.

km 1972.2 / mile 1225.5 Border City Lodge. Motel and restaurant. Tel. 907-774-2211.

km 1977.8 / mile 1229 Log Cabin Alaska Visitor Center. Information about Alaska, open daily, 7 a.m. to 7 p.m., summer only.

km 2020.5 / mile 1249.3 Deadman Lake US Forestry Campground. 2.4 km / 1.5 miles off the highway. No drinking water, 18 RV and tent sites, boat launch, swimming and fishing.

km 2011.8 / mile 1250.1 Rest stop with picnic tables.

km 2017.4 / mile 1253.6 Frontier Surplus RV Park. Tel. 907-778-2274. Store with military surplus goods. State Highway Maintenance Camp. No services.

km 2022.5 / mile 1256.7 State Lakeview Campground, 8 small sites. No large RVs.

km 2034.2 / mile 1264 Naabia Niign Campground. Tel. or Fax 907-778-2297. RV park and camping, grocery store and a native craft shop; gas.

Junction to the village of Northway. This community of about 400 is 11 km / 7 miles off the Alaska Highway. All basic services.

A moose crossing the Alaska Highway.

km 2094.8 / mile 1301.7 Tetlin Junction. The Taylor Highway #5 branches off the Alcan to the small Alaskan Yukon River village of Eagle, and to Dawson City in the Yukon.

- 40 Mile Roadhouse service station. Tel. 1-907-883-5120. Car and tire repairs, towing, and car wash.

__Remember that the Alaska / Yukon Border to Dawson City is only open from 8 a.m. to 8 p.m. Alaska Time.__

TOWN OF TOK

km 2115 / mile 1314.5 Town of Tok. Tok has a population of 1250 and offers all services. **Alaska State Troopers** call 911 or 1-907-883-5111. **Ambulance** call 911 or 1-907-883-2300. **Public Health Clinic**, call 1-907-883-4101. **Tok Mainstreet Visitor Center**. Tel. 1-907-883-5775 / 5887. Open daily May 1st to October 1st from 7 a.m. to 9 p.m. You can't miss this grand log building, offering art shows, trip planning and free coffee.

Tok is home to a **Public Lands Information Center** which sells State Park Passes with all the information you might need. It is open May to September, daily from 8 a.m. to 8 p.m. and winter from 8 a.m. to 4:30 p.m, or write to Box 359, Tok, AK 99780. Tel. 883-5667. There is an **Alaska Youth Hostel** just outside Tok. Tel. 883-3745.

Distances from Tok: Dawson City 301 km / 187 mi.; **Eagle** 278 km / 173 mi.; **Inuvik** 1084 km / 674 mi.; **Los Angeles** 5445 km / 3384 mi.; **Miami** 8217 km / 5106 mi.; **Whitehorse** 637 km / 396 mi.; **Anchorage** 527 km / 328 mi.; **Fairbanks** 331 km / 206 mi.; **Skagway** 811 km / 504 mi; **Haines** 719 km / 447 mi.

Whitehorse

The S.S. Klondike resting on the Yukon River banks in Whitehorse.

WHITEHORSE

Introduction

Before 1957, the name Whitehorse was spelled White Horse and plenty of stories exist about the origin of the name. Before Miles Canyon was dammed just upstream from the city, a rough set of rapids made life difficult for early fur traders and prospectors. At least one of the first river runners must have been reminded of a white horse's mane while watching those foaming white waves rush through the narrow canyon. The first prospectors came across the Chilkoot Trail and down the Yukon River in 1880-81. Having braved the rapids, they may have paused for a few days where Whitehorse is located now, to collect themselves and dry their belongings.

Early settlements during the madness of the 1897-98 Gold Rush were on the east side of town, where the suburb of Riverdale is stretched out now. It was in Riverdale where,

The S.S. Klondike. Photo courtesy of J. Joyce.

the following year, roads and building sites were surveyed and blasted out of the wilderness. The west side of the river, where downtown Whitehorse is today, was largely granted to the White Pass & Yukon Railroad for their terminus. It was then called "Closeleigh", after the Close Brothers, the main financiers of the railroad project. The name Whitehorse was given to the growing town on April 21, 1900. In July 1900, the railroad between Skagway and Whitehorse was completed, and river boats picked up where the railroad tracks ended, giving the town a permanent lease on life. Until construction of the Alaska Highway in 1942-43, Whitehorse never had a population of more than 500, as most people moved quickly on toward the gold fields of the Klondike. The construction of the Alcan changed all that. The town's population expanded to over 8000 for a few years, but in the 1950s decreased to about 3000.

On March 31, 1953, Whitehorse became the Capital of the Territory. In 1974, the city limit was expanded from 6.9 square km (2.7 square miles) to 421 square km (162 square miles), creating one of the largest metropolitan areas in North America. The population now approaches 24,000; which is about two-thirds of Yukon's total. The next largest town is Dawson City (the former capital), with about 2000 people; followed by Watson Lake with roughly 1850. Another 13 settlements spread across the Yukon have an average population of about 370 each. Yukon's population as of 1996 was about 32,000, sharing a total of 483,450 square km or 186,660 square miles. This makes the Yukon somewhat larger than California, which has a thousand times the population!

Most of the city spreads out west of the Yukon River. At this point the river is in its infancy; it is quite narrow with very clear-blue waters. The remainder of the city climbs out of this wedge-like valley, up and over steep embankments into the forested hills beyond. The airport is situated, high and dry, on the embankment overlooking the river valley. For those flying into Whitehorse, the great sensation persists that the runway might drop off the cliff at any moment, and onto this blue ribbon of water stretching toward the horizon. In 1920, the International Airport was just a clearing in the woods.

There are 45 hotels, motels, B&Bs and one private hostel in the city. There are numerous restaurants with all types of fast food from a "Bistro Saigon", to an "Imaginary Horse". There are quite a few gourmet and fine dining places to satisfy one's hunger pangs; fifty-three restaurants at the latest count. There is an indoor swimming pool, four movie screens, and various theatre groups, shopping centres, health food stores and just about any other service one might desire.

A new **Yukon Territory Visitor Centre** has been opened downtown at 2nd and Lambert, or call, visit or write to **Tourism Yukon** P.O. Box 2703, Whitehorse, Yukon, Canada, Y1A 2C6. Tel. 667-5340, Fax 667-3546. Their offices are located in the Visitor Centre. The Whitehorse **Chamber of Commerce** office is located downtown at 302 Steele, in a pleasant looking log house, open year-round from 9 a.m. to 5 p.m. Tel. 667-7545 or fax to 667-4507. For specific information about Whitehorse, call the **city office** at 668-8687. See the Alaska Highway chapter for important phone numbers and listings of businesses along the Alcan in the Whitehorse area.

LODGING

Hostel / Hotel:

Roadhouse Inn & Saloon. Tel. 667-2594, Fax 668-7291. On 2nd Ave. close to the Greyhound bus depot. Budget motel and hotel rooms from $40. Hostel bunks for $19 per person. There are 3 rooms with 4 beds each and 2 rooms with 2 beds each.

Motels/Hotels:

Highcountry Inn. Tel. 667-4471, Fax 6676457, or 1-800-554-4471. Full service hotel, next to the indoor pool on 4th Ave., from $36 to $80.

Best Western Gold Rush Inn. Tel. 668-4500, Fax 668-7432. Full service hotel, 411 Main Street, from $60. Toll-free from Yukon, Alberta, BC, NWT 1-800-661-0539. Toll-free from Alaska 1-800-764-7604.

Edgewater Hotel. Tel. 667-2572, Fax 668-3014. Full service hotel, 101 Main Street, from $65. Near the Yukon River in the down town area.

Westmark Klondike Inn. Tel. 668-4747. Fax 667-7939. Full service hotel at 2288 2nd Ave, summer only. For toll-free reservations, use the numbers below.

Westmark Whitehorse Hotel. Tel. 668-4700, Fax 668-2789. Full service hotel, at 2nd and Wood. Toll-free reservations for both above hotels: Western Canada 1-800-999-2570 and USA 1-800-544-0970. Rooms for about $100.

Yukon Inn. Tel. 667-2527, Fax 668-7643. Toll-free 1-800-661-0454. Full service hotel at 4220 4th Ave. Costs approximately $100.

Town and Mountain Hotel. Tel. 668-7644, Fax 668-5822. Toll-free call 1-800-661-0522. CAA/AAA approved, 401 Main Street, from $79.

Regina Hotel. Tel. 667-7801, Fax 668-6075. Full service hotel, 102 Wood Street, from $66. Heated underground parking.

Stop In Family Hotel. Tel. 668-5558, Fax 668-5568. Close to shopping centre, 314 Ray Street, from $60. Hot tub and sauna for guests use.

Stratford Motel. Tel. 667-4243, Fax 668-7432. On corner of Jarvis and 4th. Toll-free numbers are the same as of the Best Western Gold Rush Inn, rates from $59. Convenient location and drive-up rooms. Norcan car rental operates out of the motel.

Bonanza Inn. Tel 668-4545, Fax 668-6538. 4109 4th Ave, rates from $55.

Two-O-Two Motor Inn. Tel. 668-4567, Fax 667-6154. 206 Jarvis Street, rates from $45.

Chilkoot Trail. Tel. 668-4190. On 4th Ave, rates from $50.

Capital Hotel. Tel. 667-2565, Fax 668-4651. 103 Main Street, rates from $50.

Pioneer Inn. Tel. 668-2828, Fax 668-2848. 2nd Ave., from $45.

"The 98". Tel. 667-2641. 110 Wood Street, from $45.

Not to forget those five motels and hotels next to the airport and along the Alaska Highway, all of which have been mentioned in the Alaska Highway chapter.

Bed and Breakfasts in Whitehorse:

Town and Country B&B. Tel. 633-3523. Fax 667-6442, no smoking.

The Drifters B&B. Tel. 633-5419, from $55, no smoking.

Highland Home B&B. Tel. 633-5804, Fax 668-5705, from $65; open year-round.

Up North B&B. Tel. 667-7905, Fax 667-6334, from $50. Next to the River; canoe rental, German spoken.

Scandia B&B. Tel. 633-5421, from $50, no smoking.

Hawkins House B&B. Tel. 668-7638, Fax 668-7632, from $85. French and German spoken.

Casey's B&B. Tel. 668-7481, from $70. Downtown.

International House B&B. Tel. 633-5490, Fax 668-4751. From $55. Off the Alaska Highway. No smoking.

Downtown B&B. Tel. 668-5293.

Bakers B&B. Tel. 633-2308, from $45; 3 km from the city in Porter Creek.

Ballymena B&B. Tel. 633-6010. Outside town, dog sled rides.

Barbs B&B. Tel. 667-4104. In suburb of Riverdale.

Country Blue Bed B&B. Tel. 667-7095. In Pineridge subdivision.

Evergreen B&B. Tel. 633-2747, Fax 633-3322, from $55. In Porter Creek. E-mail: jwebster@yknet.yk.ca.

Flora Danica B&B. Tel. 668-2806. In Granger subdivision.

Four Seasons B&B. Tel. 667-2161. Fax 667-2171. In Riverdale, French spoken.

Garlands B&B. Tel. 633-2173, Fax 633-4313. In Porter Creek.

Haekel Hill B&B. Tel. 633-5625, Fax 633-5630. Overlooking Yukon River in Porter Creek. E-mail: bear@yknet.yk.ca. Open year-round. Canoe and bike rental.

Blue Gables B&B. Tel. 668-2840, Fax 668-7120. Bike Rental.

Valley Magic B&B. Tel. 667-2132, in Riverdale.

Lou's B&B. Tel. 663-6575, in Riverdale.

Diane's B&B. Tel. and fax 663-4592, from $60. Near the Takhini Hot Springs, canoe rental.

Hearts Content B&B. Tel. 667-4972. Outdoor hot tub and no smoking; 20 min. by car from Whitehorse.

Do you want to **rent a cabin** anywhere in the Yukon? 'Wild Treats Vacation Properties' rents cabins for a minimum of one week. Call or fax them at 633-3322 for their catalogue.

The only **camping** or tenting place within walking distance (1 km) from downtown is the beautifully located **Robert Service Campground**; on Robert Service Way next to the Yukon River, with 48 walk-in tenting sites; open May to September, $11 per site. Tel. 668-3721, Fax 667-6334. A perfect place to leave from by canoe, going down the Yukon River to the Gold Fields of the Klondike. All RV parks have been mentioned in the Alaska Highway section of this book.

RESTAURANTS

Most restaurants are located within the immediate downtown area. All larger hotels operate one, if not two, restaurants and at least one lounge on their premises. The others are divided between the usual fare of fast food places, hip places with organic soups, and gourmet dining places, which will satisfy the most discriminating eater. The quality of food ranges from not bad to quite good - just like the prices. Only the downtown Tim Horton's, on 2nd Avenue, is open 24 hours a day. The author would like to highlight a few of them because of their decor, atmosphere, imaginative food, AND their non-smoking policy.

No Pop Sandwich Shop. Corner 4th and Steele. Tel. 668-3227. Not much to look at from the outside, but the inside is cozy and small, with local art on the wall, and well prepared food. No smoking.

Talisman Restaurant. Opposite CIBC Bank on 2nd. Tel. 667-2736. Looks much better from the inside than the outside. Large non-smoking section with local art on the wall, food from all over, and very attentive service.

Pandas Fine Dining. 212 Main Street. Tel. 667-2632. One of the finer eating places in town, from schnitzel to salmon steak. German spoken.

Angelo Restaurant. Strickland and 2nd, on the 2nd floor. Tel. 668-6266. Greek-Italian food with good views.

Tung Lock Seafood Restaurant. 404 Wood Street. Tel. 667-6138. Chinese and Vietnamese cuisine.

Sam and Andy's. 506 Main Street. Tel. 668-6994. Mexican and Canadian food. Bar.

Mexican Deli on corner Hanson and Third. Open Mon. to Sat. from 10 to 5:30 p.m. Tel. 668-5858.

Parthenan Restaurant. On 204 B Main Street. Greek-Canadian Food. Tel. 668-4243

Chocolate Claim. 305 Strickland. Tel. 667-2202. Soups, salads and coffee bar, sweets. No smoking.

The Java Connection on Third Ave. is around the corner from the mail delivery office. Best cafe in town and perfectly brewed cappuccinos. Also cakes, soups and sandwiches. No smoking. Tel. 668-2196

The Blackstone Cafe & Midnight Sun Coffee Roasters. Wood and 3rd. Meals and coffee. Tel. 667-6598.

Dallas 2 for 1 Pizza. 1116 - 1st Ave. Tel. 633-3336. Open seven days from 4 p.m. to 1 a.m. Will deliver.

Klondike Rib and Salmon BBQ. Corner Second and Steele. Open only in summer. Tel. 667-7554.

The Deli - Sausage Factory. 203 Hanson Street. Tel. 667-7583. Specializing in imported European foods, and sausages made on the premises. Small eat-in section. Those wanting to travel the Yukon's river's, or wilderness hikers, can fax ahead to order packages of long-lasting food. Fax 633-4147.

Alpine Bakery. 411 Alexander Street. Tel. 668-6871. One cannot miss this large log structure. Their breads are some of the best outside Europe, baked with 100% certified organic ingredients. There are also different types of cheeses and locally made preserves made from Yukon berries. Local art is for sale. They will bake long-lasting breads for wilderness travellers, if ordered in advance. Fax them at 668-6101. Open Tuesday to Saturday from 10 a.m. to 5:30 p.m. Shorter hours in winter.

<u>Buying Food</u>: There are two large grocery stores almost next to each other. **Food Fair, in the Yukon Centre**, and the much larger **Extra Food, in the Qwanlin Mall** next door. Extra Food has a large bulk food selection, which river travellers might find convenient. The Canadian Superstore, in the Mall, carries no groceries, but instead has a wholesale section for bulk sweets - to keep those bears happy! The 'Wharf', opposite the High Country Inn on 4th Ave., sells fresh salmon, frozen lobster and any fish in between. Tel. 667-7473.

24 hour food stores: Riverdale Groceries on 2nd and Lowe near the Yukon River Bridge, and **Tags Food And Gas** next to the 'Golden Arches' on 4th Ave.

The liquor store is located in the Yukon Centre. There is a deposit payable on each beer or liquor bottle and can. Deposits can be returned at liquor stores Yukon-wide. Summer hours are: Thursday and Friday 9:30 a.m. to 8 p.m, other days until 7 p.m., closed Sunday. Hours open are reduced in winter. Off-sale beer and wine can be purchased in most saloons.

OTHER SERVICES

<u>Camping Equipment</u>:

Northern Outdoors on 208 Main Street. Tel. 667-4074.

Sportslodge, Hougen Centre on Main street. Tel. 668-6848.

Both Canadian Tire, and **Canadian Superstore** in the Qwanlin Mall have large selections of sports and camping gear. If time permits, call the **Mountain Equipment Co-op** store in Vancouver for their free catalogue: 1-800-663-2667.

<u>RV and Car Repairs</u>:

Philmar RV Service Centre. Parts and repairs. Tel. 668-6129. Mile 912 on the Alaska Highway.

Happy Daze RV Centre. Parts. Tel. 667-7069. 127 Copper Road.

Pine Creek Motors RV Repairs. Tel. 668-2958. Alaska Highway-Carcross Junction.

The Spring Shop. RV Parts and Service. Mile 922 Alaska Highway. Tel. 633-4712.

If you need help with your Volkswagen, try **John's Auto Repair**, 2052 2nd Ave., downtown. Tel. 668-4550. There are many car repair shops downtown on 4th Ave., with the **Canadian Tire** repair shop being the largest.

Drive-thru-Oil Change. On 411 Ogilvie Street. Enviro Lube is open Mon. to Sat. normal hours. Call 668-5823.

> **RV parking for extra large motor homes** in the down town area (no overnight parking allowed) is next to the Visitor Centre; or next to the Roadhouse Inn where Black St. meets 2nd; or the western end of Main St.

<u>Telephone:</u>

Area Codes: Yukon and western NWT, (403), **will change Oct. 1997 to (867)**. It is (250) anywhere in B.C., except it is (604) in the vicinity of Vancouver. Alaska is (907). **The first 3 digits of Inuvik's tel. numbers will change October 1997 from 979 to 777.** For information about toll-free 800 numbers (all 888 numbers are toll-free too) in the Yukon call 1-800-555-1212. **Credit card** calls (Visa and Mastercard) can be made by first dialing '0'. The newly built Visitor Centre might install a telephone booth where payment can be made after your call has been completed.

<u>Postal Service:</u>

In the Qwanlin Mall at the Coffee Tea and Spice store. Open during store hours. Fax number 668-4737.

At Main and 3rd, below Shoppers Drugmart. Fax number 668-5847.

Both postal outlets can send and receive faxes. From $1 per page, depending upon destination or origin. Both will keep faxed messages for about one week. Fax messages can also be send from most other postal outlets, hotels and copy stores.

The Delivery Centre for ALL General Delivery mail is at the Wood Street Delivery Centre, on Wood Street and the corner of Third Ave. It is open Monday to Friday from 8 a.m. - 6 p.m. No sale of postage stamps. Mail has to be addressed to you c/o General Delivery, Whitehorse, Yukon; Postal Code Y1A 3S7 for names from A to L and Y1A 3S8 for names from M to Z. For Postal Codes of other communities call 1-800-267-1133, for service in English; and 1-800-267-1122, for service in French.

<u>Banks:</u>

Five of Canada's major banks have branches in Whitehorse. **Canadian Imperial Bank of Commerce (CIBC)**. Tel. 667-2534 (toll-free 1-800-661-0412); **Royal Bank of Canada**. Tel. 667-6416; **Bank of Nova Scotia**. Tel. 667-6231; **Toronto Dominion (TD) Bank**. Tel. 668-5575; **Bank of Montreal.** Tel. 668-4200. All five banks are located along Main Street and all offer Instant Bank and a 24 hour Automated Teller Service accepting INTERAC and PLUS SYSTEM, <u>except the Bank of Montreal, which accepts INTERAC and CIRRUS. This means only the Bank of Montreal in Whitehorse</u> **(and only in Whitehorse)** <u>will accept MASTERCARD / EUROCARD for cash advances at their tellers or in their cash machines. This has led to many a crisis in places like Dawson City - trust me!</u> All Whitehorse banks are open Monday-Thursday from 9:30 a.m. to 4 p.m. and Fridays to either 5 or 6 p.m.

Western Union has three Money Transfer offices in the Yukon. **In Whitehorse**, at Cashplan Financial; 201 Hanson Street, Whitehorse, YT, Y1A 1Y3, Telephone 667-2274, Fax 667-2509. **In Watson Lake**, at the Gateway to Yukon RV park and at the **Morley River Lodge** at Mile 777, Alaska Highway.

Maps:

Jim's Gifts and News shop on 4137 4th Ave. sells topo maps and guide books of the Yukon, Northern B.C. and Alaska. It's also an art and crafts supply store. One 1:250.000 map costs $9.04 including GST. Tel. 667-2606.

Sub-zero Army Surplus Store. 4230A 4th Ave., opposite McDonald's, sells most topo maps covering the Yukon, plus some camping gear, outdoor clothing and fishing gear. Tel. 667-2753. See also 'maps' on page 25.

Bike Rental, Repairs and Sales:

Element Sports. 4198 4th Ave. Near shopping centre. Tel. 393-3993. Renting bikes for $30 per day.

Wheels and Brakes Cyclery. 4168 4th. Ave. Tel. 633-3760. $20-$30 per day depending on the quality of the bike. During winter, both sell snow related merchandise. **The Canadian Tire Store** at the Mall sells bikes and parts.

Cameras and Film Supplies:

Hougens Photography. 305 Main Street in the Hougens Centre. One-day developing. Tel. 668-6808.

Photo Vision. At 205A Main Street. Tel. 667-4599 with another branch in the Qwanlin Mall. One-day developing and sometimes good deals on slide film. The store at the Mall develops slide film. Tel. 667-4525. All three businesses give away those small film containers - perfect waterproof containers for spices or fishhooks.

Native Parkas, Clothing and Crafts:

Yukon Native Products. See Native Parkas and Anoraks being sewn on site in the Yukon's largest Indian arts and crafts shop, 4230 4th Ave. Tel. 668-5955, Fax 668-6466.

Indian Craft shop. 504A Main Street. Tel. 667-7216.

The North West Company Trading Post. 2195 2nd. Ave, next to the bus depot. Native Clothing, local handicrafts- crafts and gold jewelry. Tel. 667-7717.

Gift shops selling natural Yukon gold jewelry:

Gold Originals by Charlotte. 204A Main Street. Tel. 668-7928. German and French spoken.

Murdoch's Gem Shop. 207 Main Street. Tel. 667-7403. Largest selection of gems in town.

Pot O' Gold. 4129 4th Ave. Tel. 668-2058. Yukon-made crafts, as well as gold nugget jewelry.

Laundromats and Dry Cleaners:

Norgetown Laundry. 4213 4th Ave. Open daily from 8 in the morning to 9:30 at night. Tel. 667-6113.

The **Family Hotel** on 314 Ray Street has public washing machines. Almost all hotels and RV parks have a coin laundry service, and some are open to the public. For dry-cleaning services go to **Qualita Drycleaners** on 3161 3rd Ave. Tel. 667-2789.

Health Food Stores:

Yukon Health Food Centre. 504A Main Street. Tel. 667-2306. A small store selling health related foods.

Three Beans Natural Foods. 308 Wood Street. Tel. 668-4908. Fresh organic fruits and vegetables, as well as other organic products, bulk foods and special foods for hikers. Freshly made juices. Open Mon.- Sat. 9 to 6.

Fishing and Angling:

'**Learning to Fly**', on 407A Ogilvie Street, has everything you will possibly need to catch your dinner. Tel 668-3597 and Fax 668-5916. They also organize day or week-long fishing trips, rent cabins and boats, and sell fishing licenses for the Yukon, Alaska and British Columbia.

Public Indoor Swimming Pool and Workouts:

The Lions Pool. On 4th Ave., next to the High Country Inn Hotel costs $3.50 for an adult per swim-hour, and less for children. Includes showers, sauna and a whirlpool. Times vary for adult swimming, family swimming, line swimming, etc. Call them at 668-7665. Open year-round.

Peak Fitness Centre. 2nd and Strickland Street. Tel. 668-4628. Fitness training, workouts, cardio equipment, massage and sauna. Open every day.

Golf Course: Mountainview Golf Course. Alongside the Yukon River, just off Range Road. Open daily from May 1st to September 30th, 7:30 a.m. to 8 p.m., 18-hole grass greens, par 72. Rentals. Tel. 633-6020.

Medical Care

The **Whitehorse General Hospital** is located on the east side of the Yukon River opposite the Rotary Peace Park. Their non-emergency telephone number is 667-8700. In emergencies dial 911 or 668-4444.

Private Clinics:

Pine Medical Centre. 5110 5th Ave. at Main. Tel. 668-4353.

Medical Clinic. 406 Lambert Street. Tel. 667-6444.

East West Health Centre. 208 Alexander Street. Tel. 633-6157. Acupuncture.

Branigan Clinic. Alternative Medicine. 106 Lambert. Tel. 667-6491.

Riverfront Physiotherapy. 102A Main Street. Tel. 668-4886.

The Chiropractic Clinic. 306 Hoge Street. Tel. 667-7308.

Canyon Mountain Medical Centre. 3059 3rd Ave. Tel. 633-3044.

Therapeutic Life Centre. Call 667-2424 for appointment. Massage, Acupressure, Shiatsu etc.

Dental Health Care:

Klondike Dental Clinic II. 202A Strickland. Tel. 668-3909. 8 a.m. to 3:30 p.m. Mon.-Friday. French spoken.

Northern Dental Clinic. 106 Main Street. Tel. 668-6818 or call toll-free 1-800-661-0509.

Pine Dental Clinic. 5110 5th Ave. Tel. 668-2273, Fax 668-5121. Czech speaking dentist.

In Dawson City: Dr. Helmut Schoener Dental Clinic. Tel. 993-5538. Mon. to Wed. 9 a.m. - 5 p.m. Closed for lunch from noon to 1 p.m. German spoken. In emergencies call 993-6347. A simple filling costs about $80.

Taxis:

- **Yellow Cabs call 668-4811**. Taxi drivers accept Visa and Mastercard

- **5th Ave. Taxi call 668-4111**. Drivers accept Visa credit cards only.

- **Yukon Taxi Service call 667-6677**. Taxi drivers accept Visa and Mastercard.

- *For taxi companies from other communities in the Yukon see page 21.*

Raven Recycling at 138 Industrial Road, Whitehorse, tel. 667-7269, collects recyled items from surrounding communities and you can drop off your items at their location, 24 hours a day.

Women's Centre: Victoria Faulkner Women's Centre. Tel. and Fax 667-2693, for women and their children who need a safe place to stay. The Centre is located on 207D Elliot Street.

Social Services: Mary House: call 668-2611 for emergency accommodation and help. **Salvation Army**: tel. 668-2327. Check out their Second Hand Store on 4th and Black. Open Tues. to Fri. 1-5 and Sat. from 10 to 2 p.m. **Hospice Yukon Society**: tel. 667-7429. **Sexual Assault**: tel. 667-4000. **Alcohol and Drug Treatment**: tel. 668-5225.

Other Community Service Groups: Big Brothers and Sisters: tel. 667-7911. **Elks of Canada**: tel. 667-2201. **Girl Guides of Canada**: tel. 667-2456. **Kiwanis**: tel. 633-2102. **Lions and Lionesses**: tel. 633-2102. **Rotary**: tel. 633-5479 / 668-5439. **Royal Canadian Legion**: tel. 667-2800. **Scouts Canada**: tel. 668-5006. **Telephone Pioneers of America**: tel. 633-4039. **Women's Business Network**: tel. 668-3600. **The Law Line**: free basic information, call toll-free from outside Whitehorse, tel. 668-5297. **Association Franco - Yukonnaise**: tel. 668-2663, fax 668-3511. **Humane Society Yukon**: tel. 668-8382 or call their **PETLINE 668-7387.**

Whitehorse Public Library: Inside the Yukon Government Building on 2nd Ave. Tel. 667-5239. Open weekdays noon to 9 p.m., and Saturday from 1 p.m. to 9 p.m. A very comfortable place with a huge selection of northern-based books.

Book Shops:

Mac's Fireweed Books. 203 Main Street. Tel. 668-6104, Fax 668-554. Toll-free Yukon only, 1-800-661-0508. The largest book shop in the Yukon, with a very good selection on northern books, also sells Western Canada, Alaska and Yukon guide books in German, and European newspapers.

The Broke Bookworm. On 210 Ogilvie St. near the shopping centre. Large selection of 2nd hand books.

Sirius - Science and Nature. 4194 4th Ave. Tel. 668-2875. This store sells 'Astronaut Food', spotting scopes and binoculars of all sizes, nature books and lots of other interesting 'stuff'.

The Heritage Branch of the YTG **Tourist Department** has various books and publications in print about Yukon archaeology, geology, native history and other topics. Write for a publication list to the Heritage Branch, Department of Tourism, Government of Yukon, Box 2703, Whitehorse, Yukon, Y1A 2C6. Fax 1-403-667-2634.

ACTIVITIES IN WHITEHORSE

Art Galleries

Captain Martin House. 305 Wood Street. Tel. 667-4080. A non-profit Yukon Art Society with locally produced arts and crafts.

Yukon Arts Centre. Theatre and Public Art Gallery. Tel. 667-8575. Near Yukon College, suburb of Takhini.

Yukon Gallery. 2093 2nd Ave. Tel. 667-2391. Artworks by internationally known northern artists.

Stonesthrow Gallery. 108 Lambert Street. Tel. 667-4281. Studio Gallery. 404 Ogilvie St. Tel. 667-7599.

Arctic Memories. 4194A 4th Ave. Tel. 633-2111. Gallery, photo art works, and developing.

Movies, Museums, Theatre, Entertainment:

Qwanlin Twin Cinemas (4th Ave.) and **Yukon Cinema** (Wood St.) are two separate movie houses, with two screens each. Both are in the downtown area. Call 668-6644 for movie listings. Tuesdays are half-price days.

Yukon Arts Centre. For current plays, concerts and performances, check the newspapers; the Visitor Centre; or Hougens Box Office, (tel. 667-4222) in the department store on Main Street, upstairs. Tickets are available two weeks before performances. Call 667-8575 for information and reservations. There are many small independent theatre groups performing irregularly throughout the year.

Hutshi Productions. Our Story, First Nation Storytelling Theatre. Opens at 7 p.m. every night except Sunday, opposite the McBride Museum on 1st Ave. Call 668-4869 for more information.

McBride Museum, on 1st and Wood Street, has 465 square m / 5000 square feet of exhibits from prehistory to the present. Open daily in the summer. Call 667-2709, Fax 633-6607

Old Log Cabin Church Museum. Built in 1900 by Rev. R.J. Bowen for the Church of England. Displays and exhibits range from the pre-contact life of native Yukoners, to the Alaska Highway construction. Located at the corner of 3rd Ave. and Elliot. Tel. and Fax 668-2555. The museum is open only in summer. Episcopal services are held Sunday's at 11 a.m.

The Yukon Transportation Museum is located next to the airport and is open daily in summer; it encompasses the history of dog-sledding, early river boats, bush aviation, and the Chilkoot Trail. Tel. 668-4792. Take note of what may be the world's largest weather vane at the entrance to the airport. The shell of a Douglas DC-3, mounted on a rotating pedestal, always points its nose into the wind.

The Yukon Beringia Interpretive Centre is also next to the airport. The museum highlights the history of pre-historic Yukon - the landscape, flora and fauna and the First People. Open 8 to 8 in the summer, seven days a week, with reduced hours in winter. Call to arrange for group tours at other times. $6 per adult and less for youth, seniors, families and groups. Tel. 667-8855 or Fax 667-8854. E-Mail yktour @yknet,yk.ca. For more specific information, call the paleontologists office of the Heritage Branch. Tel. 667-8089. Fax 667-8007. E-Mail jstorer @ gov.yk.ca.

Historical Walking Tours of Whitehorse leave daily in summer from the Donnenworth House at 3126 3rd Ave. at Wood Street (next to Chamber of Commerce Office), tel. 667-4704. Tours are available in German and French. The office is open year-round Mon. to Fri. and offers information on the history of Whitehorse.

SS Klondike Sternwheeler Tours. At the southern end of 2nd Ave., near the Yukon River. The SS Klondike used to be the largest river-boat plying the Yukon River. It was built in 1929, sank in 1936, was rebuilt in 1937, and was retired in 1950. Tours leave every half hour and cost $3.25 for adults, and $2.25 for students and seniors. Please call 667-4511 in summer or, year-round, 667-3917 or 667-3910.

Frantic Follies Vaudeville Stage Show is held at the Westmark Hotel, nightly from June to September. It is a one and half hour show for the whole family. $18 for adults, $9 for under 12 years old. Tel. 668-2042.

The 1940s Canteen Show is held at the Gold Rush Inn Hotel nightly in summer. The show is a nostalgic re-creation of a WW II USO Show, with dance, music and comedy. $16.50 adults and $8 for under 12. Call 668-4500.

The Yukon Experience Super Slide Show is held at the Yukon Inn Hotel daily from June 1st to August 31st at 11 a.m., 2, 7, and 8:15 p.m. It is a great introduction to the Yukon's magnificent outdoors. Tel. 667-2527.

Yukon Permanent Art Collection - in the foyer of the Yukon Government Building on 2nd Ave. 8:30 a.m. to 5 p.m. on weekdays.

<u>Other Things to do</u>:

Guided Nature Walks Around Whitehorse are organized by the **Yukon Conservation Society**, a non-profit organization working to preserve Yukon's flora and fauna. The walks are free and leave from their office daily in summer. It is a perfect way to learn more about local and natural history and about what grows and moves around you, especially should you be striking out into the Yukon's wilderness. Tours are available through the archaeological site of Canyon City (see Alaska Highway chapter). Their office is at 302 Hawkins Street. Call them for more information and hours, at tel. 668-5678 or fax 668-6637. Donations are welcome, and check out their publication 'Hikes and Bikes' around the Whitehorse area, with 35 trails from easy to difficult.

Yukon River Cruises, on the **MV Schwatka**. A two hour boat tour through historic Miles Canyon. Please call 668-4716 for departure times and prices.

Yukon Gardens, off thee Alaska Highway are open daily from April to September, offering scenic walks through flower beds of wild and domestic flowers, trees and shrubs. Tel. 668-7972.

The Yukon Wildlife Preserve includes elk, moose, caribou, bison, goats and other animals that roam in this huge preserve just outside the city. Daily tours are available, please call for times and prices, tel. 668-3225.

Emerald Lake near Carcross.

Signpost Forest in Watson Lake (above).

Giant gold pans at the village of Carcross (below).

Motoring along the Alaska Highway, north of Fort Nelson (above). Paddlers on the Yukon River (below).

A Yukon River island (below).

Whitehorse Fishway is located at the end of Nisutlin Drive in Riverdale, on the eastern side of the Yukon River. This fish ladder was built in 1959, in order to provide access for salmon, which were unable to continue past the hydroelectric dam to their spawning grounds. There is a viewing deck to observe king salmon and other salmon species navigating the 366 m (1200 foot) long wooden ladder. Between 50 and 1500 salmon pass through the fishway each summer. Open daily from 9 a.m. to 5 p.m., May 25th to July 1st; and 8 a.m. to 10 p.m., from July to the end of September. Tel. 667-4263 or 633-5965. For specific information call the Yukon Fish and Game Assoc. at 667-4263, or the Department of Fisheries and Oceans at 667-7821.

Northern Splendor Reindeer Farm offers viewing and feeding of reindeer; is open seven days a week. It is just off the Klondike Highway at Mile 10.5, toward Dawson City. For more information call 633-2996.

Organized bus tours to some of the locations above are available from Grayline Tours at the Westmark Hotel. Call them at 668-3225 for their program.

"A Taste Of 98" Yukon River Tours offers either three hour river trips from Whitehorse, or all-inclusive float trips, lasting up to 2 weeks, to as far as Dawson City, on a pontoon craft. Tel. 633-4767 or Fax 668-2633.

Atsua Ku Riverboat Adventures offers three hour long, to overnight boat tours downstream from Whitehorse, including a barbecue. There are First Nations cultural activities and nature watching; from $41 to $80 per person, depending on the length of the trip. Call 668-6854 or write to Box 5494, Whitehorse, YT, Y1A 5H4.

Youcon Voyage gives tours on the catamaran MV Youcon Kat. Trips depart for 2 1/2 hour sight-seeing boat trips down the Yukon River or week-long trips to Dawson City. Call them at 668-2927 or 668-1252, Fax 667-7379.

Yukon Archives. Discover Yukon's history through documents, audio visual records and photographs dating back to 1845. Want to know if one of your forebearers might have taken part in the Gold Rush? This is the place to find out. It is open Tues. and Wed. from 9 to 5 p.m.; Thurs. and Fri. from 1 p.m. to 9 p.m. and Sat. from 10 a.m. to 6 p.m. Yukon Archives, Box 2703, Whitehorse, Yukon, Y1A 2C6. Tel. 667-5321 or Fax 667-4253.

Tour the Yukon Legislative Assembly Building, Monday to Friday at 2 p.m. No charge.

Whitehorse and Yukon-wide Radio Stations.

CHON FM (98.1) Northern Native Broadcasting - can be listened to throughout North America on 5.41 MHz Transponder 12 Anik E-Q. Tel. 668-6629, Fax 668-6612.

CKRW Radio. In Whitehorse 610 AM. Elsewhere in the Yukon 98.7 FM, and throughout North America via Satellite Anik E-I, transponder 18, 6.8 MHz. Tel. 668-6100 and Fax 668-4209. Call 667-7891 "Tradertime", a daily radio program where listeners may call in to buy or sell - a canoe? Call them for air times.

CKYN Radio 96.1 FM is broadcasting out of Visitor Centres Yukon-wide, with information for visitors.

CBC Yukon Radio 570 AM. Regional and international news on the hour with road reports and weather. CBC frequencies elsewhere in the Yukon are as follows: **Atlin** 90.1 FM; **Beaver Creek** 690 AM; **Carmacks** 990 AM; **Faro and Burwash Landing** 105.1 FM; **Dawson City** 104.9 FM; **Elsa** 560 AM; **Haines Junction** 106.1 FM and 103.5 FM;

Mayo 1230 AM; **Old Crow and Stewart Crossing** 101.1 FM; **Pelly Crossing** 100.1 FM; **Ross River** 990 AM; **Teslin** 940 AM; **Swift River** 970 AM; **Watson Lake** 990 AM; **White River** 93.3 FM.

Weather Information: For the Whitehorse Region call 24 hours, tel. 668-6061.

YUKON BASED PACKAGE TOUR COMPANIES

Grayline Tours. Package bus and river tours connecting Skagway with Dawson City, Eagle, Juneau and Fairbanks in Alaska and Whitehorse. Tel. 668-3225, Fax 667-4494. Or 1-800-544-2206.

Rainbow Tours. Tel. 668-5598, Fax 668-5595, or toll-free 1-800-661-0468.

Princess Tours. Call 633-6592 or fax 633-2197.

Midnight Sun Tours. Van camping and B&B tours. Hiking and river tours. Call 668-6361.

Beringia Tours. Packaged or individual 'soft' adventure tours. Tel. 668-7391. Fax 668-4359.

ABC International Travel / Tour. Network of independent Yukon tour operators. Tel. and Fax 667-4837.

Emerald Travel Tours. Charter and tour service by van or bus throughout Alaska and the Yukon. Tel. 633-3778 or Fax 633-5460.

ADVENTURESOME THINGS TO DO AROUND WHITEHORSE

Horseback riding:

Sky High Wilderness Ranches. Box 4482, Whitehorse, YT, Y1A 2R8. Wilderness horse adventure tours either by the hour, day, or longer; also winter camping dog team trips. Tel. 667-4321, Fax 668-2633.

Whitehorse Riding Stable. At mile 912.5 on the Alaska Highway, tel. 633-3086. Hour, half or full day rides in the Miles Canyon area south of Whitehorse.

C.J. Trail Rides. Tel. 667-4169. Trail rides, children's farm, sleigh rides by the hour or overnight. At mile 8 on the North Klondike Highway toward Dawson City, near Takhini Hot Springs.

Biking Tours:

Frontier Spirit Biking Tours. Box 5390, Whitehorse, YT, Y1A 4Z2. Tel. or Fax 667-1032. Bicycle tours lasting from 6 to 10 days.

Mountain and River Nature Travel. 211 Main Street. Box 31122, Whitehorse, Yukon, Y1A 5P7. Tel. and Fax 667-4590. Fully supported bike tours throughout the Yukon.

Ridgeline Mountainbike Tours. 2157 A 2nd Ave., Whitehorse, YT, Y1A 1C6. Tel. and Fax 667-6501.

Wildwater Rafting Tours:

Tatshenshini Expediting Ltd. 1602 Alder Street, Whitehorse, YT, Y1A 3W8. Tel. 663-2742, Fax 633-6184. Day trips to 12-day adventures on the Tatshenshini and Alsek.

Nahanni River Adventures. Box 4869 Y, Whitehorse, YT, Y1A 4N6. Tel. 668-3180, Fax 668-3056. Guided rafting trips on the Nahanni, Yukon and Tatshenshini.

Eco Summer Yukon Expedition. Box 5095, Whitehorse, YT, Y1A 4Z2. Tel. and Fax 633-8453. Rafting on the Tatshenshini, Alsek and Firth River in the northern Yukon, including Herschel Island.

Cloudberry Adventures LTD. Box 6115, Whitehorse, Yukon, Y1A-5L7. Tel. 668-7700. Fax 668-7711. E-Mail cloudberry @ hypertech.yk.ca. Guided wilderness kayak and canoe trips into the Coal River Ecological Reserve, Atlin Wilderness Park, and other parks. Rentals for unguided trips, and kayak and canoe courses.

Skiing

Mt. McIntyre Recreation Centre offers world class cross-country skiing facilities. Contact them at: Box 4879, Whitehorse, YT. Tel. 667-2500.

Whitehorse Ski Club. Mt. Sima offers downhill skiing from about mid-December to mid-April; there is a rope tow and a chair lift. Tel. 668-4557.

Downhill Ski Shop. On 4168 4th Ave. Tel. 633-3000 or Fax 633-3760.

Dog sledding:

Doggone Sledding and Woodworks. Tel. and Fax 668-5547. R.R. I, Site 20, Comp. 100, Whitehorse, YT, Y1A 4Z6. Guest cabin. Trips can last one day or one week. Handling and training are emphasized.

Cadillac Kennels Dogsled Adventures. Box 4845, Whitehorse, YT, Y1A 4N6. Tel. 667-7040, Fax 668-3073. Guided six day dog sled trips, with accommodation provided.

Wanderlust Wilderness Adventures. Box 5076, Whitehorse, YT, Y1A 4S3. Fax 668-2633. Wilderness homestead vacations with guided dog sled trips, by a Yukon Quest race veteran; also summer hiking / river trips.

For many other wilderness operators, check with the **Wilderness Tourism Association of the Yukon,** Box 3960, Whitehorse, Yukon, Y1A 3M6, or call 1-800-221-3880. Internet: www.wtay members.yk.net.

For Canoe rental companies, see the next chapter, the Yukon River.

ANNUAL FESTIVALS IN WHITEHORSE:

MAY. Annual Sourdough Stompers Square and Round Dance Jamboree. Dates change, please call 633-2256 for more information.

JUNE. June 21 Annual Summer Solstice Dance. Contact tel. 668-4921.

Mid to end of June. Yukon International Storytelling Festival. Don't miss it! Traditional Storytellers from all across the North, as well as other parts of the world, share what is as old as the human language. Call 633-7550.

Mid-June. Dun Na Kwe Ye (People Celebrating). Contact Kwanlin First Nation, tel. 667-6465.

JULY. July 1st Canada Celebration at the Rotary Park with the Annual Great Yukon River Rubber Duck Race.

Mid-July. Whitehorse Rodeo. Call 633-5300.

End of July. Annual Ladies Golf Classic. Mountainview Golf Course.

AUGUST. Discovery Weekend is always on the weekend nearest August 17th. There are all kinds of festivities, including the World's Longest Bathtub Race, over 750 km from Whitehorse to Dawson City. For more information call 667-2148.

End of August. Peter Gzowski Invitational Golf Tourney.

SEPTEMBER. First week. Klondike Trail of '98 International Road Relay. From Skagway to Whitehorse.

FEBRUARY. Mid-month. Annual Yukon Quest Dog Sled Race from Whitehorse to Fairbanks, or visa versa. Contact tel. 668-4711.

Mid-month. Frostbite Music Festival. Contact tel. 668-4921.

End of month. Yukon Sourdough Rendezvous. Winter Carnival Yukon-style. Call 667-2147 for more information, or call the Whitehorse Chamber of Commerce at 667-7545 for exact dates and times of these events, or the many others not mentioned or not yet thought of.

TRANSPORTATION

Car and RV Rentals operating out of Whitehorse:

Avis Car and Truck Rental. 306 Ray Street. Tel. 667-2847, Fax 667-6464. Toll-free 1-800-879-2847.

Budget Rent A Car. 4176 4th Ave. Tel. 667-6200, Fax 667-2732. Toll-free 1-800-268-8900, with one way rentals to Dawson City. Check-out their late summer and fall one-way rental specials from Whitehorse to points south, $39.95 per day with no km limit and no drop-off charge; to Edmonton, Calgary and Vancouver only.

Hertz Rent A Car. Toll-free 1-800-263-0600.

Norcan Car and Truck Rentals is at mile 917.4, at the corner of Two Mile Hill. Tel. 668-2137. Toll-free 1-800-661-0445. Offers one-way rentals to Dawson City.

Rent A Wreck. Whitehorse Shell Centre. Tel. 668-7554.

Sears Car and Truck Rentals. 4178 4th Ave. Tel. 667-6220 and Fax 667-2732.

Tilden Interrent Car and Truck. 9038 Quartz Road. Tel. 668-6872, Fax 668-3974, or call 1-800-387-4747.

Ambassador Motorhomes Rental. Office at mile 912, Alaska Highway. Tel. 667-4130. Fax 604-946-3680 One-ways from Vancouver and Edmonton.

Klondike Recreational Rentals. Motorhomes, Trucks and Campers. P.O. Box 5156, Whitehorse. Office in Porter Creek. Tel. 668-2200, Fax 668-6567. One-ways between Kamloops in BC, to Whitehorse or back. They also rent canoes, but only with their cars.

Cana Dream. 110 Copper Road, Whitehorse, YT, Y1A 2Z6. Tel. 668-3610, Fax 668-3795. One-way rentals between Whitehorse, Calgary, Vancouver and Toronto.

Whitehorse Motors Trucks and Camper Rental. 4178, 4th Ave. Tel. 667-7866, Fax 667-6246. Open year-round.

Remember - when driving, turn off propane to all your appliances!

Airlines serving Whitehorse and the Yukon: Whitehorse Airport has a small duty free section, a gift shop, restaurant and lounge. You can rent vehicles from Budget, Hertz, Norcan or Tilden at the airport. There is infrequent daytime bus service to downtown Whitehorse.

Canadian Airlines International: daily flights between Whitehorse and Vancouver. Flight Arrival and Departure: tel. 668-4466. Reservations and Information: tel. 668-3535. Toll-free 1-800-665-1177. Fax 294-2066.

Alkan Air: Air charters only from 1997. In Whitehorse call 668-2107, or toll-free 1-800-661-0432.

Air North has scheduled DC-3 service from Whitehorse to Dawson City (tel. 993-5110) and on to Fairbanks, Alaska (1-907-474-3999), Old Crow, (tel. 965-3603) and Juneau in southwestern Alaska (tel. 1-907-789-2007). Flights also go to Inuvik in the NWT. In Whitehorse call 668-2228 for reservations and freight inquiries, toll-free from Western Canada 1-800-661-0407, and from Alaska toll-free 1-800-764-0407. Consider their Klondike Explorer Pass, it is valid for 21 days and connects all their destinations for Can$550 or US$470. Starting in 1997, their elderly DC 3's are being replaced with newer aircraft.

NWT / Air Canada has daily flights to Vancouver, and Saturday flights to Edmonton. Operates year-round. Call 1-800-661-0789 for reservations and flight information.

Royal Airlines has flights to Vancouver, Yellowknife and Edmonton on Tues. and Fri. Call 1-800-663-9757

First Air makes flights to Yellowknife and other points in the NWT and Eastern Canada on Mon., Wed. and Fri. Call 1-800-267-1247.

Canada 3000 charter airlines might fly into Whitehorse starting in 1997. Check with your travel agent.

Ranger Air Charter offers chartered services to anywhere in the Yukon, northern BC and Alaska. In Whitehorse call 633-4368 or Fax 667-2684.

FLYING IN THE YUKON

There are numerous **fixed wing (wheels, floats, skis) and helicopter charter services** operating out of Whitehorse, and almost any other community in the Yukon. All of them offer sight-seeing trips around Whitehorse, or to anywhere else you might wish to go. Most bush planes are permitted to carry canoes, but wind drag will, of course, reduce the overall payload. If you want to fly to a remote corner of the Yukon, check what plane the charter might be using. The average fixed wing aircraft has a payload from 450 kg to 1400 kg, and a DC-3 can carry up to 2300 kg (100 kg equals 220 lb.). Bush planes charge by the distance travelled, and helicopters charge by the hour they are in the air; about $800 to $1000 per hour. Helicopters, too, can carry canoes, and their average payload is approximately 500 kg or 1100 pounds - about 2 passengers and their freight. Contact Tourism Yukon for a listing of all charter airlines.

Flying the Alaska Highway: It certainly must be a trip of a lifetime for the general aviation pilot. There are many official and not so official landing strips along the Alaska Highway and elsewhere in the Territory - remote mining camps and wilderness lodges come to mind. Please obtain the Canada Flight Supplement and Alaska Highway Strip Chart (1:500,000 scale) from Transport Canada (AANDHD), Ottawa, Ontario, K1A 0N8, or call 1-613-991-9970. Also ask for the booklet 'Flying the Alaska Highway in Canada' (TP 2168).

Bus Lines:

Greyhound Bus Line leaves daily at 12:30 (times change, please check) in summer for Dawson Creek, and will stop at many of the highway lodges along the road. Bicycles need to be boxed and made as small as possible, and - no, they do not take canoes. One-way from Whitehorse to Vancouver is about $290; there are often special fares at different times of the year. In Whitehorse, the bus depot is at 2192, 2nd Ave., tel. 667-2223, Fax 633-6858 and toll-free nation-wide 1-800-661-8747.

Atlin Express leaves from the Taku Hotel for **Atlin** every Monday, Wednesday and Friday at noon, via Carcross and Tagish; $25 one-way and $40 return. Atlin to Whitehorse, leaves the same days, at 06:00. Whitehorse call 668-4545, Atlin 1-250-651-7617, Fax 1-250-651-7742.

Norline Coaches leaves from the bus depot for **Dawson City** every Monday, Wednesday and Friday at 09:00, from June 1st to September 1st only. The rest of the year the bus departs on Wednesday and Friday only. Arrives in Dawson City at 15:30, leaves for Whitehorse the same day at 16:00, arrives at 23:15. One-way costs $68, children age 3 - 10 are half price, seniors are 10% off, plus GST. In Whitehorse call 668-3355 or 633-3864 and in Dawson City call 993-5057. The Dawson City office of Norline does not accept credit cards. Bus stops along the Klondike Highway are at **Braeburn Lodge** (radio 2M3987); **Carmacks Hotel** in Carmacks (tel. 863-5221); **Pelly Crossing; Stewart Crossing** (tel. 996-5201) - from there to Elsa, Keno and Mayo by taxi, $60 per person; **Moose Creek Lodge** (radio JL39570) and **Klondike Highway Lodge** at the junction with the Dempster Highway (tel. 993-6892).

Alaska Direct Busline offers trips to **Skagway** and other points in Alaska. It leaves from the Regina Hotel at 112 Wood Street, for Skagway daily in summer at 08:00. One-way $35. The winter schedule is based on the ferry arrival times. The bus goes to **Haines Junction** (Kluane National Park) every Tuesday, Friday and Sunday at 07:00. ($20). This bus goes on to Anchorage. In winter only the bus departs on Wednesdays at 07:00. In Whitehorse, tel. 668-4833. In Anchorage, tel. 1-907-277-6652, fax 1-907-388-1951, toll-free 1-800-770-6652.

Alaskon Express operates summer services to Skagway, **Haines** and other points in Alaska. The Whitehorse to Skagway route departs daily at 16:30; US$54 one-way. Whitehorse to Haines leaves on Mon., Wed. and Fri. at noon; US$82 single, with a transfer in Haines Junction. Whitehorse to **Anchorage** leaves on Sun., Tue. and Thur. at noon, with an over-night stop in Beaver Creek, which continues at 08:45 the following day; US$190 with overnight not included. The Whitehorse office is at the Westmark Hotel, tel. 668-3225. Departures are from the Greyhound Bus Depot. Order their timetable from Grayline of Alaska, 300 Elliot Ave. W., Seattle, WA, 98119. Toll-free reservations call 1-800-544-2206, Fax 1-206-281-0621.

White Pass and Yukon Route is a combination bus and train ride to **Skagway**. It leaves Whitehorse daily in summer at 08:00 from Atlas Travel at the Westmark Hotel, and costs one-way US$92. In Whitehorse call Atlas Travel at 667-7823. For reservations and a brochure call toll-free 1-800-343-7373, tel. 1-907-983-2217, fax 1-907-983-2734.

North West Stage Lines has scheduled year-round service to Beaver Creek via Haines Junction and Destruction Bay. It ceased services in 1996 due to bus failure. New services depend on the purchase of a new bus. Call the Gold Rush Inn Hotel at 668-6975 or 668-7240 for updates.

Vangorda Transport out of Faro. Tel. 997-2790, Fax 994-2039. Charters only.

Watson Lake Bus Line. Tel. 536-7381, Fax 536-7391. Charters only.

Arctic Tour. Out of Inuvik every Tuesday and Thursday at 08:00 to Dawson City. Tel. 1-403-979-4100, Fax 1-403-979-2259.

Area code - 403 will change to 867 AND 979 (Inuvik) will change to 777 in October 1997

Gold City Tours departs out of Dawson City every Tuesday and Thursday at 08:00, to Inuvik. Tel. 993-6424, Fax 993-5261. The above two bus lines are charters, and need at least four passengers (max. 14) for the Dawson - Inuvik run.

Silver Trail Tours has taxi and bus service out of Mayo. Tel. 996-2240. Charters are available.

Whitehorse Transit Buses is the local bus service in the city of Whitehorse. Tel. 668-8381, Fax 668-8388.

WHITEHORSE

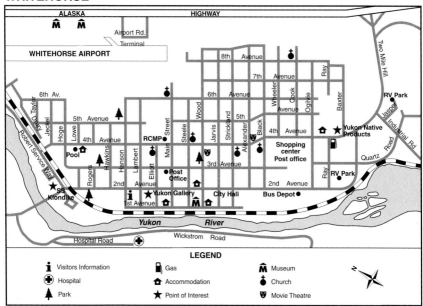

Yukon River frontage in Whitehorse. The building in the center is the historic train station.

Yukon River

The Yukon River, flowing fast and free (almost) to the Bering Strait.

INTRODUCTION

A large number of people visit the Yukon to canoe, raft or kayak down one of the many rivers in the Territory. The most popular is the **Yukon River**, followed closely by any of its many tributaries. The most commonly 'floated' river is the Yukon itself, an up to two week trip over 750 km or 470 miles, between Whitehorse and Dawson City. It can be done by just about anyone with enough common sense to keep a canoe afloat and cookies out of the tent. A less difficult option would be to go down the **Teslin River**, a tributary of the Yukon River. This route bypasses Lake Laberge and saves 60 km / 37 miles of, at times, strenuous lake paddling. The put-in is at Johnson's Crossing on the Alaska Highway, 135 km / 84 miles south of Whitehorse. That trip covers roughly 790 river kilometres (490 miles) to Dawson City, taking up to two weeks.

The **Big Salmon River** is also a tributary of the Yukon River and can be considered easy paddling with some class II sections. The put-in is at Quiet Lake on South Canol Road, 235 km / 146 miles from Whitehorse, or 98 km / 61 miles from Johnson's Crossing. The river distance from Quiet Lake to Dawson City is around 770 km / 480 miles, and will take about two weeks. All three trips may end in Carmacks on the Klondike Highway, but most river travellers continue to Dawson City. If you only have one week, you might consider the float from Carmacks to Dawson City. Reading through the Yukon River description might help determine what section to canoe.

CANOEING

Canoe Rentals:

Up North Boat and Canoe Rental. Tel. 667-7905, Fax 667-6334, 86 Wickstrom Road, Box 5418, Whitehorse, YT, Y1A 5H4. Rental prices: Whitehorse - Dawson City, 16 days, $299 per canoe. Down the Teslin River to Dawson City costs the same as above. Big Salmon River - Dawson City, 19 days, $349 per canoe. From Whitehorse to Carmacks is 320 km, eight days and $199 per canoe. Always included are three paddles, two life-vests and waterproof buckets. Camping gear can be rented. Transport to the various put-in places is extra - about $100 for all equipment and people to Quiet Lake. Up North offers B&B accommodation for departing and arriving river travellers. German is spoken.

Kanoe People. Tel. 668-4899, Fax 668-4891. Box 5152, Whitehorse, YT, Y1A 4S3. Their office is located downtown, next to the river. The prices are somewhat higher than at Up North, with the same services

A river kayaker approaching Dawson City.

except that guided river and fishing tours are also offered. Kanoe People rent a ten metre long (32 foot) Voyageur Canoe, big enough for 16 paddlers - it can be rented for $160 a day, or $960 a week.

Prospect Yukon. Dave Guhl, Box 5323, Whitehorse, YT, Y1A 4Z2. Tel and Fax 667-4837. A smaller renter with only a few canoes, kayaks and inflatables; $297 from Whitehorse to Dawson City. Dave speaks some German.

Log Cabin Adventures Yukon. Tel. 633-3566, Fax 688-7526. Renting canoes for $20 a day. Will also organize all-inclusive canoe, hiking and camping trips as well as winter vacations. Write to R.R. 2 Site 15, Comp. 125, Whitehorse, YT, Y1A 5W9. German spoken.

Wolf Adventure Tours. Tel. and Fax 399-4723. Canoe rentals and guided river tours; transportation to rivers provided. Address: R.R. 1, Site 20, Comp. 261, Whitehorse, Yukon, Y1A 4Z6. German is spoken.

Yukon Tours. Tel. 667-7790, Fax 667-6303. German is spoken. Sight-seeing tours by canoe, van and float plane. Canoe rental and guided river trips to Dawson City. Write to 200 - 307 Jarvis, Whitehorse, Yukon, Y1A 2H4.

Klondike Recreational Rentals. Tel. 668-2200, Fax 668-6567. Box 5156, Whitehorse, YT, Y1A 4S3. If you rent a car or camper with the company, a canoe can be rented as well.

Access Yukon. Tel. 668-1233, Fax 668-5595. Canoe rental and transportation to the rivers. German is spoken. Write to 212 Lambert Street, Whitehorse, YT, Y1A 1Z4.

Listers Rental Ltd. Tel. 668-2776, Fax 668-2474. Address: 125 Copper Road, Whitehorse, YT, Y1A 2Z7. Canoes, motorboats and ATV's for rent. Canoes go for $275 from Whitehorse to Dawson City. This Yukon-based company also rents motorboats, ATV's, snowmobiles, chain saws and such.

Big Bear Adventures. Box 5210, Whitehorse, Yukon, Y1A 4Z2. Tel. 633-5642. Fax 633-5630. $20 per day canoe rental. German, French and Dutch spoken.

Canoe rentals in other communities

Dawson City

Dawson City River Hostel. Tel. 993-6823 (summer only). Canoe rental for $20 a day. The hostel also rents one-way canoe's from Dawson City to Eagle and / or Circle in Alaska. The distance to Eagle is 170 km / 105 miles, costing US$110 for 4 days. To Circle it is 440 km / 275 miles, costing US$270 for 10 days. The hostel rents the canoes for the above trips for Eagle Canoe Rentals out of Eagle, Alaska. Tel. 1-907-547-2203.

Dawson Trading Post. Tel. 993-5316. Canoe rentals for $30 a day. They will provide transportation and also organize wilderness trips.

Atlin

Sidha Tours. Tel. and Fax 250-651-7691. Box 368 V, Atlkin, BC, VOW 1A0. Renting canoes and kayaks.

Norseman Adventure. Tel. 250-651-7535, Fax 250-826-2559. Box 184, Atlin, BC, VOW 1Ao. Renting canoes and houseboats.

Carmacks- Canadian Wilderness Travel. Tel. 863-5404, Fax 863-5405. Box 114, Carmacks, Yukon, Y03 1C0. Canoe rental and transfers, as well as guided wilderness trips. German spoken.

Faro- Horizons North. Tel 994-2878, Fax 994-3154. Box 736, Faro, Yukon, Y0B 1K0. Canoe and motorboat rental, fishing trips and guided wilderness tours.

Mayo- Moose Bay Adventure. Tel. and Fax. 667+1068. Box 153, Mayo, Yukon, Y0B 1M0. Fishing and hiking wilderness trips; canoes for rent on request.

All canoe rental prices include three paddles and two life-vests. The prices quoted are always for one canoe and not per person, and some of the renters might rent camping gear for an extra fee. If you feel insecure about that special paddle stroke, most rental companies will give you a chance to practice. The quiet back waters of the Robert Service Campground are ideal to get your feet wet in a safe way. All rental companies will drive you to what ever take-in point you choose. Prices for that service depend on the company and driving distances.

The Yukon Canoe and Kayak Club is a non-profit all volunteer organization offering safety and skill courses all summer long and they will organize river trips of various lengths. Call or write to them at: Box 5546, Whitehorse, YT, Y1A 5H4. Or E-mail: bear@yknet.yk.ca. Tel. 633-5625, Fax 633-5630.

If you are looking for a partner, or for a group of people paddling your river, the canoe rentals might be helpful, but also check at the Robert Service Campground and/or leave a note on the notice board of the Visitor Centre. No one should travel on Yukon rivers if one feels insecure in a canoe. On the other hand - nobody should deprive her or himself of the trip of a lifetime due to a lack of expert paddling skills. The rivers of the Yukon can be deadly, and people do die in the icy cold waters. Plenty of common sense, coupled with enough maturity not to do "macho things" in the middle of a fast flowing river, should get anyone to their destination. About 3000 to 5000 people each summer canoe, kayak or raft from Whitehorse to Dawson City, and who knows how many on all the other rivers. REMEMBER, it is a real wilderness out there; even though you might not be all alone. Responsibility for your safety AND others in your party depends on no one else but YOU. Ice cold water, sweepers, log jams, drifting logs, and wildlife, command respect, and constant attention to your surroundings is always important. Why would anyone be out there in the wilderness without those attributes! Consider this: on a scale of dangers, smoking definitely beats any river trip in the North.

All canoe rental companies periodically have to pick up their canoes from Dawson City. By calling the individual company, you may return your own canoe this way too, or use the cheaper service of **Frontier Freightlines** out of Dawson City who charge $30 for returning your canoe to Whitehorse. Tel. 993-5402.

Buying a canoe

Depending on your plans, buying a second-hand canoe might make more economic sense than renting one - even buying a brand new one can be a good idea. There is a good buyer's market for canoes in Dawson City; you need your own canoe anyway should you want to go past Circle, in Alaska. To sell your canoe, or any other boat, try the hostel in Dawson City. There always seem to be guests in the hostel waiting for that "special" deal to start their river trip into Alaska. Second-hand canoes in Whitehorse are not a dime a dozen - especially in early summer, when they are in high demand. Trying hard enough might bag you one for $200 - $300. For that price you might get an older Coleman or a fibreglass canoe needing a patch or two. Most rental companies sell older canoes, but often at a price close to a brand-new one. Both Whitehorse newspapers, the daily **Whitehorse Star** and the bi-weekly **Yukon News** have large - for sale - sections where canoes or other boats might be found. Also, check the blackboards at the Visitor Centre, the many coffee shops, and at camping gear businesses. Put up your own "want ad". Brand-new canoes can be found at the **Canadian Tire Department Store** or at the **Hougens Centre** on Main Street; both in Whitehorse. Each spring, Canadian Tire gets a truck load of 15 and 17 foot (4.5 m and 5 m) Colemans priced between $700 and $900, and Hougens stocks up with a few quality canoes, like

Old Town, for around $1200. Also, check with the **Cloudberry Canoes and Kayak Store** on 103-100 Main Street. They stock high quality Swift Canoes and Kayaks, as well as Nimbus Kayaks and all the accessories. Call them at 668-7700 or Fax 668- 7711.

RAFTING

It has become quite popular to build one's own raft out of logs, clean steel drums, inner tubes, whatnots, or any combination of the above, then float down the Yukon River - just like those gold-seeking adventurers did one hundred years ago. Rafts of all shapes, materials and float-worthiness have been spotted on the river; some have cabins on top or a tent, with maybe a stove, table and other trappings of the good life. Of course, some logistics have to be conquered, and some knowledge of the inner workings of a wild-running Arctic river to be mastered, before the "ship" can be let loose. As potentially easy as the Yukon can be to float, it is as potentially deadly, with the icy water, sweepers, log jams and deadheads that are part of any northern river - and help can be hours, if not days away. Since rafting is a team job, bring a group of your best friends and make certain you have at least one carpenter, a person who not only knows how to build a rudder, but also knows how to steer a contraption the weight of a dump truck. Then construct it - using logs definitely is the most authentic way. There are two ways to get logs for your raft - legally and illegally. The latter means you and your friends find yourself some deadfall (since green trees have the buoyancy of a submarine) near a river or Lake Laberge, arm yourself with the necessary tools, and start cutting. This could mean the end of your vacation, since a fine of up to $5000 is more than likely. The wood cutting permit for a tree of between 18 and 28 cm (7 - 11 inches) diameter costs 15 cents, and since roughly 20 trees would do the job, the possession of a legal wood-cutting permit would cost you less than a glass of beer.

The permit can be obtained from the field operation office of the Federal Government: 200 Range Road, not far from the intersection of the Alaska Highway and Two Mile Hill. Their tel. number is 667-8078 and fax 667-4125. Field officers there can assist you in locating forest burn-sites, since partially burned trees can be fairly dry. No permits are issued for cutting within city limits, nor the first 30 m or 100 feet away from any body of water. For tree cutting on territorial land a permit from the Lands Branch of the YTG (Yukon Territorial Government) is required. Their office is on Burns Road opposite the Whitehorse Airport. Tel. 667-8129 and Fax 667-3641. Alternatively, go first class by buying the logs directly from a sawmill for about $10 to $20 per log, depending on size. Make sure the logs are dry - seasoned for about one year after cutting. Be sure to get a receipt, in case a field officer needs convincing that your logs are not illegally cut! The construction company Kilrich, along the Alaska Highway, will deliver to anywhere within city limits for $12 a load. Their 6 by 6 (18 by 18 cm) 16 foot / 5 m long logs cost about $30 a piece. You might even be able to sell them again at the end of your trip. Call them at 668-5958 or fax 668-3682.

THE YUKON RIVER FROM WHITEHORSE TO DAWSON CITY

Start your river trip from either the **Robert Service Campground** or the **Rotary Park** near the Yukon River bridge. A river traveller has about 320 km / 200 miles before Carmacks, the next settlement, is reached. It is only 176 km / 110 miles by road between these two places, but by canoe it will take one week. Carmacks is the first and only place along the river where new provisions can be bought - and where the journey can be abandoned.

When drifting away from Whitehorse, one can hardly imagine that in the early summer of 1898 thousands of boats of all types floated toward Dawson City filled with men (and some women) dreaming of wealth and riches awaiting them at the end of their trail. The gold-seekers back then certainly had very little in common with today's river traveller, except for the search for adventure. Today's adventurer will find many remnants of those "wild" days along the riverbanks, from abandoned cabins and wood-cutting camps, to the remains of once proud paddle-wheelers, with their machinery rusting away in the bushes. The Yukon River is a river of history; a river of dreams. It also is a wild river, running free and untamed for 3000 km until emptying its frigid waters into the Bering Strait.

Lake Laberge lies approximately 40 km / 25 miles from Whitehorse, about a day's trip downstream if one has left early enough in the day. The Yukon River flows very quickly past Whitehorse, averaging 10 km/h, and even faster after the spring thaw in June, or after heavy rains. In these first kilometres, the river carries only one tenth of the volume that it later pushes past Dawson City, and only a fraction of what later gets discarded into the Bering Sea. Lake Laberge is over 50 km / 30 miles long with an average width of between 2 and 4 km (1.5 to 2.5 miles). Regardless of which side one chooses, the crossing should take from 2 to 4 days - longer on a log raft. It is very important to remember that the calm waters of Lake Laberge can transform within moments into a raging sea, with waves that reach a height of two metres or over six feet. Once one has selected a side of the lake, one should stay on that side. Lake Laberge is nestled in a long narrow valley where the wind, as in a wind tunnel, can build up very quickly. The right (east) side of the lake is generally the shorter, less inhabited and, in spite of the steeper shore, has very good camping sites. The left (west) side has many bays and flat rocky beaches, but is more settled and has more private property. The **Deep Creek Territorial Campground**, with 22 RV/tent sites, is your best bet, and has road access back to Whitehorse - should you have forgotten to buy your week's supply of marshmallows!

Richthofen Island, across from the campground, was named after the German Baron von Richthofen, a respected geographer during the 1880s. Lake Laberge was named after a Michael Laberge from Quebec who, in 1867, surveyed the Yukon for a possible overland telegraph line route between New York and Paris. **Lower Laberge**, at the northern end of the lake, is where the river starts to make life easier again for those paddling. Some of the cabins in this former river steamer camp have been renovated, and it is an excellent place to camp, with outhouses and fire rings. The remains of the river steamer Casca add further character to this site.

The next 50 km/30 miles, between **Lower Laberge** and the abandoned river village of **Hootalinqua**, are not only considered the most beautiful stretch of river along the entire length of the Yukon River, but its historical value has earned it the distinction of being a Canadian Heritage River. This stretch of river is curvy and narrow, with icy clean-blue waters. Many river steamers met disaster in this part of the river during the Gold Rush, but for modern travellers the river poses no problems. **Hootalinqua** used to be a native village, police outpost, trading centre and river steamer stop, but has been uninhabited since 1950. It is located just downstream from where the Teslin River adds plenty of water, and many more river travellers to the Yukon. This is a very pleasant tenting spot with some limited facilities - some of the cabins have been partially renovated. **Shipyard Island**, just below Hootalinqua, is a nice place to camp, and also is home to the river steamer Evelyn, later renamed Norcom, which was built in 1908 in Seattle and abandoned on this island in 1931. _Please remember that all wooden relics, artifacts and machine-parts are protected by law._

After a further 50 km / 30 miles, the river traveller arrives at the village of **Big Salmon** where, for thousands of years, local Tutchone Indians enjoyed their seasonal fishing camps until they were pushed aside by the stampede of gold-seekers en route to the Klondike. The village is partially being used again by the native people of this area, and river travellers are asked to respect their privacy. The village of **Little Salmon** is next, connected by a short gravel road to Highway #4. Carmacks is only a day or two further down the river. **Carmacks** has all services- from hot showers to cold beer. Some will end their river journey here; others will start out from Carmacks, but the majority will continue to float northward towards Dawson City (for more information about Carmacks see the Klondike Hwy chapter).

The notorious **Five-Finger Rapids** are about

Five Finger Rapids.

40 km / 25 miles below Carmacks. Four rock islands in the middle of the river await the river traveller and, be assured, no dangers exist for those using the channel <u>FARTHEST TO THE RIGHT</u>. Point the bow of your canoe straight toward the channel, stay in the centre, and if the water level of the river is low you won't even notice the rapids - well - you will, but only a little. At high water levels, the high standing waves on either side of the channel might look a bit more threatening but, nevertheless, the ride will be over in seconds and some of you might wish to go through it again. In any case - <u>DO NOT</u> take any of the other channels unless you are equipped with the proper gear and white water experience. River travellers have lost everything, and some have lost their lives in these rapids. Of course, during the Gold Rush years, the rapids were regarded very seriously, especially by those who were floating on large, awkward, slow moving log rafts and by large paddle wheeler steamships, many of which were badly damaged trying to navigate the rapids. Today's log rafters still need to take special care floating through the Five Finger Rapids. For river steamers going back upstream, a pulley and cable system existed which allowed them to be winched upstream through the rapids.

One further set of rapids, the **Ring Rapids,** await the river traveller just downstream from the Five Fingers. The story here is the same - stay on the right side of the river and you will get nothing more than a bit of fast water. When the white foaming water of the Ring Rapids comes into view, it seems as though the entire width of the river is a boiling mess, and only in the so-called last minute does a calm channel appear on the right. Many river steamers were damaged in this area during the Gold Rush. The most dangerous rock obstacles were blasted out of the river by frustrated steamship crews, making the river a lot safer for modern-day explorers.

Minto Landing again offers access to the Klondike Highway, and to the government campground located there. From Minto Landing, it is a further 320 km / 200 miles to Dawson City. The historic site of **Fort Selkirk** is the next established tenting site along the river. Fort Selkirk was built by Robert Campbell during the years 1848-52. For many years this was a busy trading post - until it was burned to the ground by a group of coastal Chilkat Natives, whose trading with the inland natives had been disrupted by White traders. The Gold Rush brought back life to Fort Selkirk. It became a focal point on the river, with schools, hotels, police barracks and many other services. In later years, it even became a plane-stop on the Whitehorse-Dawson City air route. The highway between these two cities bypassed Fort Selkirk and drained all reason for being from this settlement. Today, many of the original buildings have been restored, and various short river tours to Fort Selkirk are offered from either Carmacks, Minto, or the village of Pelly Crossing. River travellers will find this settlement a very rewarding stop-over point worth a couple of days stay.

Many of the **creeks further downstream** were inhabited during the river steamer days, and some of them still are. People live off gold mining, trapping or commercial salmon fishing, and some of the "creeks" are occupied year-round. It is easy to realize that these 'refugees from civilization' treasure their private life very much and visits from inquisitive river travellers might not be wanted. If a creek is evidently inhabited, it would be rather rude to pitch one's tent in the front garden. On the other hand, many residents would be very pleased by a visit, and the hospitality of some river residents is legendary. One way to match-up a (possibly) lonely river traveller with a (possibly) lonely river dweller, is by stopping to ask if you can buy fresh vegetables or freshly caught salmon from them. If you have brought current magazines or newspapers down the river with you, an immediate friendship could be cemented.

The White River: Well, nobody could miss the White River emptying its truck loads of sandy, gritty silt into the fairly clean waters of the Yukon River. **Stewart Island** lies a few kilometres downstream within a maze of islands at the Stewart River junction with the Yukon River. The island has been lived on continuously since 1849, and before that was used seasonally by the aboriginal peoples. It is assumed that, during the Russian

Historic Stewart Island. Every year the waterfront moves closer to the buildings.

possession of Alaska, their fur-traders worked this far upstream, but the Gold Rush was the real boom-time for Stewart Island. Nowadays, only one family lives on the island as, year by year, more of the island's frontage, where most of the buildings happen to be, is slowly being reclaimed by the mighty powers of the fast moving river. Sometimes cabin space is offered for rent to river travellers, but it can not be counted on - stop and ask.

Henderson Creek is just below Stewart Island on the right. Not much remains there, but there is still evidence of ongoing gold mining. It was on the northern arm of this tiny creek where **Jack London** lived part of eight months during the winter of 1897-98, in the cabin in which he inscribed: *"Jack London miner author, Jan. 27, 1898"*. In the 1960s the cabin was authenticated, dismantled and turned into two separate cabins. One now stands in Dawson City, and the other at the Jack London Square in Oakland, California. Incidentally, the log with Jack London's signature went to Oakland. Where the cabin once stood, 20 km / 13 miles or so upstream from the mouth of Henderson Creek, nothing remains except a promise that one day soon another cabin will be built to the original specifications, with original tools, to become the proud centrepiece of the newly-created Jack London Historical Park.

It is a further 110 km / 70 miles to **Dawson City** - the city of dreams and promises to modern day adventurers, as well as to the Gold Rushers. By this point in one's journey downstream, dreams of clean clothes, a hot shower and a properly cooked meal are perhaps as strong as were the dreams of thousands of gold-seekers about gold and immeasurable riches. Most of their hopes were dashed in the reality that it was too late. The creeks had all been staked, the gold had all been divided; all that remained was the adventure. For modern paddlers, Dawson City is the 'Big Apple', a dream come true after a long and exciting journey.

Dawson City.

Even before any buildings come into sight, you will know you have arrived at the last major urban area along the river, as the **Moosehide Rock Slide** still greets the river traveller. The clean blue waters of the Klondike River drain into the Yukon River on your right, and you must quickly decide which side of the river to steer toward - before the swift moving water slides you past town. Stay to the left, upstream from the ferry landing where, just a short walk up the embankment the tent sites and cabins of the **Dawson City River Hostel** await. If time permits, the hostel manager can help to retrieve your canoe or kayak. A short distance past the Yukon River Ferry, one finds the **Territorial Government Campground** with 98 tent sites, some of them right on the water's edge. If the canoeist decides to paddle along the right side of the river to Dawson City first, the task of crossing the river to the hostel and camping areas is easily manageable. See the Dawson City chapter for more information about Dawson City.

A tree cut by a beaver on a Yukon river island.

One final word to river travellers: many of you will unload, clean-up, pack-up and head back home, and many of you will wish to dispose of surplus material; leftovers from the river trip. Much of it, such as sugar, spices, rice - or boating and camping equipment, can be used by someone else. The owner of the hostel collects innumerable clothes, wetsuits, tents in almost perfect shape, all kinds of food items - mostly thrown away, or left behind at a tent site in the government campground, or somewhere in town in a garbage can. If you can, please drop off whatever is re-usable at the hostel, where some food items will be used in the hostel kitchen, but most are collected for distribution to places like the local women's shelter. Clean clothing can also be dropped off at the hostel, or directly to the charitable second-hand store of the St. Paul's Church at the corner of Front Street and Church. Thank you.

Five Finger Rapids highlighting the right channel, at the end of April.

View from the Top of the World Highway across the Yukon River, Dawson City and the Klondike Valley.

River travellers on the Klondike River.

YUKON RIVER

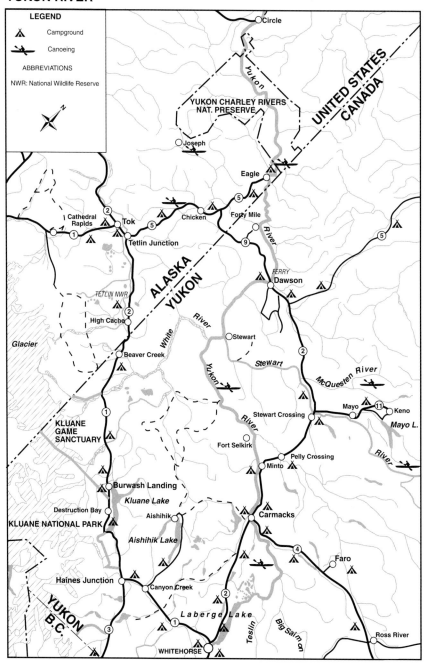

LEGEND

Campground

Canoeing

ABBREVIATIONS

NWR: National Wildlife Reserve

Campbell Highway

A First Nation native of the Yukon River Territory.

INTRODUCTION

This highway, mainly gravel, connects Watson Lake with Carmacks on the Klondike Highway (#2). For those travelling to Dawson City, 32 km / 20 miles will be shaved off the journey on this highway - but driving via Whitehorse will give the traveller a better surfaced road and more services. There are no services between Watson Lake and Ross River - a distance of 362 km or 225 miles, and some preparations are advisable.

This 582 km / 362 mile long highway was completed in 1968, and was named after Robert Campbell who, as a trader for the Hudson Bay Company, was the first White man to travel in this part of Canada by boat and on foot. In early 1840, he and his Indian companions travelled the Liard River from Dease Lake to Frances River, which originates in the lake of the same name along the Campbell Highway. Their journey continued up the Finlayson River, and on to the Pelly, which empties into the Yukon River. In 1848, he established Fort Selkirk at the confluence of the Pelly and Yukon rivers. After the destruction of Fort Selkirk (see Yukon River chapter) in 1852, Robert Campbell returned east to Minnesota - completing one of the most remarkable journeys of all time. Between November 30, 1852, and March 13, 1853, he covered a distance of 5310 km / 3300 miles solely on snow shoes. He never returned to the Yukon, and died in Winnipeg on May 9, 1894.

CAMPBELL HIGHWAY NO. 4 - FROM WATSON LAKE TO ROSS RIVER

km 0 / mile 0 Watson Lake. For information about Watson Lake see the Alaska Hwy chapter.

km 10.8 / mile 6.7 From here the road starts climbing to a plateau, and then follows the eastern bank of the Frances River.

km 58 / mile 36.1 Rest stop at Frances River Bridge.

km 81 / mile 50.3 Simpson Lake Government Campground, 10 RV and tent sites with shelter, boat launch, fishing.

km 110 / mile 68.4 Junction with the Nahanni Range Road #10. The Nahanni Range Road is a narrow gravel road with no services along its entire length. There is a YTG maintenance camp 3 km / 1.8 miles past the junction on highway #4, where information about highway #10 can be found. The road was completed in 1963, in order to provide access to the tungsten mining town of Cantung - now commonly known as Tungsten. This open pit mine started working in 1960, and lasted until 1986, when the town of 500 was shut down. The road is maintained to km 134 / mile 83.3; past that point you are on your own.

THE NAHANNI RANGE ROAD #10

km 85 / mile 52.8 Nahanni Range Government Campground, 10 RV and tent sites with kitchen shelter.

km 134 / mile 83.3 The highway is maintained to this point. Those who want to continue need a rugged All-Wheel Drive vehicle to navigate around numerous wash-outs, and the risks are entirely the driver's. For those well prepared, this highway offers a true car-based wilderness experience, with good fishing in numerous creeks, beautiful scenery and truly wild wildlife.

km 201.2 / mile 125 Tungsten. This former mining town is not completely abandoned. A year-round caretaker crew lives at Tungsten; which is located 9 km / 5.6 miles past the Yukon border. Do not miss the Cantung (Tungsten) Hot Spring, about 1 km (southeast) from town and adjacent to the airstrip. A pronounced sulphur odour points the way. The water temperature approaches 40°C or 105°F.

Nahanni National Park is very close to Tungsten, and the park is accessible by water via Flat Lakes, which is the source of Little Nahanni River. From there on, persons must be very confident in their white water skills. It is possible to fly in to Flat Lakes from Watson Lake - a distance of 225 km / 140 miles. For more information about this National Park, write to Nahanni National Park Reserve, P.O. Box 348 (EK), Fort Simpson, NT, X0E 0N0. Tel. 1-403-695-2310 or 1-403-695-3151, Fax 1-403-695-2246. Various Yukon-based wilderness tour operators organize wildwater rafting trips down the South Nahanni River.

BACK TO HIGHWAY #4

km 110 / mile 68.4 Junction of Nahanni Range Road with Campbell Highway.

km 113.2 / mile 70.3 Tuchita River Yukon Government Highway Maintenance Camp. No services, but help in an emergency can be found here.

km 175.6 / mile 109.1 Frances Lake Government Campground, 24 RV and tent sites with shelter, boat launch, fishing. Robert Campbell reached this lake in 1840. He named it after the wife of the governor of the Hudson Bay Company. In 1842, he established a trading post at the lake, but it was abandoned in 1851. River travellers who can handle rapids of class III to IV, can float down **Frances River** from here back to the village of Upper Liard, 12 km west of Watson Lake. It is a distance of about 200 km or 125 miles, with many take-out points along the route. There is a wilderness lodge on Frances Lake that can be contacted via mobile radio 2M 3180 Murray Channel, or by calling Watson Lake at 667-2028. There is no road access.

km 240 / mile 149 Finlayson Lake Historic Site. The lake is 10 km long and was named by Robert Campbell after one of the directors of the trading company. The waters of the lake drain into the Mackenzie River which empties into the Arctic Ocean. North of the lake, all rivers, such as the Pelly River, flow into the Yukon River and on to the Bering Sea. There is an observation platform, and rest stop with panels giving information about the area.

km 264.5 / mile 164.4 Little Campbell Creek. Campbell followed this creek into the Pelly River.

km 274.2 / mile 170.4 Big Campbell River Bridge. Campbell built a trading post here, but it burned down in 1849.

km 312 / mile 193.9 Hoole Canyon Bridge and confluence of Hoole and Pelly Rivers. For those who are river running the Pelly, true excitement is offered in Hoole Canyon with potential class IV rapids - depending on the amount of water and the season. Most river trips start at Pelly Lakes, and only a float plane can get you there. Then it's about 500 km / 310 miles to the village of Pelly Crossing on the Klondike Highway.

km 346.6 / mile 215.4 Junction with a private road to the **Ketza River Mine.**

km 354.4 / mile 220.2 Junction with the Canol Road #6. Going south, this road meets up with the Alaska Highway at Johnson's Crossing and, going north, heads toward the Yukon / NWT border. The village of Ross River is located 10 km / 6 miles away from the junction on the northern arm of the Canol Road.

Village of Ross River. The community of Ross River has a population of about 400, consisting mainly of the Kaska Indian people. Located on the southwestern bank of the Pelly River, the town is connected to the other side of the river by a foot bridge and a government vehicle ferry. The ferry operates daily in summer from 8 a.m. to noon, and from 1 p.m. to 5 p.m., there is no charge. In emergencies call: **RCMPolice** 969-5555 and the local **hospital** at 969-2221. **CBC** radio can be found on 990 AM. The **Ross River Airstrip** has a length of 1676 m / 5500 feet and is at an elevation of 734 m / 2408 feet. Tel. 969-2241. The river, flowing north past town, was named by Campbell, after a chief trader of the Hudson Bay Co. (HBC).

Services in Ross River:

The Welcome Inn. Tel. 969-2218, Fax 969-2325. Rooms, restaurant, lounge with off-sales and coin laundry. Service station with car and tire repairs.

Sooley's B&B. Tel. and Fax 969-2905.

Dena General Store. Selling groceries and a post office is located on the premises. Tel. 969-2280.

Ross River Service Centre. Tel. 969-2212, Fax 969-2108. Service station with repairs, groceries and hardware store.

Banking services by CIBC. Mon., Tues. and Fri. from 9:30 to 1 p.m. Tel. 969-2212.

Self-contained RVs and motorhomes can park for the night near the foot suspension bridge.

Ross River Dena Cultural Exchange is a one week long festival of traditional native activities and sports. It takes place at Coffee Lake, near Ross River from about mid to late July. Please call 969-2279 for more information.

Ross River is a staging point for various mining companies and mineral prospectors. For wilderness trips with a local operator, contact **Kosers Yukon Outback**, General Delivery, Ross River, YT, Y0B 1S0. Telephone or Fax 969-2908 or Tel. 969-2210 / 2726.

NORTH CANOL ROAD TO THE YUKON / NWT BORDER

The ferry across the Pelly River operates from about mid.-May to the middle of October. Cyclists can use the foot bridge. The highway was built partly as a military access route during World War II, and the fear of Japanese attacks on Alaska. The Canol (CANadian Oil) Road and oil pipelines to Whitehorse were built to access the rich oil fields near Fort Norman, along the lower Mackenzie River in the NWT. Beginning in April 1944, the 4 inch (10 cm) wide pipeline carried 3000 gallons (about 11.4 kL) of oil per day . The road was opened in September that year, but the pipeline was abandoned after the war. On August 18, 1990, the Canol Road was declared a National Historic Site. Some of the Yukon's most spectacular scenery can be found on either side of the highway. At the Yukon / NWT border, the road becomes largely impassable for cars - but becomes a hiker's dream, and mountain bikers and motor cyclists may continue for some distance on the road. The **Canol Road Heritage Trail** continues to Norman Wells on the Mackenzie River, over a distance of 372 km / 230 miles.

km 0 / mile 0 Ross River. It is 462 km / 287 miles, to the end of the road and back. Carry plenty of extra gas and supplies. There are no services of any kind, and even though the highway is maintained, wash-outs can occur after heavy rain. For bicyclists this is a dream road - you almost have it all to yourself. Kilometre posts along the highway indicate the distance from the Alaska Highway.

km 0.6 / mile 0.4 The large stockpile to your right (east) is barite from a defunct mine. Barite is a frequently occurring mineral found in sedimentary rock. Barite is Greek for "heavy" and can be used as a lubricant for oil and gas wells.

km 1 / mile 0.6 The road to your left (west) leads to the former site of the native village of Ross River. Present day Ross River only dates from 1964. 400 m further is a second access road.

km 10.9 / mile 6.8 Tenas Creek. For the sake of cyclists, many, but not all, the creeks are listed. The water is generally fit for drinking, but nevertheless should be treated or boiled.

km 27.3 / mile 17 Deep Creek. All bridges on this highway are one-way.

km 33.6 / mile 20.9 Marjorie Creek. A bit further is a road to Marjorie Lake.

km 45.2 / mile 28.1 Orchie Lake with a boat launch to the west.

km 51.3 / mile 31.9 Gravel Creek.

km 53.7 / mile 33.4 Flat Creek.

km 59.4 / mile 37 Beaver Creek.

km 67.2 / mile 41.8 180 mile Creek.

km 70.6 / mile 43.9 Tay Creek.

km 74.5 / mile 46.3 Blue Creek.

km 94.3 / mile 58.6 Caribou Creek.

km 99.4 / mile 61.8 Pup Creek.

km 104.7 / mile 65.1 Dragon Lake Campsite with litter barrels, good fishing and rock hunting. There is a boat launch further down the road.

km 112 / mile 69.6 Look for the wreckage of a **Twin Pioneer aircraft** and other leftovers from the road construction days.

km 113.9 / mile 70.8 Air landing strip.

km 114.2 / mile 71 Twin Creek Government Road Maintenance Camp. No services, but help is provided in case of emergencies.

km 120.8 / mile 75.1 Mt. Sheldon is a prominent feature ahead. The 2114 m / 6937 foot high mountain is named after naturalist Charles Sheldon. There is a string of three beautiful lakes to your right called Lewis, Field and Sheldon Lakes.

km 124.9 / mile 77.6 Riddel Creek.

km 128.4 / mile 79.8 A narrow road leads down to **Sheldon Lake.**

km 133.1 / mile 82.7 Sheldon Creek. The highway climbs out of Ross River Valley.

km 143.7 / mile 89.3 The highway drops into the South Macmillan Valley and river system. Drive carefully, as it is steep at times.

km 147.1 / mile 91.4 Moose Creek.

km 151 / mile 93.8 First of many **military vehicles** that have been dumped here.

km 158.5 / mile 98.5 South Macmillan River. This is a popular river to float. It's about 750 km / 470 miles to Dawson City. There are a number of class II to IV rapids, but all are fairly easy to portage, and most are on the first 20 km / 12 miles of the river.

km 169.4 / mile 105.3 View of Selwyn Mountains ahead. Keele Peak at 2975 m / 9760 feet is the most prominent mountain in this range.

km 178.6 / mile 111 Itsi Creek.

km 180.5 / mile 112.2 Wagon Creek.

km 182.8 / mile 113.6 South Macmillan Bridge No. 1. This is the second access point for river travellers. It is also a good picnic place. James Macmillan was the sponsor who had supported Campbell's journey.

km 185.2 / mile 115.1 Eleven km / 7 mile long access road to a Barite mine.

km 191.2 / mile 118.8 An abandoned maintenance camp and **Jeff Creek Bridge.**

km 195 / mile 121.2 Hess Creek.

km 205.2 / mile 127.5 Ascent to **Macmillan Pass,** at an elevation of 1366 m / 4480 feet.

km 208.2 / mile 129.4 Macmillan River Bridge No. 2 and more abandoned army vehicles, with possible access to the South Nahanni River and Nahanni National Park. This route has to be carefully researched, and is not for the foolhardy.

km 215 / mile 133.6 Sekie Creek and location of a work camp.

km 219.5 / mile 136.4 Airstrip landing to the left. For the next 11 km / 6.8 miles the highway crosses the Macmillan River many times.

km 232 / mile 144.2 Yukon / Northwest Territory Border. The road is not maintained past this point, but stories have been told of ordinary cars making it a further 20 to 30 km (12.5 to 20 miles). Proceed at your own risk. Hikers and cyclists have the road all to themselves! Enjoy, but keep the cookies out of the tent!

A few more words about the Canol Heritage Trail: Those wanting to hike the Canol Trail need to be aware of one thing - the total length of the trail, from the Yukon / NWT border to Norman Wells along the Mackenzie River covers about 370 km. That's 230 miles with no services and no help. There are numerous river crossings and wash-outs, and weather that can quickly change from one extreme to another. Food drops need to be organized, hiking gear and stamina needs to be top-of-the-line, and any type of recklessness might be paid for dearly. Cyclists and motor bikers have done this trail, but need to be warned that each year more and more of the former road is washed away, more river sections need to be forded and more boulders the size of a car need to be scrambled across. Only about the first 100 km / 62 miles are passable by those who have brought wheels - after that it's going to be hellish! Ideally, this trail should be done by a larger group of people with the resources to establish food drops either by small plane or helicopter, and who can assist each other in some of the possibly dangerous river crossings. The Twitya River, for example, is too deep to wade across. Hikers either need to swim across, or bring some sort of a floating device. For more information about the trail, and the free hikers guide, write to the SAHTU TOURISM ASSOCIATION, P.O. Box 115, Norman Wells, Northwest Territories, Canada X0E 0V0. Telephone 403-587-2054, Fax 403-587- 2935.

THE SOUTH CANOL ROAD FROM ROSS RIVER TO THE ALASKA HIGHWAY

It is 224 km / 139 miles to Johnson's Crossing and there are no services along the highway.

km 0 / mile 0 Junction of Canol Road and Campbell Highway.

km 1.9 / mile 1.2 Jackfish Lake; used by float planes.

km 6.1 / mile 3.8 Look for Hoodoos. They are caused by erosion; and contrary to some tall tales, they do not move during the full moon.

km 7.2 / mile 4.5 Lapie River Bridge No. 2. The road follows the canyon for the next few miles. It's a narrow winding road. Watch for rocks.

km 16.9 / mile 10.5 Look-out over the **Lapie River Canyon.**

km 47.3 / mile 29.4 Lapie River Bridge No. 1. The Lapie Canyon run is a favourite one for white water enthusiasts. Only go with those who know the canyon - there are some potentially very dangerous spots. Lapie was the Iroquois companion of Robert Campbell. This spot is 173 km / 107 miles from the Alaska Highway.

km 55.2 / mile 34.3 Access to Lapie Lakes. Good camping sites.

km 65 / mile 46.4 Rose River Bridge No. 6. From here to Rose River Bridge No. 1, it is an exiting day trip by canoe or kayak for those who know how to handle class III rapids. The best time is early summer.

km 114.7 / mile 71.3 Rose River Bridge No. 1.

km 121.2 / mile 75.3 Quiet Lake Yukon Government Maintenance Camp. No services. From here it is 99 km / 61.5 miles to the Alaska Highway.

km 121.6 / mile 75.6 Quiet Lake Recreation Site. Seven picnic sites with hand pump water, boat launch, fishing. It is the put-in for river travellers running down the **Big Salmon River** to Carmacks, which is 350 km / 217 miles away. Dawson City is 400 km / 250 miles further. The Big Salmon is a class II river and is okay for beginners, if all the others in the party are not beginners as well. The Big Salmon is one of the more popular rivers (after the Yukon and Teslin Rivers) - and it shows! Please keep a clean camp, take out your own garbage, and pick up garbage left behind by others. For the next 21 km / 13 miles the road follows the lake.

km 143.2 / mile 89 Quiet Lake Government Campground, 17 RV and tent sites with three sites for tents only, shelter, boat launch, fishing and swimming. You can begin a trip on the **Big Salmon River** here, but more lake paddling is necessary. Quiet Lake can be anything but quiet - be warned that high winds can whip up whitecaps within seconds. In 1881, the Big Salmon River was first travelled by four Juneau prospectors. The Tagish name for the river was Ta-Tlin-Hini, which means "big salmon". Earlier names given to this major tributary of the Yukon River were "Lyon" and "d'Abbadie." From the campground to the Alaska Highway it is 77 km / 48 miles.

km 152.5 / mile 94.8 Access road to the Nisutlin River, with a few tent sites, tables and outhouse. The Nisutlin is a flat, curvy and quiet river, rated class I along its entire length. "Nisutlin" means "quiet" in Tlingit. It is about four days, or 140 km / 87 miles back to Teslin on the Alaska Highway. Starting from here and going all the way to the Yukon River delta is one of the longest continuous paddle trips in North America - approximately 3200 km or 2000 miles, and it will turn any novice into an expert.

km 170.9 / mile 106.2 The side road leads to **Sydney Lake**, with some good tenting spots.

km 220.2 / mile 136.8 Junction with the Alaska Highway. Johnson's Crossing, with a service station, RV parking, tenting and cafe, is to the right and across the Teslin River Bridge.

THE CAMPBELL HIGHWAY FROM ROSS RIVER TO FARO AND CARMACKS

km 354.4 / mile 220.2 Junction of Campbell Highway #4 and Canol Road #6 near Ross River.

km 363 / mile 225.5 Ross River Road Intersection.

km 364.2 / mile 226.3 Lapie Canyon Government Campground, 14 RV and tent sites and 4 tent only sites, shelter, trails.

km 380.3 / mile 236.3 Danger Creek. Not what one might think - the creek was named after a horse!

km 426 / mile 264.7 Scenic viewpoint overlooking the mining community of Faro.

km 427.3 / mile 265.5 Junction to Faro, turn right (north). The village is located 10 km / 6 miles off the highway. About one third of the way to Faro, follow the signs to your right to the **Faro Airport**, and the **Johnson's Lake Government Campground**. There are 15 RV / campsites with a shelter, a boat launch, fishing and swimming. It's a further 6 km / 4 miles to Faro from the Government Campground. Next, you will cross the Pelly River where gold can be panned from sandbars - good luck!! Watch out for the fast current, though. Faro is just ahead, and so is the local sanitary land fill - better known as 'dump'. Faro's dump is famed the Yukon over as a prime but sad viewing area for grizzly bears.

FARO

The community of Faro is named after a card game, and was established in 1968 as Canada's largest lead-zinc mine. On June 13th, 1969, a forest fire destroyed most of the newly-built town, but it was rebuilt before the summer was over. The mine's fortunes have gone up and down. It was shut down in 1982, opened again in 1986, and closed again in 1993. The mine was opened for business in 1995, but the next closure may be in early 1997. Through all these years, the town of Faro survived, often only as a half-asleep ghost town, and sometimes as a thriving, bustling mining community. These days, tourism is doing its bit to keep Faro alive and there are some fascinating things to do in and around Faro. The population can fluctuate wildly, but about 500 people call Faro their permanent home. It's 356 km / 221 miles to Whitehorse and 534 km / 332 miles to Dawson City.

Some telephone numbers: RCMPolice: 994-5555. Fire: 994-2222. Hospital: 994-4444. Or call '0', the operator, to connect you. **CBC** radio is at 105.1 FM and CKRW on 98.7 FM. The **Faro Airstrip** is 914 m / 3000 feet long, gravel and at an elevation of 717 m / 2351 feet; fuel is available. Call 994-2791. **Visitor Centre**: Open daily in summer. Call 994-2728 or Fax 994-3154. Located across from the RV Park.

Faro Wilderness Association has more information about the Faro area. Write or call them at P.O. Box 389, Faro, YT, Y0B 1K0. Telephone 994-3239, Fax 994-3311. **Banking** at Toronto Dominion on Mon. from 10 to 5 p.m., Tues., Wed. and Thurs. from 10 to 2 p.m. and Friday from 10 to 6 p.m.

<u>**Where to stay - things to do:**</u>

Redmonds Motel and restaurant. Tel. 994-2430, Fax 994-3055.

Sally's Roadhouse. Motel. Restaurant, lounge, store and laundromat. Tel. 994-3109, Fax 994-2710.

Faro Hotel. Tel. 994-2400 and Fax 994-3251. Open year-round.

John Connolly RV Park. Tel. 994-2728, Fax 994-3154. 10 fully serviced RV sites.

Wongs Restaurant. Their telephone number is 994-2111.

Wits End Gallery. Quite a special place. Call ahead for opening times. Tel. 994-3344

Shane Wilson Carvings. Antler, horn and mastodon carvings for sale. Call 994-2060, fax 994-2560 or visit at 136 Dawson Drive.

Faro's other services are: service stations, a grocery store, government liquor store, video rental, post office, library, recreation centre with indoor swimming pool, tennis and squash court, and even a movie theatre, and two churches. Faro is famous for its wildlife viewing, especially grizzly bears. The townsfolk built a viewing deck with a cabin about 6 km / 4 miles out of town, with almost guaranteed viewing of fannin sheep, moose, caribou, wolves or grizzlies. There are many hikes of varying length in the vicinity of Faro, and most lakes and creeks nearby offer some of the best fishing in the Yukon. Good fishing may be found at Cousin's Lake, Pelly River, Blind Creek, Elephant Lake for graylings and / or salmon, Fisheye Lake for rainbow trout, and Swim Lake for lake trout.

The Faro / Ross River Annual Summer Arts Festival is held in early June, with exhibitions, storytelling, BBQs, and activities for all. Call Miranda Wilson in Faro at 994-2060, for more information and exact dates. Canoe rentals are available in Faro for floats all the way to Dawson City. The Pelly River between Faro and its confluence with the Yukon is rated Class I to II. Various wilderness adventure guides operate out of Faro.

Tour companies:

Faro Wilderness Adventures. Box 204, Faro, YT, Y0B 1K0. Tel. 994-2055.

Faro Yukon Fishing Tours. Box 625, Faro, YT, Y0B 1K0. Tel. 994-2339.

Horizon North Ltd. Box 736, Faro, YT, Y0B 1K0. Tel. 994-2878, Fax 994-3154. Canoe and motorboat rental, fishing trips and guided wilderness tours.

Snowy Mountain Safaris. Box 736, Faro, YT, Y0B 1K0. Tel. 994-2878, Fax 994-3154. Winter tours only.

Vangordo Transport offers charters and bus tours out of Faro, call 994-3790 or fax 994-2039; and so does **Faro - Ross River Taxi,** call them at 994-2433 or radio 2 M 8358.

We continue on the Campbell Highway toward Carmacks: The road between Faro and Carmacks is part gravel, part asphalt.

km 460 / mile 285.5 Magundy Airstrip. Summer only.

km 481.7 / mile 299.3 Lena's Place. Food and lodging. Mobile radio, YJ2 5865.

km 483 / mile 300.1 Drury Creek Government Campground. 6 RV / tent sites, shelter, boat launch, fishing. **Yukon Government Road Maintenance Camp**. No services except in emergencies.

km 510 / mile 316.9 Little Salmon Airstrip. Length 549 m / 1800 feet.

km 517.3 / mile 321.4 Little Salmon Lake Government Campground, 12 RV and tent sites with shelter, boat launch and fishing. The Little Salmon River can be paddled from the campground, for a 50 km / 31 mile, 1 to 2 day trip (class I - II) to Little Salmon Village on the Yukon River, or a further 60 km / 38 miles to Carmacks. There are many take-out points along the road.

km 559 / mile 347.3 Junction with Frenchman - Tatchun Road. This gravel side road, with a total length of 46.2 km / 28.7 miles, is curvy and narrow, and thus requires slow driving. Thousands of years ago, the Yukon River used to run where these two lakes are located, before carving its present longer route via Carmacks. Some years ago, there was a proposal to dam the Yukon River, diverting it back into its age-old berth, in order to create a huge hydro-electrical power source. Happily this idea was shelved. The road passes the Frenchman and Tatchun lakes, providing a short-cut to the Klondike Highway and Dawson City. There are three Government Campgrounds on this road.

A gold mining operation.

- km 8 / mile 5 Frenchman Lake Campground, with 10 RV and tent sites.

- km 15 / mile 9.3 Nanutak Campground, with 10 RV and tent sites.

- km 41.4 / mile 25.7 Tatchun Lake Campground, with 20 RV and tent sites.

The distances to the three campgrounds from the Klondike Highway are: **Tatchun Lake** is at km 8.4 / mile 5.2; **Nanutak** at km 33.3 / mile 20.7 and **Frenchman Lake** at km 41.9 / mile 25.9. Both lakes are beautiful clear-water lakes, with great boating and fishing.

km 562.4 / mile 349.5 Access to Little Salmon Village and the Yukon River. There are no services at the end of this 1.4 km / 0.9 mile road.

km 573.2 / mile 356.2 Rest stop overlooking Eagles Nest Bluff and Yukon River. This bluff (cliff) was an important landmark for crews of river steamers. It was here, on September 25, 1906, where one of the worst paddle-wheeler accidents occurred. Even though it was against regulations, Phil Murray, a deckboy of the steamer Columbia, was shooting at squirrels. Surprised by a fireman, he stumbled while handing over the rifle, the gun discharged and accidentally hit a pile of three tons of gunpowder and explosives. The explosion totally destroyed the steamer, killing six of the crew.

km 595.4 / mile 370 Carmacks Airstrip. The gravel runway is 1585 m / 5200 feet long at an elevation of 539 m / 1770 feet. Carmacks is 8 km / 5 miles away.

km 600.2 / mile 373 Junction with the Klondike Highway #2. To your left (south) it's 3.2 km / 2 miles to Carmacks, which offers all services (see Klondike chapter for information on Carmacks). The distance to Whitehorse is 178 km / 111 miles. Turning right at the junction (north), it is 360 km / 224 miles to Dawson City.

Klondike Highway

The Discovery Claim on Bonanza Road near Dawson City.

WHITEHORSE TO CARMACKS

It is 9 km / 5.6 miles from Whitehorse to the junction of the Alaska and Klondike Highways. See Alaska Highway chapter.

Distances from Whitehorse: Carmacks, 178 km / 111 miles. **Dawson City,** 536 km / 333 miles. **Faro,** 356 km / 221 miles. **Inuvik,** 1222 km / 759 miles. **Stewart Crossing,** 354 km / 220 miles. **Tok,** - via the "Top of the World Highway", 837 km / 520 miles.

km 0 / mile 0 Junction of Alaska and Klondike Highways. The Klondike Highway is asphalted north to Dawson City, except where construction or re-aligning of the highway creates dust and / or mud. Kilometre posts along the highway reflect the distance travelled from Skagway. This road was built in the 1950s to connect Whitehorse with the silver mines in Mayo and Keno. Only as recently as 1960, was the road extended to Dawson City. The completion of the highway effectively halted all river steamer traffic on the Yukon River. The modern highway closely follows the original trail between both cities.

km 3.7 / mile 2.3 Takhini River Bridge. The Takhini River is quite popular with river travellers, and has occasional class II - III rapids. The float usually starts at Kusawa Lake Campground, and it is a multi-day affair. The Yukon River is a stone's throw away from the bridge.

km 6.1 / mile 3.8. Junction with Takhini Hot Springs Road. It is 10 km / 6.2 miles on a paved road to the hot springs. Before arriving at the hot springs, you will find access to the **Yukon Wildlife Preserve;** and **Country Cabin B&B,** tel. 633-5011, open year-round. **Takhini hot springs,** tel. 633-2706, are open year-round, and have a constant water temperature of 47°C/117°F. The pool itself averages 38°C or 100°F. Minerals contained in the water are mostly calcium, magnesium, and iron, with a slight odour of sulphur. RV park and tenting with restaurant, cafe, coin laundry. Towels and bathing suits are for rent. Horseback riding in summer, and groomed cross-country ski trails in winter. Tenting sites are $8, and with hook-ups $10.

km 15.5 / mile 9.6 Policeman's Point Road with access to **Heart's Content B&B.** Tel. 667-4972. The B&B is located 15.3 km or 9.5 miles from the highway.

km 16.2 / mile 10 Ten Mile Road accesses **Tahini-Wud B&B.** Tel. and Fax 667-4169.

km 17.2 / mile 10.7 Shallow Bay Road offers access to **Northern Splendor Reindeer Farm.** Open 7 a.m. to 6 p.m. in summer. Tel. 633-2992.

km 20.4 / mile 12.7 Horse Creek Road.

km 24.2 / mile 15.3 Dog Sled Inn B&B. Tel. 667-2901. Open year-round.

km 32.8 / mile 20.4 Access road to Lake Laberge and the Gov. Campground 3 km / 1.8 miles away, 22 RV and tent sites with shelter and boat launch. Boil the water to purify it. On the road there are several businesses, including a bakery and a canoe rental. The campground is a convenient take-out point for one to two day canoe trips from Whitehorse, or as a starting point for river trips downstream toward Carmacks or Dawson City. Lake Laberge is a 64 km / 40 mile long, narrow lake between 2 and 4 km wide. The Yukon River enters the lake at its southern end, bringing with it many happy boaters. Due to pollution, fish should not be eaten, nor the water be used for anything but getting your feet wet - at least until further notice. Once the river spills out of the northern end of the lake, fish and water are fit to be consumed again; however, the water still should be either treated or boiled. Boaters should be aware that high winds can whip up the surface of the lake into a froth within seconds. Unless your boat is a big one, always stay close to shore.

km 48 / mile 29.8 Fox Lake and Cranberry Point B&B. Mobile radio - JJ3 9257. Fox Lake Channel.

km 56 / mile 34.8 Fox Lake Government Campground, 30 RV and tent sites, three tenting only sites. Shelter, boat launch and good fishing for burbot, lake trout and grayling. Watch for muskrats feeding on aquatic vegetation.

km 70.5 / mile 43.8 Little Fox Lake. Rest stop with beach.

km 89.5 / mile 55.6 Breaburn Lodge. Mobile radio 2M 3987. Service station, B&B, cafe and camping. Open year-round. On the other side of the highway is the **Cinnamon Bun Landing Strip.** The airstrip derives its name from the lodge's famous enormous cinnamon buns. It is 914 m / 2998 ft long on gravel; elevation 716 m / 2349 feet - the landing strip, of course, not the cinnamon bun! The Whitehorse - Dawson bus stops at the lodge Monday, Wednesday and Friday at 09:30, headed for Dawson City, and at 20:45, to Whitehorse.

km 106.7 / mile 66.3 This rest stop showcases an interesting geological feature - the Whitehorse Trough Conglomerates. The conglomerates were deposited by underwater landslides and volcanic mud flows about 185 million years ago (Jurassic times). This geologic action formed huge sheaths, or fans, up to 1 km wide and 100 m thick, extending for almost 400 km / 250 miles from Carmacks to Atlin in the south. The rounded boulders near the rest stop are eroded volcanic mountains, which were deposited here in ancient times when there was a huge lake right where you are parking. The Fingers of the Five Finger Rapids in the Yukon River are formed by these conglomerates. This is a great place for rock-hounds.

km 115.2 / mile 71.6 Rest stop on both sides of the road at Twin Lakes.

km 116.4 / mile 72.3 Twin Lakes Government Campground, 8 RV and tent sites with shelter, boat launch, fishing.

km 131 / mile 81.4 Rest stop at the historic remains of a roadhouse built in 1899. The Montague House was one of 55 roadhouses built at approximately 30 km / 19 mile intervals along the Whitehorse - Dawson City Trail. They provided shelter and food for travellers on the stage coach trail.

km 163 / mile 101.3 The Nordenskiold River is to the west - the river flows into the Yukon River near Carmacks. The coastal Chilkats used this river to approach the interior Indians for trading. The native name for the river is "Thuch-en-Dituh", meaning "meeting place". Schwatka, of the US Army, named this river after Baron Nils Nordenskiold, a famous Swedish explorer.

CARMACKS

km 165.3 / mile 102.7 Village of Carmacks. The population is about 500, and Carmacks is not only the largest, but also the busiest stop on this highway.

For emergencies call: RCMPolice: 863-5555. **Fire:** 863-2222. **Nurse:** 863-4444. **Ambulance:** 1-667-3333.

CBC Radio is at 990 AM; for news and weather on the hour. **Banking** services by CIBC on Tues. and Thurs. from 11 a.m. to 2 p.m. Tel. 863-5015. **Visitor Information** is located in the 'old Telegraph Office'. Open daily in summer. Tel 863-6271. Fax 863-6606

The community of **Carmacks** is named after George Washington Carmack, who was born Sept. 24, 1860, in Port Costo, California. In 1885, he went north on a quest for gold, crossing the Chilkoot Trail with some other men in April of that year. Prospecting and panning his way down the Yukon River, he started to live with members of the Tagish Tribe and, to some extent, adopted their life-style. Forming a friendship with Skookum Jim Mason and his sister Kate, he built a cabin near the Five Finger Rapids, in order to develop coal seams nearby. That was in 1893. It was Carmack, Skookum Jim and Tagish Charlie, three friends and partners, who found what turned out to be one of the biggest gold discoveries ever, on Rabbit Creek, the 16th of August 1896 - afterwards re-named Bonanza Creek. Carmack died on June 5, 1922, in Vancouver, BC. In many accounts of the gold discovery written after 1896, George Carmack was pictured as a lazy White man, a "drifter" who did not work for a living but associated with natives instead of other "White folks". It has been suggested that Carmack was one of the few adventurers from the South who saw the native people of the Yukon as equals - living with them, learning their ways and sharing their life. It also seems to be true that Kate, Carmack's wife, was with those three when the gold strike was made, and it has been suggested that maybe it was she who found the gold.

Where to stay:

Carmacks Hotel. Tel. 863-5221, Tel. & Fax 863-5605. Service station with general store, bakery and camping supplies, hotel, motel with restaurant and lounge. Also offers coin laundry with showers, boat tours to Five Finger Rapids and Fort Selkirk. Bus stops to Dawson City at 11:15, and Whitehorse at 21:00 every Monday, Wednesday and Friday.

Sunset Motel. Tel. 863-5266, Fax 863-5260.

Mukluk Manor B&B. Tel. 863-5232

Carmacks Community Campground is located right alongside the Yukon River. Do not leave your belongings unattended! Tel. 863-6271. Fax 863-6606.

Other services:

High Noon Cafe. May not be open. Call or Fax to 863-5714 to find out.

Northern Tutchone Trading Post. Tel. 863-5381, Fax 863-5611. The Trading Post is located at the north end of the bridge, and has a service station with minor car repairs, a general store with a post office, and CIBC banking services. Open year-round. Tourist Information tent and native craft shop.

Canadian Wilderness Travel. Tel. 863-5404, Fax 863-5405. Box 114, Carmacks, YT, Y0B 1C0. German spoken. Adventure tours, Yukon River tours and canoe rental.

Five Finger Tours. Box 56, Carmacks, YT, Y0B 1C0. Tel. 863-5001.

Gold Rush River Tours. Box 134, Carmacks, YT, Y0B 1C0. Tel. and Fax numbers same as Carmacks Hotel. Yukon River tours to as far as Fort Selkirk.

Create your own tour! Take the 11:15 bus to the Five Finger Rapids Recreation Site, with an overlook and stairways down to the rapids. Then take the bus back to Carmacks at around 21:00. Tell the driver about your intentions, and pack lunch and something to drink. It is 23 km / 15 miles one-way, and this trip works only on Mon., Wed. and Fri. from June to the end of August. The other months it is Wednesday and Friday only.

Walk the Carmacks Boardwalk, which is 2 km long and follows the Yukon River, and offers viewing platforms and benches. The walk is wheelchair accessible. At the south end of the bridge, look for the trailhead to Coal Mine Lake. It is a 4 km / 2.4 mile round trip.

The Carmacks Roadhouse Heritage Site, built in 1903, was one of the many roadhouses along the Whitehorse - Dawson City Trail. The building is being restored.

There is a summer only **public pool** on Victoria Crescent.

River travellers who arrived in Carmacks with rented canoes can drop them off at designated places. Those with their own canoes, and no vehicle, can check with the rental companies for space, or call **Frontier Freightliners** in Dawson City, tel. 993-5402 for their next truck passing through. You can start your Dawson City bound river trip in Carmacks, or rent a canoe for a day or two to shoot the Five Finger Rapids. A take-out is at Tatchun Creek, about 40 km / 25 miles (by river) from Carmacks.

km 168 / mile 104.4 Junction with Campbell Highway #4 to Faro, Ross River and Watson Lake. The distance from Carmacks to Faro is 180 km / 112 miles; to Ross River 232 km / 144 miles and to Watson Lake 602 km / 374 miles (See Campbell Highway chapter).

km 189 / mile 117.5 Five Finger Rapids Recreation Site is a rest stop with a viewpoint and a long flight of steps (220 at latest count) down to a viewing deck overlooking the rapids. With luck, there will be river travellers lining up to shoot the opening closest to the viewpoint. All the other channels are dangerous. During the Gold Rush, negotiating steamers over these rapids proved to be quite a hazard, and many of the early stampeders lost all their possessions here, and some lost their lives.

km 191.3 / mile 118.9 Tatchun Creek Bridge. The road just past the bridge (west of the road) leads to the Yukon River. **Tatchun Creek Government Campground** (east of the road), has 12 RV and tent sites with shelter and fishing. Tatchun Creek is off-limits for fishing from August 1 to September 30.

km 192.5 / mile 119.6 Junction with the Frenchman - Tatchun Road. There are three government campgrounds on this 40 km / 25 mile long gravel road that connects to the Campbell Highway. The Tatchun Road is a beautiful stretch of highway in autumn. *(See previous chapter for information on these government campgrounds).*

km 238.2 / mile 148 Minto Resorts Ltd. In Whitehorse call 633-5251. RV park and campground with snack bar, ice, showers and coin laundry. This resort is located next to the Yukon River, offering 80 km / 50 mile round-trips by boat to Fort Selkirk. This six hour excursion leaves daily at 10:00; $50 per person.

km 239.1 / mile 148.6 Minto Landing Government Campground is 2 km/1.2 miles off the highway, alongside the river. It is a convenient put-in and take-out point for river travellers. During its heyday, Minto Landing used to be a busy trading post, native village, and river steamer stop. Paddle-wheelers delivered construction material for the building of the Klondike Highway, but once the highway was built, Minto as a community vanished. The Minto Airstrip is 1524 m / 5000 feet long, and at an elevation of 472 m or 1550 feet.

PELLY CROSSING

km 272.6 / mile 169.4 The Village of Pelly Crossing has mostly a native population, of about 300. **RCMPolice**: 537-5555. **Nursing Station**: 537-4444. If no answer at either number, call toll-free 1-403-667-5555 or call the operator at "0". **CBC** radio is located at 100.1 FM.

The village is the take-out point for upper Pelly River travellers, or a starting point for canoe trips to Fort Selkirk, or north to Dawson City. The river was named by Robert Campbell for Sir John Henry Pelly (1777-1852), then Governor of the Hudson Bay Co.

The Klondike Valley and Highway from Crocus Bluff. Dawson City.

Midnight sun from the Dempster Hwy (middle).

Midnight Dome in Dawson City on June 21, Solstice Day (bottom).

View across Dawson City and the Midnight Dome from the Top of the World Highway, at the end of August.

An early native name for the Pelly was "Ayan" or "Lyon", after a native tribe from this area. Driving north and across the bridge, stop at the overlook just up the hill. There are good views across the village and the Pelly River Valley.

Services in Pelly Crossing:

Selkirk Gas Bar, Tel. 537-3307, Fax 537-3016, 24 hour access to the gas bar with Visa / Mastercard cardlock. Store, cafe, campground and a post office (tel. 537-3614). Open all year. **Norline Coaches** stop here, continuing on to Dawson City at 12:15, and returning to Whitehorse at 20:00 on Mon., Wed., and Fri. Also visit the **Heritage Centre**, which has native crafts and art.

Pelly Crossing Campground is on the south side of the bridge. No charge. Firepits and shelter. A **swimming pool** is open in summer only, call 537-3151 for hours open.

Banking services by CIBC on Tues. and Thurs. from 10 a.m. to 3 p.m. Tel. 537-3515. **Pelly Crossing Airstrip**, length 914 m / 3000 feet, at an elevation of 570 m / 1870 feet, is 3.5 km / 2 miles north of the village.

km 298.5 / mile 185.5 Access road to Jackfish Lake, with good fishing.

km 314.8 / mile 195.6 Access road to Wrong Lake, with good fishing.

km 333.4 / mile 207.2 Ethel Lake Government Campground is 29 km / 15 miles off the highway on a gravel road, with 14 RV and tent sites, a boat launch, fishing and swimming. Nearby, and not accessible by road, is the **McArthur Wildlife Sanctuary**. Many species of wildlife, including fannin sheep, as well as various hot springs, can be found within the sanctuary. Check with **Crooked Creek Wilderness Tours**; General Delivery, Stewart Crossing, YT, Y1A 4N1. Tel. and Fax 996-2721; for guided horseback tours and other wilderness trips in this area.

STEWART CROSSING

km 344.2 / mile 213.9 Village of Stewart Crossing. An important highway stop with a population of about 50. There is a Government Highway Maintenance Camp in the community.

The Stewart River is named after James G. Stewart who travelled on this river for the first time in 1849 - he was an assistant to Robert Campbell. Stewart Crossing started out as a trading post in 1868, and functioned as a major re-fuelling stop for river steamers. Dawson City is four to five days away by canoe, via the historic Stewart Island at the confluence of the Stewart and Yukon Rivers.

Services in Stewart Crossing:

Stewart Crossing Lodge. Tel. 996-2501. Service station with car and tire repairs, propane. Motel with restaurant and cafe. Camping and RV parking. The lodge is being rebuilt, and might not be open for the 1997 season. The service station will be open for business. **The Norline Bus** stops here Mon., Wed. and Fri. at 13:20 for Dawson City, and at 18:30 for Whitehorse. **Mayo Taxi Service** meets these buses, for trips to Mayo, Elsa and Keno. To verify, call 996-2240 or Fax 996-2225.

Hilda's RV Park. Tel. 996-2714. RV ($10) and tenting ($3) sites with showers and a snack bar.

Whispering Willows RV Park. Tel. 996-2411. Grocery store, cafe, and car repairs with gas. Hook-ups.

Check with the Silver Trail Kiosk for information about Mayo, Elsa and Keno, if you are heading that way.

km 345 / mile 214.4 At the northern end of the Stewart River Bridge, is the junction with Silver Trail Road #11. To the right, the road leads northeast to **Mayo** - 52.8 km / 33 miles; to **Elsa** - 98 km / 61 miles, and to **Keno** - 112 km / 70 miles.

Let's follow the **Silver Trail Road** as far as Keno. The road is paved to Mayo, and is well maintained gravel beyond the town. The area around Mayo used to be one of the richest silver producing mining regions in Canada. Gold was found at the mouth of the Mayo River in 1902, and silver deposits were discovered at Keno in 1919, and at Elsa in 1929. The first man to prospect this area was Alexander McDonald from New Brunswick. In 1887, he came across a large lake, naming it after a friend - Captain Alfred S. Mayo, who was the owner of a small steamboat called the New Racket. Mayo was born in Maine, and in his younger life used to be a circus acrobat. Alfred S. Mayo was a founding member of the Yukon Order of Pioneers.

km 0 / mile 0 Junction of Klondike and Silver Trail Highways.

km 22 / mile 14 Hungry Mountain Farm and Research Station. Visitors welcome. Tel. 667-1054 in summer.

km 44.1 / mile 27.4 Rest stop with picnic tables.

km 50.2 / mile 31.2 McIntyre Park with nine picnic sites overlooking the Mayo River.

km 50.3 / mile 31.3 Mayo River Bridge. Fishing from bridge.

km 51.3 / mile 31.9 Junction. To the right (south), the road goes to Mayo. To Elsa and Keno, keep to the left. It is 2 km / 1.2 miles to Mayo.

MAYO

The **community of Mayo** has a population of about 500, and is home to the Na Cho N'y'ak Dun Mayo Indian Band.

Some telephone numbers:

RCMPolice: 996-5555. **Fire:** 996-2222. **Ambulance:** 996-2345. **CBC** radio can be found at 1230 AM. **Banking: CIBC** is open Tues., Thurs. and Friday from 10 a.m. to 2 p.m. and their tel. number is 996-2039. The **Visitor Centre** and town office are in the **Binet House**. The Interpretive Centre not only offers information about the Mayo area, but has an extensive display on environmental and geological features of the district. You can obtain more information by writing to Box 160, Mayo, YT, Y0B 1M0. Tel. 996-2317, Fax 996-2907. Information about the Mayo, Elsa, and Keno district is available from the **Silver Trail Tourism Association**, Box 268, Mayo, YT, Y0B 1M0. Tel. in summer 996-2929, in winter 996-2024, Fax 996-2907. **Air North** connects Mayo with scheduled flights to Whitehorse and Dawson City. The airstrip is located 6.5 km / 4 miles out of town. The length of the runway is 1478 m / 4850 feet, at an elevation of 503 m / 1650 feet. Tel. 996-2334. There is a **taxi / bus** service to Stewart Crossing which connects with Norline Coaches. Call 996-2240 for the schedule.

Other services in Mayo include a restaurant, cafe, hardware and grocery store, post office, government liquor store, library, swimming pool, and a service station. Ask at the Visitor Centre for individual crafts people who sell their art from their homes.

Where to stay:

Bedrock Motel. Tel. 996-2290, Fax 996-2728. 12 units from $70, with restaurant, public showers, coin laundry.

North Star Motel. Tel. 996-2231, Fax 996-2934. From $55 single to $65 double. All units have kitchenettes. Open year-round and 24 hours a day.

Country Charm B&B. Tel. and Fax 996-2918. $45 single & $50 double. No smoking, no pets. Summer only.

Mayo B&B. Tel. 996-2221, Fax 996-2810. Near Five Mile Lake just outside Mayo.

Holly's Place B&B. Tel. 996-2029.

Moose Bay Ventures. Tel. and Fax 667-1068. This adventure operator offers wilderness cabins near Mayo, with photo and hiking excursions, as well as canoe rentals.

It is an easy float from here down either the Mayo or Stewart River to Stewart Crossing, 60 km / 38 miles away.

Annual Festivals in Mayo:

Third week of March. Winter Carnival; from moose calling to nail pounding and tea boiling.

July 1st Canada Day Celebrations. Slow-pitch tournament and kids games. For the above two events, call Gordon at 996-2600.

Mid to late July. Mayo Motorsport Weekend. Timed races, BBQ and family events. Call Daren at 996-2290.

Early to mid-August. Annual Mayo Mountain Maniac Triathlon Race combines swimming, biking and running. Call Gordon at 996-2600.

Mid-September. Terry Fox Charity Run. All can participate. Call Joan at 996-2237 for more information.

MAYO TO KENO

km 52.8 / mile 32.8 Access to **Mayo Airport.**

km 55.5 / mile 34.5 Country Charm B&B. See listing under Mayo.

km 56.2 / mile 35 Access road to **Mayo River Hydro Dam.**

km 57.6 / mile 35.8 Five Mile Lake Government Campground, 20 RV and tent sites with shelter, playground, boat launch, fishing, swimming and hiking trail.

km 58 / mile 36 Five Mile Lake Recreation Site. Day use only.

km 69 / mile 42.9 Junction. To the left is the **Minto Lake Road** which leads 19 km / 12 miles away to Minto Lake, which offers good fishing for trout and grayling. **To the right** is the **Duncan Creek Road**, which leads to the large and beautiful mountain-framed Mayo Lake. Watch for the **Duncan Creek Golddusters** along the road - a working gold mine offering guided tours and gold panning. Mayo Lake is a very good fishing lake, but be wary of high winds. From Mayo Lake, the Duncan Road continues on to Keno City and Elsa via a narrow gravel road. **Straight ahead** the road continues to **Elsa.**

km 77.2 / mile 48 Halfway Lake and the Silver Trail Lodge. Lodging and food in summer. Call mobile radio YSR 9044.

km 78.8 / mile 49 Mount Haldone Lions Shelter. Follow signs to a 6.4 km / 4 mile long trail to the summit.

km 88.3 / mile 54.9 Junction with South McQuesten River Road. It is 8 km / 5 miles to the river and a non-maintained camping site. From there, it is an 120 km / 75 mile canoe float to where the river crosses the Klondike Highway en route to Dawson City. At high water, sweepers (tree's that have been washed off river banks 'sweeping' the river) can be hazardous.

km 97 / mile 60.3 The community of Elsa was established as a mining camp when large calumet silver-lead deposits were discovered in 1929. Production did not get under way until 1939, but the mine shut down in 1989 because of depressed silver prices. There is only a small number of permanent residents in Elsa.

KENO

km 112 / mile 69 About 25 people live in Keno City, a former silver mining centre that was moth-balled in 1989 when United Keno Hill ceased operations. Keno's location is breath-taking, with commanding views and many hiking trails nearby. Keno got its name from a popular gambling game. In 1919, a miner by the name of Louis Bouvette found the first rich silver deposits. He called his first staked claim "the Keno". Until 1989, hundreds of people lived in Keno, but nowadays it's down to just a handful - many of them making a living from tourism.

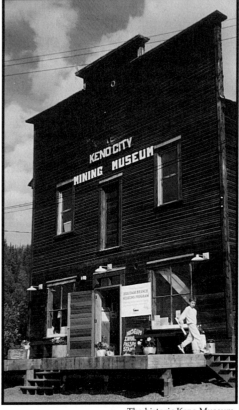

The historic Keno Museum.

<u>Where to stay and what to do</u>:

Keno City Hotel. Tel. 995-2312. A unique place, especially the bar. The hotel has a coffee-shop, but only limited food service. Public showers and a coin laundry.

Keno City Campground. Tel. 995-2792, 7 sites with shelter, and a wood stove, firewood and water. Open from June 1, to the end of August.

Keno City Snackbar. Tel. 995-2409. Open daily in summer from 10 a.m. to 6 p.m.; soups and sandwiches.

Keno City Mining Museum. Tel. 995-2792. Open daily in summer from 10 a.m. to 6 p.m. No admission charge. Mining implements dating from the turn of the century. This beautifully maintained wooden structure was build in the 1920s and used to be Jackson Dance Hall. The building was rescued from neglect as recently as 1994, and turned into a museum. The museum is one of the more fascinating historical sites the Yukon has to offer.

Hike or drive up to Keno Hill, formerly called Sheep Hill. The distance to the summit is 10.5 km / 6.5 miles.

The Duncan Creek Road can be taken back to the **Silver Trail Road,** completing the loop to **Mayo** and back to the **Stewart River Bridge** on the **Klondike Highway.**

STEWART CROSSING TO DAWSON CITY

km 361 / mile 224.4 Access to Stewart River, with information panels on the history of the river.

km 368.7 / mile 229 Moose Creek Lodge. Mobile radio JL3 9570. Fax 996-2139. RV park and log cabins for rent (from $45), cafe. A very pretty and rustic place. Open May to September.

km 369.3 / mile 229.5 Moose Creek Government Campground, 30 RV and tent sites, with 6 tenting only sites. Shelter, playground, fishing and hiking trails.

km 390.6 / mile 242.7 McQuesten River Bridge. River trips that started near Elsa can end here, or continue on to Dawson City. **Spruce Grove RV Park,** 11 RV and tenting sites, with three overnight cabins for rent. Cafe and picnic sites. The river is named after Leroy Napoleon McQuesten, who was born in 1836, in Litchfield, New Hampshire. He worked the gold fields north along the Fraser River in British Columbia during 1858. Arriving in the Yukon in 1873, he became a major player in the Yukon's history as a trader and prospector. Earning his wealth by "grubstaking" others, he was called the "Father of the Yukon". He left the Yukon in 1898, a rich man.

A prospector working the area around Mayo Lake.

km 398.3 / mile 247.5 Partridge Creek Farm and B&B; $45 to $65, closed Saturdays. Dial 1311 and ask the operator for Radio 2M 3168 Stewart Channel. Organic vegetables in season.

km 401.2 / mile 249.3 McQuesten Airstrip is two kilometres off the highway to the west. The length of runway is 1524 m / 5000 feet, elevation 457 m / 1500 feet.

km 419 / mile 260.4 Access to Barlow Lake.

km 432.6 / mile 268.2 Gravel Lake is just to the east.

km 438.5 / mile 272.5 Rest stop.

km 464.9 / mile 288.9 Rest stop.

km 465.6 / mile 289.3 Tintina Trench rest stop and scenic viewpoint offers views across the Klondike River Valley, and for most of the year, the snow-capped Ogilvie Mountains. This trench, visible evidence of the geologic theory of plate tectonics, extends across Alaska and the Yukon. The word "Tintina" means "Chief" or "Major", indicating a chief or major fault line - named by R.G. McConnell in 1901-02.

km 479 / mile 297 The southern arm of the **Klondike River** is to your right (North).

km 485.4 / mile 301.6 Junction with **Dempster Highway #5 to Inuvik. Klondike River Lodge.** Tel. and Fax 993-6892. Motel and restaurant with RV parking, grocery store. Service station with all repairs and propane. Open year-round from 7 a.m. to midnight. **Norline Coaches** briefly stops here at about 15:00, headed for Dawson City; and at 16:30 for Whitehorse. Driving north along the Dempster Highway, the next fuel is available in **Eagle Plains** 372 km / 231 miles away. To **Inuvik** it is 726 km / 451 miles (See Dempster Highway Chapter). From the junction, it is a one day canoe float from the Klondike River Bridge, just off the junction, to Dawson City, about 50 km or 31 miles away. Transportation and canoe rentals are available in Dawson. By road it is a further 42 km / 25.6 miles to Dawson City.

km 500 / mile 311 Farmland and subdivision of **Henderson Corner.**

km 502.3 / mile 312 Subdivision of **Rock Creek,** with fire station.

km 507.3 / mile 315.2 Klondike River Government Campground, 38 RV and tent sites with shelters, and trails to the river.

km 508 / mile 315.7 Dawson City Airport. One runway 1524 m / 5000 feet long, at an elevation of 369 m / 1211 feet. Fuel is available. Scheduled flights to Fairbanks, Alaska, Whitehorse, Inuvik, Old Crow and Mayo. **Flight service station**, tel. 993-5338. **Airport Manager,** tel. 993-5547. **Customs,** tel. 993-5455.

km 510.3 / mile 317.1 Hunker Creek Road is a mining road that loops around **King Solomon Dome**, goes on to the Bonanza Creek Road, and comes back to this highway. It is a total distance of 96 km / 60 miles. It is a narrow, twisting dirt road through working gold mining territory. Drive slowly and carefully, and please respect the privacy of working gold claims. **Goldbottom Mining Tours,** tel. 993-5023, is 13 km up the Hunker Road, this company offers escorted tours through an authentic and working gold mine. Open daily, except Sundays, from 11 to 7 p.m. A full tour is $12 and gold panning is $5 per person. Their gift shop offers nuggets for sale, and a B&B is under construction. The road following the ridges on either side of the **King Solomon Dome** area (1239 m / 4048 feet) has some pull-outs for overnight parking. The **Dominion Creek** and **Sulphur Creek Roads** loop will add a further 72 km / 45 miles of driving distance. There are no services on either loop road, and large motorhomes might find the driving difficult - especially after heavy rains when the road is slippery. Over 80% of the 26 km / 16 mile long Hunker Creek has been mined, dredged, and turned over - and more than once. Gold is still being mined here and on other creeks in the area.

Albert (Andrew) Hunker, born in Wittenberg, Germany, was the first person to stake a claim on Hunker Creek. When he and his Swedish friend, Charles Johnson, heard of the gold strike on Bonanza Creek, they rushed to the Klondike Valley hoping to find some open ground to stake along the creek. Miners then had 60 days to register a claim with a mining recorder, the nearest one being at Fortymile Village, a fair distance downstream from Dawson City. They found some open ground to stake on Rabbit Creek, but with time to spare, they kept on going - up another creek of the Klondike River. There, on September 11, 1896, and 20 km / 12 miles up a small creek, they both found their 'Eldorado'. Hunker staked the Discovery Claim, and the creek was subsequently named after him. Apparently, they met with Henderson, the original discoverer of gold on Rabbit Creek (Bonanza Creek), and told him about the Gold Rush and that most of the rich ground had already been staked. Henderson was working a claim near the Hunker Valley, but by then it was too late - he had missed out on one of the richest gold strikes in modern history.

km 513.2 / mile 318.9 Access to the subdivision of **Bear Creek.**

km 514.3./ mile 319.6 Entrance to Bear Creek - Parks Canada Heritage Site. Open daily in summer from 9:30 a.m. to 5 p.m. Admission charge is $5; less for kids, families and groups of 10 or more. The 25 hectare / 62 acre Bear Creek Complex was built in 1905 to support the work of up to a dozen huge gold dredges. The Yukon Consolidated Gold Corporation Ltd. was one of various large companies that had turned the Klondike Mining District from an individual effort of thousands working their tiny claims to one where a large corporation owned whole valleys. Bear Creek Co., which could build almost any kind of machinery from scratch in its foundry, blacksmith shop, and machine tool workshops, ceased operation in 1966. Parks Canada now operates the Bear Creek Complex, offering tours and movie showings of a gold dredge at work (See Dredge #4 and Yukon Ditch). Driving the last miles toward Dawson City, notice the vast piles of rocks and gravel littering both sides of the highway. They are the marks of gold dredges which deposited their washed-out gold bearing gravel, which look like claw-marks of an alien monster.

-**Bear Creek B&B** is beautifully located near the entrance to the Heritage Site. Tel. 993-5605. Fax 993-6532.

km 520.3 / mile 323.3 First access road into the **Callison Industrial Park**, with a propane distributor, welding shops, saw mill, heavy equipment repairs, and the trucking company **Frontier Freightliners**. There is access to the **Ridge Trail** at the end of the industrial road. The trailhead skirts a gravel pit to the left.

km 520.6 / mile 323.5 Second access road to Callison Industrial Park. **Blattler Services** on the corner, repairs RVs and other cars. Certified mechanics, welding. Tel. 993-6232.

km 522.2 / mile 324.5 Bonanza Creek Road is a well-maintained gravel road which follows the famous Bonanza Creek to **Dredge #4** and the **Discovery Claim**, 14.8 km / 9.3 miles from this junction. There are no services on this road other than a gold panning business and mining companies. See page 150.

- **Guggieville RV Park**, Tel. 993-5008/5319, Fax 993-5006, 100 RV and campsites fully serviced. Showers and coin laundry, RV wash and supplies, small store. Gold panning instructions. $13.75 for serviced site; $8.75 un-serviced.

- **Trail of 98 Restaurant.** Tel. 993-5664, Fax 993-5943. Un-serviced RV parking and tenting, and mini golf. Open from 7 a.m. to 11 p.m.

km 522.5 / mile 324.7 Dawson City RV Park and Campground. Tel. and Fax 993-5142. Full service station with repairs, car wash, and propane. Rooms for rent from $42 and 70 RV and campsites, from $10. Free gold-panning, and a small grocery store. Showers.

- **Northern Kat**. Tel. 993-5710, Fax 993-5089. Complete RV, motorcoach and car repairs with welding, full wash and vehicle storage, 24 hour self-serve credit card fuel access.

km 522.7 / mile 324.8 Klondike River Bridge. Robert Campbell might have mentioned this river as "Deer River" in 1851. Native names include "Chandik" and "Thron-Duck" or "Tron Deg" meaning either "Deer" or "Hammer Water", after a native custom of driving stakes into the water, in order to form fish traps. This was too complicated for miners tongues, so the name slowly changed to "Clunedik" and then from "Clundyke" to "Clondyke", finally settling on "Klondyke". "Klondike" became the official name in 1898. It has been said that the three friends, George Carmack, Skookum, Jim Mason, and Tagish (Dawson) Charlie, a nephew of Jim, had no luck fishing for salmon on the Klondike River; so instead of fishing, they decided to trek up

Rabbit Creek, hunting for moose and panning for gold as they went. Skookum Jim Mason's native name was Keish, meaning Wolf, and Skookum means 'strong' - which he was. Apparently, Jim's sister Kate, who was married to George Carmack, and Jim's wife, Mary also were at the fish camp. It is likely that all five of them trekked up Rabbit Creek, but these two women are hardly mentioned in any historical account, which figures - it was a man's world out there and, to a large extend, it's history was written by men.

The Klondike used to be a rich salmon spawning river, and in recent years some obstacles have been removed to try to re-establish the salmon. Just across the bridge you will notice many gravel ponds. They are dredging ponds left behind by the mammoth gold-washing machines that needed to dig their own float ponds, while scooping their way through gold-bearing gravel. A short distance ahead (to your right or east) is a rest stop with a Dawson City map and information panels. Adjacent to the rest stop is what might look like a gravel pit, but actually is a gold mining operation. If operating, the miners might offer sluice box tours and gold panning demonstrations.

km 524 / mile 325.6   Access Road to the Midnight Dome, and 9 km / 5.6 miles of paved and, at times, steep road to the landmark of Dawson City. It is a great drive; bike or hike up to the 887 m / 2911 foot Midnight Dome, ("Dome" - because it is a rounded hill) with marvelous views over the city, the gold fields and the Yukon River Valley. The hill was once called "Moosehide Hill" or "Mooseskin Mountain", referring to the shape of the rock slide which fans down the side of the hill above Dawson City. It resembles a moose hide left to dry in the sun. During the Gold Rush, the hill became known as "Midnight Dome", because of the custom of picnicking on top during the night of the longest day of the year, June 21st. It still is a great place to picnic.

km 524.5 / mile 326   Entering Dawson City. To your left, walk up to the dam that shields the city from spring flood waters, and observe the Klondike River emptying into the silty waters of the Yukon River. To your right, or behind you, towers **Crocus Bluff**, with its rocky face beloved by local rock climbers. The area next to the Bluff will be home to a new RV Park by 1998.

The first major street leading into town is **5th Ave.** - past the diesel-run Yukon Electric Power Plant to your left, and the **Gold Nugget Motel** to your right. Just across from the motel you'll see the **public water pump** where, for one Loonie ($1), you can fill your tanks for one minute - this is no car wash though, and you will need your own water hose. Next is the **public swimming pool, the museum** and the **Victoria Gardens** adjacent to it, and the **hospital** behind the gardens. The **bus depot** is located in the **Chevron gas station** to the left, followed by the **school** and the **post office** opposite. Keep on driving and you will pass the **fire station**, and soon enough you will see the only RV park which is located right in town - at 5th and York. The **RV Park** will close at this location after the 1997 season.

If you decided to follow **Front Street (or 1st Ave.)** you will soon pass the **RCMP** building to your right, and the impressive looking **Commissioners Residence** - dating from the time Dawson City was the capital of the Yukon. The main shopping strip will soon catch your eye, and so will the beached **Sternwheeler Keno**. When you see a large log building, you have arrived at the **Visitor Centre**, and the ferry across the river is only a few blocks ahead. **The ferry across the Yukon River runs 24 hours a day and on demand** - roughly every 15 to 20 minutes, for the five to seven minute crossing. On the other side are three businesses: **Dawson City River Hostel** which is an affiliated Canadian Hostel, but privately run, with cabins and tenting; the **Government Campground**; and a full-sized **golf course** a few kilometers from the ferry landing. See the next chapter for more about Dawson City.

Dawson City

A Dawson City bar scene.

INTRODUCTION

Dawson City is located at Latitude 64 degrees, or 247.8 km / 154 miles south of the Arctic Circle. This little town was once a very big one, and known as "The Paris of the North", but now it has only about 2000 permanent residents. This number sky-rockets every spring, as hundreds of gold miners and their families, tourism related workers from all over the country, and scores of job seekers descend on the valley. Visitors from all over the world fill the dusty (or muddy - as the case may be) streets from June to August, giving Dawson City the appearance of a city on a roll. Still, it doesn't come close to the number of people who filled the even more dusty or muddy streets during the short

Dawson City, a view from across the Yukon River.

period between the summer of 1897 and 1899, when an estimated 30,000 to 40,000 fortune hunters crowded the streets looking for riches, for work, and eventually, for ways to get back home, since all available ground had been staked.

> By the way - for a very entertaining but highly inaccurate history of the Klondike, check out various volumes of a certain Scotland born fellow by the name of Scrooge McDuck. Yes, remember, Uncle Scrooge? He made his trillions in the Klondike, and the slim volume 'King of the Klondike' (and others) is proof of it or at least, fun to read.

A few numbers:

RCMPolice: 993-5555. If no answer call 1-403-667-5555. **Ambulance**: 1-667-3333. **Fire**: 993-2222. **Fire: non emergency** 993-5434. **Nursing Station**: 993-4444. If no answer call 1-403-667-3333. **Dawson Medical Clinic**: 993-5744. The nursing station and the clinic are located in the same building on the corner of 6th and Church; both are open from 8:30 to noon and 1 to 5 p.m. Monday to Friday. **Dawson Dental Clinic**: 993-5538. In emergencies only, call Dr. Helmut Schoener, tel. 993-6347. German spoken. The Dental Clinic is open Mon. to Wed. 9 - noon and 1 to 5 p.m. Located within the clinic complex.

TIP - To Turn-in-Poachers Yukon wide call: 1-800-661-0525. **Dawson City Women's Shelter**: For women and their children who need help. Call 993-5086. **Dawson City Chamber of Commerce**: tel. 993-5274, Fax 993-6817. **Gold City Travel Agent**: tel. 993-6424.

Klondike Sun Newspaper: 993-6318. Local news, published every 2nd Friday of the month. Or surf through their pages on the World Wide Web at: http://www. yukonweb.wis. net community / dawson / klondike_sun.

Visitor Reception Centre. Tel. 993-5566. Open daily from mid-May to mid-September from 8 a.m. - 8 p.m. There are many historic displays, movie clips and slides about Dawson City and its history. German and French are spoken. It is located on Front Street, on the lower floor of the large log building.

Klondike Centennial Information Centre. Tel. 993-1997. Information on a "Decade of Centennials" until 2004. Their office is located at 1082 3rd Ave.

Dempster Highway Information Centre. Toll-free 1-800-661-0752. Or call 993-6167, Fax 993-6334. On Front Street opposite the Visitor Centre. Offering complete information about the Dempster Highway, Inuvik and the Northwest Territories, with displays and movies.

Klondike Visitor Association. Tel. 993-5575, Fax 993-6415. On the second floor of the Visitor Centre log-building. Can be contacted year-round at Box 389, Dawson City, Yukon, Y0B 1G0.

The Association operates:

- Diamond Tooth Gerties Gambling Casino. Admission charged.

- Jack London Cabin and Museum. No charge.

- Palace Grand Revue and Gaslight Follies Show. Admission charged.

Klondike National Historic Sites. Tel. 993-5462, Fax 993-5683. Box 390, Dawson City, Yukon, Y0B 1G0. Historical sites include:

- Bear Creek and Gold Dredge Camp.

- The renovated Gold Dredge #4 on Bonanza Creek.

- Fort Herchmer Police Barracks and Tour.

- "Dawson as they saw it" exhibit in Harrington's Store.

- Guided Tours of Palace Grand.

- The 1901 built Post Office, no charge and there is limited postal service.

- Robert Service Cabin and Poetry Readings.

- The Steamer Keno on Front Street (being renovated).

- Walking Tours through historic Dawson City.

The admission fee for all National Historic Sites is: $5 per site, per adult with children; family, groups and seasonal rates available. Under 12 no charge. The Robert Service Poetry Readings have an additional charge.

ACCOMMODATION IN DAWSON CITY

Dawson City River Hostel. Tel. 993-6823. Box 32, Dawson City, Yukon Y0B 1G0. Off the ferry in West Dawson, one hundred metres to the left. A privately run affiliated Canadian Hostel with four rooms for two guests and four rooms for up to five guests - in log cabins. Tenting sites and group tenting area with a common-room cabin, fire pit, roofed outdoor kitchen with wood stove and drinking water, cold water showers and a 'prospector bath', no electricity. Bring your own sleeping bag - but linen rental is possible. Bike and canoe rental and a small store. Overnight Charge: $13 members, $15 non-members in cabins, and $8 per person per tent, and $6 each for multiple occupants. Sorry, no credit cards. The hostel opens for the season with the first ferry-run in mid-May and closes at the end of September. Bus pick-up every Mon., Wed. and Fri. at 3:30 p.m. The hostel rents one-way canoes to Eagle and Circle in Alaska.

Dawson City River Hostel.

Yukon River Government Campground. Off the ferry in West Dawson, 300 m / 1000 feet to the right; 74 RV and tent sites and 24 tenting only sites. Shelters, play-ground, boil water to purify it. The campground stretches alongside the Yukon River for about 1 km, offering some tenting sites next to the river. Boat launch, and a nice hike to the Sternwheeler Graveyard along the beach. $8 per site and tent. There is now a city-run campground close to the ferry, with no services except outhouses. Fees are for daily, weekly, and monthly stays, and those fees had not been determined by the time this book was written. The campground is mainly used by seasonal workers and can be noisy.

<u>Motels, hotels, cabins and RV parks/camping and B&Bs</u> (All are within walking distance to anywhere in Dawson City).

Downtown Hotel. Tel. 993-5346, Fax 993-5076. Toll-free from the Yukon and BC: 1-800-661-0514. Toll-free from Alaska: 1-800-764-4653. Open year-round. Full service hotel with restaurant and lounge, from $69 single.

Eldorado Hotel. Tel. 993-5451, Fax 993-5256. Toll-free from the Yukon: 1-800-661-0518. Toll-free from Alaska: 1-800-764-3536. Open year-round, full service hotel with restaurant and lounge, from $72 single.

Midnight Sun Hotel. Tel. 993-5495, Fax 993-6425. Restaurant, cocktail lounge and pub. Summer only, from $54 single.

Triple "J" Hotel / Motel. Tel. 993-5323, Fax 993-5030. Toll-free from the Yukon and BC: 1-800-661-0405. Toll-free from Alaska: 1-800-764-3555, summer only. Restaurant and lounge, rooms from $80.

Westmark Inn Dawson City. Tel. 993-5542, Fax 993-5623. Central reservation from Canada 1-800-999-2570, from USA 1-800-544-0970, summer only. Restaurant and lounge, non-smoking rooms, rates from $85.

The Dawson City Bunkhouse. On Front Street. Tel. 993-6164, Fax 993-6051. Rates from $45 without showers, to $75 with showers. Look for the "Underground Station", by international artist Kippenberger.

Klondike Kate's Cabins and Rooms. Tel. 993-6527, Fax 993-6044; has an adjoining restaurant, room rates from $55.

Whitehouse Motel. Tel. 993-5576. At the northern end of Front Street, rates from $60.

Gold Nugget Motel. At the entrance of town. Tel. 993-5445. No credit cards. Rates $46 for one or two, $50 for three.

Westminster Hotel. Tel. 993-5463, Fax 993-6029. The oldest hotel structure still standing, rates up to $45. The hotel has a lounge and saloon, which can be noisy.

<u>Bed & Breakfasts:</u>

White Ram B&B. Tel. 993-5772, Fax 993-6509. Hot tub and BBQ area, rates from $69 to $79. Visa, MC; AAA listed.

Bonanza House B&B. Tel. 993-5772/6909, Fax 993-6509. Close to the public swimming pool; rates from $69 to $79.

The Palace Grand Theatre.

Dawson City B&B. Tel. 993-5649, Fax 993-5648. Open year-round, no smoking, rates from $69 to $99. Visa, MC; AAA/CAA listed.

5th Avenue B&B. Tel. and Fax 993-5941. Next to the museum, no smoking, with rates from $62 to $72.

Northern Comfort B&B. Tel. 993-5271. No smoking, families welcome and baby sitting is available; rates from $59.

<u>RV Parks and Camping</u>:

Gold Rush RV Park. Tel. and Fax 993-5247. At 5th Ave. and York. Public showers and coin laundry. Some tent spots are available, from $12 per site. The RV park will close at this location at the end of the 1997 summer season.

All other RV parks have been mentioned in the highway section.

FOOD AND RESTAURANTS

All major hotels have their own restaurants, coffee shops and lounges. Others are:

"Klondike Kate" Restaurant. Tel. 993-6527. Corner of King and Third. One of the oldest historical buildings in town. Ethnic food and good breakfast deals, coffee bar. Open from 7 a.m. to 11 p.m. daily in summer only.

"Marinas" Restaurant. Tel. 993-6800. On 5th Ave. opposite Westmark Hotel. Steaks, pizzas, seafood and takeouts.

"Nancy's" self-service restaurant. Tel. 993-5633. On Front Street, outdoor deck eating. German - Canadian Food.

"River West Cafe" and Health Food Store. Tel. 993-6339. On Front Street between Queen and King. Soups and sandwiches, very good coffee and cakes. Organic fresh produce. No smoking.

Black Sand and Gold Cafe Shop and Tea House. Cakes and sandwiches. On 2nd and Princess. Computer time is for rent while you sip your coffee. No smoking.

"98 Drive In". Tel. 993-5226. Take-out or eat-in. Hamburgers with the works, ice cream.

"Grandmas" Subs and Pizzas. Eat-in or take-out. On 2nd Ave. next to the Downtown Hotel. Open until 11 p.m.

Yukon River Cruise & Pleasure Island Restaurant. Tel. & Fax 993-5482. Salmon BBQ and River Tour. Their office is on Front Street, inside a very pretty and rustic looking birch cabin. Their all-you-can-eat dinner tours (costing $31 for adults, less for kids) leave daily between about 5 and 6 p.m. depending on the number of reservations - which are needed. The island is located a few kilometres downstream, next to the native village of Moosehide. Their small paddle-wheeler also conducts afternoon coffee trips.

> If you think you see a gravestone next to the above mentioned cabin - you do. It's where the "Toemaster", Capt. Dick "buried" all the toes that, over the years, have been either stolen or swallowed. Read more about it in the Saloon Section of this chapter!

Of all hotel-based restaurants, the one in the Midnight Sun Hotel stays open the latest - to 11 p.m. on weekdays and 1 a.m. on weekends. Western and Chinese cuisine.

As an alternative, buy the ingredients needed for a sumptuous sandwich in any of the three grocery stores. There is no better picnic place than sitting on the dike and watching the river flow by. The dike was built after a devastating flood, which, in 1979, inundated Dawson City almost to the top of its traffic signs. Many buildings were washed off their foundations, with losses that approached $50 million. Floods may occur in Dawson City during spring break-up when ice dams the water where the Klondike and Yukon rivers meet. It does not help that the town was built on a low lying, swampy flat with the consistency of jelly.

OTHER SERVICES

Showers, Laundry, Swimming Pool

Public showers and coin laundries are on Front Street at York, just opposite the Gazebo. Open daily from 8 a.m. to 11 p.m. Showers are $2 for 5 minutes. Washing machines and dryers cost $2.50. The building burned down late in the summer of 1996 and the facilities may or may not be rebuild for 1997.

Gold Rush Campground showers and coin laundry is open 24 hours in summer. On 5th and York. Showers are $1 for 3-4 minutes. Laundry prices are as above. This facility will close after the 1997 season.

A laundromat is next to the "Marinas" Restaurant on 5th. Coin laundry is available during restaurant hours from 10 to 10.

Both out-of-town RV parks offer public showers and coin laundries. Most hotels and B&Bs offer laundry services to their guests.

Dawson City Swimming Pool and showers. Next to the museum on 5th. Open from 1 p.m. to 8:30 p.m. for public, family, adult and / or lane swims; $3.50 for adults, less for kids and families.

Public Telephones: A wheelchair accessible booth is by the Visitor Centre. Other phones are at: the Arctic Drug Store on Front Street, behind the school next to Beaver Lumber, the Bus Depot and Chevron Gas Station, inside Diamond Tooth Gerties Gambling Casino (can be noisy), the Gold Rush Campground, and inside the lobbies of all major hotels. **The Yukon's area code 403 will change to 867 after Oct. 1997.**

Car and RV Repairs:

In town:

The Gas Shack. Tel. 993-5057 on 5th and Princess. Service station, car and tire repairs and sales, propane. *This is also the bus depot.*

Out of town:

Blattler Services, located in the Industrial Park, 24-hour emergency repairs, towing. Tel. 993-6232.

Bonanza Shell. Across the Klondike River Bridge. Tel. 993-5142. Service station, propane and RV / car repairs.

Northern Kat. Opposite Bonanza Shell. Welding and all repairs. Tel 993-5710.

Van Every, in the Industrial Park. Tel. 993-5624. Tire repairs and sales, propane.

Versatile Welding, in the Park as above. Tel. 993-5072. RV and car repairs, welding and towing.

Banks: There is only one: The **Canadian Imperial Bank of Commerce (CIBC)**, at 2nd and Queen. Tel. 993-5447. Open Mon. to Thu. from 10 a.m. to 3 p.m. and Fri. 10 a.m. to 6 p.m. 24-hour bank machine accepts credit cards with Visa, Plus System and Interac logos only. NO MASTER / EURO CARD!!. The bank gives the best exchange rate for US dollars, but does not exchange any other currencies. There is a $2 charge for cashing traveller's cheques. **Note:** All businesses accept traveller's checks with no charge attached when providing goods or services.

Post Office: Opposite the school on 5th Ave. Tel. 993-5342. Open Mon. to Fri. from 8:30 - 5 p.m. Sat. 8:30 - noon. General Delivery arrives in Dawson City every Mon., Wed. and Fri., and is sorted by about 1 p.m. Mail is kept for one month and I.D. is required for pick up. The Postal Code for Dawson City is Y0B 1G0. For Postal Code information call 1-800-267-1133. For general information concerning postal service call 1-800-267-1177. To ensure mail arrives addressed correctly for you, use: (your name), General Delivery, Dawson City, YT. Canada Y0B 1G0.

Liquor Store: On Third and Princess. Open Tuesday to Saturday from 9:30 - 7 p.m. Closed on Tuesdays if a public holiday falls on a Monday - almost all public holidays fall on a Monday except religious holidays and July 1! Credit Cards are accepted.

Bike and Canoe Rental:

The hostel, across the river, rents mountain bikes and canoes. Priority is given to hostel guests, call 993-6823. Bikes $20 per day, canoes $20 per day. German spoken.

Eagle Canoe Rental. One-way rental from the hostel in Dawson City to either Eagle or Circle in Alaska. Eagle: US$110 for 4 days, Circle: US$270 for 10 days. Call or visit the hostel, or call Mike in Eagle: 1-907-547-2203.

Dawson Trading Post. Opposite Westmark Hotel. Tel. 993-5316. Canoe rental for $30 per day. Transportation extra. The Trading Post organizes wilderness tours. The store sells new and used camping gear, as well as fishing gear and licenses.

Some bike spare parts are available at the **Far North Trading Company**, at 2nd and King. Tel. 993-6704. Sells camping and fishing gear, clothing, and books, as well as other items. The hostel has a big pile of old bikes that can be plundered for spare parts, for hostel guests only, at no cost. **Bike repairs**: You're on your own. Every few weeks or so a bike repair fellow from Whitehorse sets up shop next to the Gazebo on Front Street, staying for two to four days. Call Phillipe in Whitehorse, tel. 633-5600 for dates.

Car Rentals:

Budget Rental. Call 993-5644. From $40 per day and also one-ways to Whitehorse.

Norcan Rental. Call 993-6465. Prices as above, but more choices, with one-ways to Whitehorse.

Radio Stations: **CBC Radio** on 560 AM, news and weather on the hour. **CFYT Dawson** on 98.7 FM, local programming, music. **CKYN Visitor Radio** on 96.1 FM, tourism related programming.

Photo Finishing, Books and Art Galleries:

Arctic Drugs. On Front Street. Tel. 993-5331. German spoken. Same day photo finishing, non-prescription drugs, films and cameras.

Peabody's Photo Parlour. On Front Street. Tel. 993-5209. Same day photo finishing, and you can get yourself photographed in period costumes. Also sells film and postcards

Maximilians Gold Rush Emporium. Front Street. Tel. 993-5486. Largest selection of books, magazines, newspapers, film, gifts, musical tapes, post cards and greeting cards in Dawson City. Sells the newspaper 'European', and magazines and books in German and French.

Art's Gallery. 3rd and King. Tel. 993-6967. Local arts & crafts.

Travel Agent. Gold City Travel. Front Street. Tickets and Reservations for all airlines, hotels, ferries, car rentals. Tel 993-6424. Sight-seeing tours through town, the gold fields and up to the Midnight Dome. The bus to Inuvik leaves from here, call 993-5175 or Fax 993-5261.

Library. In the school opposite the post office. Tel. 993-5571. Mon. to Sat. from 1 p.m. to either 5 or 9 p.m.

Grocery Stores:

Dawson City General Store. Front Street. Tel. 993-5475. Open 7 days a week in summer, Mon. to Sat. from 8 a.m. to 8 p.m. and Sun. 10 to 6 p.m. The store has expanded and now includes a sandwich bar.

Farmers Market. 2nd Ave. opposite the bank. Tel. 993-5410. Open daily in summer from 8 a.m. to 6 p.m.

Both places bake their own bread, have a deli and, in season, sell locally produced vegetables.

Bonanza Meat Co. On 2nd Ave. Tel. 993-6567. Meat and fish, nougat in bulk and a deli.

Yukon River ferry in Dawson City (top).   The International Outhouse Race in Dawson City (middle).

Robert Service Cabin and actor Tom Byrne in Dawson City .

Yukon river rafters and canoeists leaving the Dawson City River Hostel (above).

Captain Dick and his Sour-Toe Cocktail.   Cyclists get ready to tackle the Dempster Highway.

Off the Dempster Highway- the Tombstone Valley.   Panning for gold.

Recycling Centre: In a small lane directly behind Arctic Drugs. Drop-off place for clean and unbroken glass, clean cans, pop cans, plastic jars, pop plastic bottles, newspapers, cardboard, and household type batteries. Some items can earn a cash refund, or you may donate refundables to the volunteer-run centre. Please help Dawson City and the Yukon to recycle.

Second Hand Shop. On Church Street next to the St. Paul's Church. Open Sat. from 1 p.m. to 5 p.m., and Tues. from 5 p.m. to 9 p.m. Opening times change, please check on the post office notice board. Clothing, books and whatnots are available. It is a good place to drop off your clean and no longer wanted stuff.

The beached "Keno" in winter.

Want to rescue a dog or a cat? Call Dawson City Dog Pound at 993-5434.

TOURIST ATTRACTIONS

Pubs, Saloons and the not-so-dark night life:

You might say that pubs are bars are saloons - and in a way, you are° right. Except, that in Dawson City, after the first city streets were laid out, the first tent structure erected and the first lumber was cut for the first permanent buildings to be nailed together - those first structures must have housed saloons. With 40,000 or so gold-seekers milling about, and very, very few women, saloons provided warmth, shelter, a place to learn news, drown one's disappointments and find partners and friends. In the heyday of 1897-98, there must have been many more saloons than churches, and there were 10 churches in 1899.

Today there are nine drinking establishments in town, and they are a mighty interesting lot. All of them open at 11:30 a.m. and close at 1:30 a.m. - sometimes earlier. The legal drinking age is 19 years, and, as in all Yukon communities, public consumption of alcohol is prohibited. The two largest saloons are in the only two hotels that stay open year-round - the "**Downtown**" and the "**Eldo**". Both offer bar food, and at times live music and optional dancing. The "**Midnight Sun**" has two places - the lounge and the pub, and it's the latter which can get quite stompy, with live bands, dancing and the general type of mayhem that can be fun. The most rustic, most authentic and definitely the oldest establishments, can be found in the **Westminster Hotel**, commonly called the "Westminster" or the "Pit". Again there are two places - a pub and a saloon. They might not be to everyone's liking but - hey - there is colour in those two places and the characters who hang-out in the "Pit" certainly are among the more eccentric ones that can be found in the Klondike Valley. A notch up, and certainly a must-see place, is "**Diamond Tooth Gerties**".

"**Gerties**" as it is known, opens daily at seven in the evening between mid-May and mid-September, and the last call is at 1:30 a.m. The cover charge is $4.75 or, $12 for the whole season. You might even win the cover charge back at the gambling tables - but then, you might not. Roulette, black jack, Texas Hold-Em Poker, the wheel, and an army of slot machines await the gambler. If gambling is not to your liking, settle at a table and watch the show - "Gerties" with her Can-Can dancers will get you all hollering at 8:30 p.m., 10:30 p.m., and 12:30 a.m. "Gerties" is open on Mondays, but there are no shows, just live music. There is a bar, table service, a sandwich bar, and all staff are dressed in period dresses. The building dates back to 1901, when it was used as a home for the fraternal Arctic Brotherhood. In the summer of 1971, "Gerties" was opened as Canada's first and only legal Gambling Hall, where liquor can be served and dancing shows held. It remains unique. During the Gold Rush years, 'Gertie' was one of Dawson's leading Dance Hall Queens, and the "diamond" could be found embedded between her front teeth. Her "Gertie Girls" charged $1 for a dance, soon separating miners from their hard-earned dollars. Diamond Tooth Gerties is run by the non-profit Klondike Visitor Association and every dollar you lose will be re-invested in the up-keep of this, and other historic buildings in Dawson City. A much quieter place is the tiny saloon in the **Triple "J" Hotel** and, if you like it classy, head for the "**Keno Lounge**", on the second floor of the **Westmark Hotel**.

THE STORY OF A PICKLED TOE!

Captain Dick Stevenson (photo right) - is the founder and first member of the craziest organization on either side of the Arctic Circle: 'The Yukon Order of the Sour-toe Cocktail'. Over 12,000 members can't be wrong, and for a small fee anyone can join the club.

It used to be Captain Dick that adventurous new members could find, sitting in his favourite saloon with a small wooden treasure in front of him - but he retired from the toe-business in 1995. Now you

Toe

will routinely find Captain Bill at his favourite saloon (the Downtown Hotel) with that treasure chest on a table in front of him. In that box the seeker of thrills will find a cut-off, dried-up, preserved in salt, pickled human toe. It's not the prettiest of sights, but the toe is the major ingredient of the **Sour-toe Cocktail** - since 1973, a true Klondike tradition. Over 12,000 have been served - which proves there are a lot of adventurous spirits out there!

'You can drink it fast, you can drink it slow, but the lips gotta touch the toe'. A handsome frameable certificate is part of the deal. Wouldn't you like one prominently displayed in your living room?

The saga of the Sour-toe got it's foothold in Yukon history in 1973, when Captain Dick found a petrified human toe under the floorboards of an abandoned cabin in the Sixtymile Gold Mining District near the Alaska border. Those harsh Yukon winters have been responsible (and are responsible) for many frozen-off toes - and not only toes! In any case, he kept the toe - wouldn't you have? - showing it off to his buddies in a Dawson saloon. The "dare" was on - Capt. Dick (a real captain by the way) "had it" and so did a few others. Since there was a reporter in the crowd, it did not take long for the story to be told, and re-told, and the story grew and grew. The rest is history. Nowadays bus loads of the curious ogle and dare each-other and finally "do it". Today, it will cost you $5 for the pleasure of having a pickled human toe float in your drink (no ice, please!) and, of course, it is not the original toe any more. Occasionally a toe-swallower comes along but, as they say, as long as careless wood choppers prowl the woods and lawn cutters run wild, the steady supply of toes will be secure for years to come.

Look for a **greeting card**, including a short history of the toe on the back of the card, with very graphic photos of a toe and Captain Dick 'doing it'. It is sold in many stores around town, and in Whitehorse. Who knows - your hands might have been shaking trying to photograph the toe as it merrily floated in your glass! Also, look for a slim book written by Capt. Dick about his adventures. Captain Bill, the new "Toe Master" can be found at the Downtown Hotel Saloon from Tues. to Sat., between 3 and 5 p.m. It is a rather unholy time of the day for a stiff drink, but Capt. Bill promised this writer more liberal and extended hours starting with the 1997 season. There even might be one other Capt. Jack, John or Jenny performing the toe - ceremonies in future years! Who knows!!

More things to do in Dawson City:

Palace Grand Theatre (Gaslight Follies) was built in 1899, by one of the more colourful figures who made it to Dawson City. 'Arizona Charlie' Meadows was a famous gunslinger-showman from, you guessed it, and he was determined to make his money from those who made theirs in the gold fields. On July 1, 1899, he opened this magnificent structure with high-class shows, opera and well known entertainers. The theatre changed hands and fortunes many times before it was rescued from demolition by the newly formed Klondike Visitor Association. Every night (except Tuesday) at 8 p.m. there are turn-of-the-century type vaudeville shows for the whole family. Get your tickets early and remember - you will be asked to participate! Tickets can be bought at the **Northern Xpressions** gift shop next to the Palace Grand Theatre. Call them at 993-6217 or 993-5954 for reservations. Tickets are $15 on the main floor and $17 on the balcony. At 11 a.m. on Mon., Tues. and Wed., there is a guided tour through the theatre and a showing of the documentary film '**Gold City**'.

The Dawson City Museum is on 5th Ave. It was built in 1901, and served as the Territorial Administration Building until 1953, when Dawson City ceased to be the capital of the Yukon Territory. It is open daily in summer from 10 a.m. to 6 p.m., and there is a cafe and a gift shop. Slide shows and documentaries are shown throughout the day. Watch for the gold panning demonstrations! The research library and genealogy service is open year-round; Dawson City Museum, Box 303, Dawson City, Yukon. Y0B 1G0. Tel. 993-5291 or Fax 993-5839. The collection of narrow-gauge **steam trains** in the shelter, to the right of the museum, is what is left of the railroad that connected the city with the gold fields in the early years of the century.

Victoria Gardens, next to the museum, is a replica of a garden as it existed on this site in 1920.

The Fire Fighters Museum is on 5th Ave., next to the fire station. It displays old fire fighting equipment which was used during the many fires that partially destroyed Dawson City; on November 25, 1897; October 14, 1898; April 1899; January 1900; and many others. Open Mon. to Sat. from 11 a.m. - 5 p.m. Free admission.

Robert Service Poetry Readings. On 8th Ave. The readings are held by actor Tom Byrne, daily at 10 a.m. and 3 p.m. The cabin, Robert Service's original home until 1912, is open from 9 to 5 p.m., except during readings. Admission is $6 for adults. Robert W.

Service came to the Yukon in 1904, and to Dawson City in 1908. His second book, 'Ballads of a Cheechako' was written just a few months after his arrival in Dawson City. It was a huge success, he quit his bank job and rented a tiny cabin overlooking Dawson City, becoming a professional writer. He lived in this cabin until 1912, never to return to the Yukon. Robert Service, like no other, was able to convey the enchantment of the North and the quest of men and some women for the most elusive of all metals, gold; and the dream, shared by us all, for adventure, fulfillment and the conquest of self. Possibly some of the most widely read poems in English must be his: 'The Cremation of Sam McGee', 'The Shooting of Dan McGrew', 'The Spell of the Yukon', and 'The Law of the Yukon'. Even if poetry is not your forte, you will be enthralled. While writing poetry, Service also worked as a bank clerk, first in Whitehorse, and later at the then CIBC branch on Front Street, opposite the General Store in Dawson City. Until just a few years ago the bank, now rotting down to its foundation, was still in use. Many stores in town sell books of collected poems by Robert Service; and recitals by Tom Byrne are available on audio cassettes. Robert Service died in 1958, at the age of 84. A total of 15 novels and books of verse were written by Service, and some 2000 poems - a few of which were turned into movies.

Gold! We leapt from our benches. Gold! We sprang

from our stools

Gold! We wheeled in the furrow, fired by the faith

of fools.   *(taken from a poem by Robert Service)*

Jack London Interpretive Centre is on 8th Ave., allmost next door to Service's cabin, and is another cabin with a interesting history. It is open daily in summer from 10 a.m. to 6 p.m., with a lecture about Jack London at noon and 2 p.m. No admission charge. Tel. 993-5575. At the age of 21, Jack London was a poor lad, unknown except to the police, but with a life already worthy to be written about. With nothing to lose, he was

one of the 100,000 adventurers attracted by news of the "Big One" in the Klondike Valley. By late summer 1897, he had crossed the Chilkoot Trail. His seafaring experience made him a valuable member of any party navigating down the Yukon River. Winter caught up with him and his friends 80 miles (130 km) south of Dawson City, and they all settled in to wait out the Arctic cold season in the Stewart Island area. He must have been in many

The Jack London Cabin and museum.

cabins that winter, visiting or helping out a friend, but it was in this particular cabin, up on the northern arm of Henderson Creek, where he gave in to a very peculiar human weakness - he scribbled his name and date on one of the inside logs.

"Jack London

miner author, Jan. 27, 1898"

Two trappers found the cabin years later, in fairly good shape, but with the roof ready to collapse. They did some fixing up - it was 1936 - but only several years later did one of them remember the inscription and, returning to the cabin, cut the signature out of the log with his axe. Dick North, Yukon-based author of the territory's history and curator of the Jack London Centre, got the ball rolling and, by 1969, not only had located the slab of wood, but also had the signature of Jack London authenticated. Not much later the whole cabin was "rescued", moved to Stewart Island and, using other logs from the area, turned into two identical looking cabins - one for Dawson City and the other for the newly created Jack London Square on the Oakland, California, waterfront. Jack London stayed only one winter in the Yukon. By early summer of 1898, he was broke and ill from scurvy. He built a boat, floated down to the delta of the Yukon River and, finding a ship, worked his way back to San Francisco by shovelling coal. The rest most of us know. 'Call of the Wild' was written, and so were many other stories based on his experiences in the North. These stories made him rich and famous. Who knows what might have happened to the writer Jack London, if there had been a miner Jack London who made it rich in the Klondike.

The Whitehorse based "**Jack London Klondike Society**" is trying hard to have this cabin rebuilt at the original site, to its original size and with its original tools. It would make a perfect centre-piece for an historical park on Henderson Creek, including the single gold claim London staked for himself a short distance from the cabin site. Apparently, he never worked his claim, nor did he find any gold. For more information, or to give support please contact: Andree North, Box 5118, Whitehorse, Yukon, Y1A 4S3. Tel. 668-5531 or Fax 633-6651.

Walking tours leave the Visitor Centre up to four times a day. Please ask in person, or call 993-5566. There is at least one walking tour in French, and possibly in German. The tour includes the steamer Keno, the old Post Office, Harrington Store with a photo exhibit, and Fort Herchmer. In addition, the tour visits many other buildings which have been renovated, at least on the outside, like Lowe's Mortuary, the old Newspaper building, the Bank of British North America, and the Commissioners Residence. Some of the buildings can only be entered with a tour guide.

The River Steamer Keno, a paddle-wheeler, has been closed to the public for many years, but renovations are progressing, and the steamer might open again during the 1998 season. The Keno was one of about 250 stern-paddle wheelers that plied Yukon's rivers. In 1960, it was the last of the boats to travel from Whitehorse to Dawson City, where it was berthed on the river bank. Once renovated, it will be the crown jewel of all Dawson City sights.

DAWSON CITY

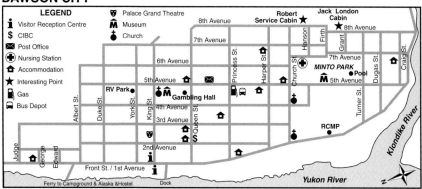

Pierre Berton House is the birthhouse of the very popular historical writer. The building has recently been renovated and is now used as a writer-in-residence retreat for deserving Canadian writers. For information and guided tours call 993-5575.

OUT TO THE GOLD FIELDS

Bonanza Creek Road. The word "Bonanza" means nothing but instantaneous wealth, and that is what some of the first to stake claims on Rabbit Creek found in the late summer of 1896. The local Han tribe called this stream "Tha-Tat-Dik". It, like other gold-bearing creeks in the Klondike, flows off a hill, and was re-named by the miners to **King Solomon Dome.** It must be noted that Carmack, Skookum Jim and Tagish Charlie were not the first to trek this creek. Robert Henderson had been prospecting in this area for quite some time. It was he who told them about the likelihood of gold on Rabbit Creek. Unfortunately, he did not stake a claim, but went on to other creeks for more prospecting. Henderson was left out when those three friends made their big strike on August 16th and staked their claims the following day. He only learned of his misfortune after all the good ground had been staked by miners who rushed in from nearby mining communities.

Bonanza Creek was phenomenally rich over its entire length of about 20 km / 12.5 miles. It is almost impossible to determine how much gold was removed. The official figures for 1896-97 were 135,440 ounces - (One ounce is about a teaspoon full, or 31 metric grams), a bit over 4 metric tons or 9000 lb., and that was years before the dredges started to arrive. The largest nugget found in the Klondike had a mass of 2.2 kg (72 troy ounces) and was nearly 15 cm / 6 inches long. Over 100 years of miners and their machines have left both sides of Bonanza Creek looking like an odd assortment of ill-kempt gravel pits. Even after all that time, pockets of gold are still being found, which those old-timers somehow must have overlooked. Be sure to stop at the many historical markers along the road. Please respect the privacy of people working their claims along this and other creeks.

Claim 33 Gold Panning and gift shop. At km 10 / mile 6.2 there is a very picturesque place where you can practice that special gold panning stroke or get instructions from the ground up, whatever the case may be. It will cost you $5 for a gold pan full of gravel, with about 50 -70 cents worth of gold hidden in the dirt. You will be shown how to get the gold out - but you do the work! Open from 9 a.m. to 5 p.m., seven days a week in summer. Tel 993-5804 or Fax 993-6260. In town there are some other businesses offering gold panning, but Claim 33 is in the most authentic location.

Gold Dredge #4. At km 12.3 / mile 7.6. The first tour is at 9 a.m., and the last one is at 4 p.m., leaving on the hour; costing $5 per adult, and less for kids, families and groups of more than 10. The shadow of this enormous wooden structure seems to fill the valley - imagine what it must have been like when in operation; especially the noise! Dredge #4 was the largest of 35 gold dredges that, at one time or another, worked the gold fields. It was built in 1912, and worked right through until 1959, when it was the last dredge to be retired. In recent years, the dredge has been restored, almost to its former glory. The cast iron buckets you see behind the dredge weigh 1515 kg or 3340 lb. each, and each one could scoop up 16 cubic feet (0.45 cubic m) of gold-bearing gravel. This dredge used 72 such buckets - moving a lot of gravel with a lot of gold - up to 22 kg or 50 pounds of gold over a working day of 24 hours. Once the gravel was inside the eight story high dredge, it was dealt with the same way as when using a gold pan. You shake and turn, and shake some more, adding plenty of water, and then the much heavier gold will separate from the gravel. That's the simple way to explain the process of gold separation - the very informative tours will explain the rest. The small Visitor

Centre shows video clips about the workings of the dredges, and do not forget to pay a visit to Bear Creek, where the electricity was produced to make these monsters run. Tours are also available in French and possibly in German. Call 993-5462 for the schedule.

Junction of Bonanza Road and Upper Bonanza Road. About 13.5 km / 8.4 miles from the Klondike Highway. The Upper Bonanza Road splits off where a narrow one-lane bridge crosses Bonanza Creek, leading the traveller into rough mining territory. The Upper Bonanza Road is a twisty, pot-holed and, at times, very narrow mining road. It is maintained, but is not suitable for larger motorhomes. After about 6 km / 3.7 miles, the road passes through the **Upper Bonanza Reserve**, an undeveloped historic mining area. Watch for signs indicating the **McCarthy's Roadhouse**. The 32 km long **Ridge Road Trail** back to Dawson City starts here; it is for hikers and bicyclists only.

From the reserve, it is another 75 km / 47 miles back to the Klondike Highway, passing King Solomon Dome, before the road joins with the Hunker Road. Watch for a radio tower to your right (north); it is on top of King Solomon Dome. A bumpy side road leads up to the dome, with commanding 360-degree views over the Klondike Mining District. The Dome is the highest hill in this area, at 1233 m / 4048 feet. Before the Gold Rush, it was just the "Dome", but after all six creeks radiating from the hill proved to be some of the world's richest, "King Solomon" was added. This 96 km / 60 mile loop makes a good one or two day trip; either by car or by bicycle, with an overnight camp-out on the Dome. Driving the **Sulphur - Dominion Creek** loop adds another 68 km / 42 miles to the trip.

Discovery Claim. At km 14.8 / mile 9.3 from the Klondike Highway. The Discovery Claim is a very unassuming place marked by a simple bronze plaque honouring those three friends who here made history on August 16, 1896. Follow the short trail down to the tiny creek and remember - all that glitters is not gold! There is plenty of pyrite (or mica) in "them thar hills". If it looks silvery and easily breaks if pinched with a fingernail, it is fools' gold. Sorry to have to tell you!

Claim No. 6. About one kilometre past the Discovery Claim. Those who want to practice the art of panning for gold can do so to their heart's content at Claim No. 6. Staked and maintained by the Klondike Visitor Association, this is the sole place in the valley where visitors can dream about striking it rich legally. Of course, there is little to no gold, especially not in the creek itself. But if you look toward the hillside behind the road, pock-marked by many others like you with their shovels and pick-axes, there are prospects - if not of riches, then, at least of a few flakes. The hostel and some of the B&Bs and hotels might provide their guests with the appropriate tools - ask them! No power tools, heavy machines or brought-from-home gold dredges are allowed - this is the Real McCoy sweatwork! **Claim No 6 is located on Eldorado Creek, a tributary of Bonanza Creek.**

The first claim staked on Eldorado Creek was on September 1, 1896. The "Eldo" is only a few miles long, but more gold has been found alongside this tiny creek than in any other comparable-sized area anywhere in the world. Gold is still being washed from its gravel. Past Claim No. 6, the road turns into a rough mining road, and it is not advised to proceed unless you have come in a 4X4 with a winch on either end of the vehicle. Mountain bikers, though, can have a great time, and it is hoped that one day soon a map will be produced to show all the roads and trails - there are many. The general area of Claim No. 6 was home to the largest settlement in the mining district - **Grand Forks**. The first buildings were constructed in 1897, and eventually 10,000 people called Grand Forks (where two "grand" little creeks met) their home. By 1903, the town was dying, and by 1921 Grand Forks was chewed up by gold dredges until there were no signs that a town had ever existed. A few remaining cabins are visible across the creek; the rotting remains of a once large bustling mining community. Beware, those cabins are very fragile.

How to stake a claim

Anyone over the age of 18, from anywhere, can legally stake a claim in the Yukon. Your first steps must be directed toward the mining recorder in Dawson City, which can be found above the post office on 5th Ave. Mining maps of the Klondike Mining District can be purchased for slightly over $1 per map, or looked at free of charge. All staked claims are marked on these maps, and claims which have expired are crossed out, meaning they can be re-staked at a cost of a few wooden 4" by 4" stakes, a black marker, the mining map, plenty of mosquito repellent, transportation to the nearest point where the elapsed claim is located, and a good set of legs. Being able to read topographic maps helps. Booklets giving instructions on legal aspects, on exactly how to stake and how to legally inscribe a claim-post, are available free of charge from a mining recorder at any of their offices in the Yukon.

A gold claim usually measures 500 by 1000 feet (152 by 304 m) and only one claim may be staked at a time, by one person, on one creek. A potential gold miner has 10 days to register his or her claim, at a charge of $10 for one year. It will take a few weeks before a mining inspector can verify the correct measurements and location of a claim. If all is in order, a legal metal tab will be issued, which the claim owner has to nail to Stake Post No. 1. The quest for gold can then begin. Of course, finding an elapsed gold claim in the Klondike is not hard, but one has to remember why it has elapsed in the first place - the most likely reason being there is no gold. But then, who really knows! For one year, the freshly-baked gold miner can fantasize about striking it rich, but if no mining related work is being done the first year, the claim will return to being public property. To retain a claim it has to mined to the tune of $200 worth of assessable shovel work. If machines are being used, different rules apply, and by then it is a more serious venture. Assessment work can be done for five years in advance.

A few words about living on your claim. The legal owner of a mining claim can build a structure by whatever means, and out of any material, so long as it is movable. Since gold is not forever, neither can be the living quarters. A tent is fine, and so is a camper trailer or a cabin on skids, but certainly not a stone castle. Mining claims that are obviously not used for mining purposes can be cancelled by a mining inspector. Further information can be obtained from your friendly mining recorder Yukon-wide. Good luck!

Tour a real Gold Mine: Over the years there have been many working gold mines trying to mine the tourists' dollar as well. Most did not survive either as a gold mine or a tourist operation for long. Now comes "**Goldbottom Mining Tours**" located 15 km / 9.3 miles up Hunker Road or 30 km / 18.7 miles from Dawson City. It is not just a working gold mine that has been in operation for many years, but also home to the authentic Gold Rush Road House - which might be turned into a future B&B. Gold mining tours, which include panning, are offered daily from 11 a.m. to 7 p.m., except Sunday, and cost $12 per person. Call or write to Goldbottom Mining Tours, Box 912, Dawson City, Yukon, Y0B 1G0. Tel. 993-5023.

Flight - Bus - Boat Tours:

Bonanza Aviation. Tel. 993-6904, Fax 993-6333. Bonanza Aviation will fly you anywhere: across the wildly beautiful Tombstone Mountain Range, or to Herschel Island and Inuvik to the north, or just short trips over the gold fields. A minimum of three passengers is required for most flights.

Trans North Helicopter. Tel. 993-5494. Heli Sight-seeing Tours over the gold fields and the Tombstone Range, or wherever else you might want to go. Open year-round.

Fireweed Helicopter. Tel. 993-5700. Charter and contract service. Space to fly up to 4 people with not too much luggage, to anywhere. Charge for one flight hour is $800.

Gold City Tours. Tel. 993-5175, Fax 993-5261. Daily sight-seeing tours through the gold fields, to the dredge, and on top of the Midnight Dome. Gold City Tours also operates the Tuesday and Thursday 08:00 bus to Inuvik at the northern end of the Dempster Highway. The bus only goes as far as Eagle Plains, being met there by another bus that left Inuvik the same morning. It is quite possible to turn this into a long day trip to the Arctic Circle, returning to Dawson City at around 20:00. A minimum number of four passengers is required; $198 one-way to either Inuvik or return to Dawson City the same day; $350 for return Dawson City - Inuvik - Dawson City.

The 'Yukon Queen' leaves every morning at 8:30, heading down-stream for the first Alaskan settlement of Eagle, four hours and 170 km / 105 miles away. After a two hour lay-over, the river boat returns to Dawson City arriving there at about 19:30. A one-day round trip fare is US$135. Their office is in the large grey building opposite the Visitor Centre. Tel 993-5599. Alternatively, travel by boat and return by chartered plane. Daily air services connect Eagle with Fairbanks. See Eagle in 'Top of the World' Chapter.

Fishwheel Charter Services. Tours by motorboat to a native fish camp downstream from Dawson City. These two hour tours leave at 10 a.m., 1, 3 and 6 p.m.; $25 per person and refreshments are served at the camp. They also organize dogsledding tours and winter camping. Call or Fax 993-6857 for information and reservations.

SPORTY THINGS TO DO AROUND DAWSON CITY

Short hiking trips nearby include the **dike walk-way** from the rock slide to where the Klondike meets the Yukon River, a pleasant 1.5 km walk. Walk up King Street, which continues into the hills beyond Dawson City. This narrow, steep road passes several **cemeteries** dating from the Gold Rush. A parking lot with information panels indicates a trail leading to **Crocus Bluff**, offering a great view over the Klondike River valley. Follow the trail back down to Front Street.

Take the ferry across to West Dawson, hike through the government campground to the very end and down to the beach. Not much further on you will come to the **Paddle-wheeler Graveyard**, where three river steamers, the Julia B, Seattle 3, and the Schwatka, are slowly rotting away. All three were beached here after the heyday of steamer travelling had passed; left to be carried away, year by year, by the spring floods. Across the river you can see the native village of Moosehide.

For those of you who are in good shape, a roughly two-hour hike up to the **Midnight Dome** awaits you, or hike further still to the **Fire Tower Dome**. Both destinations are a good day's work-out. Start your day-hike underneath the Moosehide Slide and facing it, scramble up on the right side, staying within the treed area. Soon you will come to a fairly well-trampled trail that cuts across the slide at about the half-way point. To your right the trail goes back to Dawson City, but you do not want to go there just yet. In case you are wondering why I did not send you onto this trail from the beginning -

well, wasn't it fun to claw your way up the slide? The slide, by the way, was neither caused by an earthquake, nor by gold mining activities. It is assumed that many thousands of years ago the slide was caused by the river itself. Where the town is now located, the Yukon River once must have flowed. The river slowly washed out the embankment, causing a huge rock slide which diverted the river west to where it is now. Over many years sand and silt filled the upstream side of the rock slide, which is why Dawson City sits on a wet, swampy sandflat - not the most perfect of places on which to build.

In any case, cross the slide. This trail, after about 3 km / 1.8 miles, leads to the **village of Moosehide**. Before the trail disappears into the woods, your views over Dawson City and the Yukon River are spectacular. A rock outcropping, known as "suicide leap", makes a perfect picnic place, revealing the whole valley spread out below. The trail to Moosehide is not maintained, so be careful, as there are many wash-outs that have to be scrambled across. _Permission to enter Moosehide has to be obtained from the First Nation office on Front Street BEFORE leaving on your hike._

The native Han population was banished to **Moosehide** when thousands of gold-seekers arrived and took over the traditional campsites at the confluence of the Klondike and Yukon Rivers. Moosehide had its own church and school until the 1950s, when the closure of both compelled most inhabitants to move to Dawson City. For many years, the village stood abandoned, but in recent years it has been brought back to life. Today the village is used as a spiritual centre and gathering place for meetings, pot-latches and native festivities throughout the year. There are easier and faster ways of getting to Moosehide. During ceremonies, boat transportation is provided for anyone. Check with the Han First Nation at the corner of Front Street and York. Tel. 993-5385.

To continue up to the Dome, once you have crossed the slide, look up and you will see a largely treeless slope to the left of the slide in front of you. Hike up that slope to the ridge far above the rock slide, and there you will find a trail leading to the Dome. You can't get lost so long as you do not lose sight of Dawson City to your right. It is impossible to miss the Midnight Dome (887.2 m / 2911 feet), not only because it is the highest point, but also because of the large parking lot. Don't all good hiking trails have a parking lot at the end? Once standing on the Dome, just look down toward town and follow any trail that spirals downward - Dawson City is not difficult to miss.

The Fire Tower Dome. Stand on the highest rocky point of the Midnight Dome and look east-northeast. About 50 km / 31 miles away are the usually snow-capped **Ogilvie Mountains,** with the **Tombstone Range** being the closest. A little lower, you will see a fire tower on the next Dome, roughly 3 km / 1.9 miles away. To get there, walk down the road toward Dawson City for about one kilometre, or until the first sharp right curve. To your left is a rough but usable narrow dirt road leading almost straight up to the Fire Tower Dome. Do not drive this road unless your confidence in your car is as unshakable as the hub-caps on your wheels. It is great for mountain bikers, though. There is a caretaker living in the cabin next to the tower, and his or her job is to report forest fires before they get out of hand. There are about 200 to 400 forest fires each summer in the Yukon. The caretaker might let you climb onto the tower, but a wooden platform viewpoint next to the tower will also reward you with incredible views. Carry your own food and water and BE BEAR AWARE.

Playing Golf. Canada's most northern golf course opened in 1994-95. The "**Top of the World Golf Course**" offers 9 holes (more to be added later), a driving range, a pro shop with rentals and a snackbar. Take the ferry to West Dawson and follow the highway for about 8 km / 5 miles, taking the first road to the left. Watch for signs, and stop for views along the road. Call them at 667-1472 or Fax 993-6605 for more information. Their winter tel. number is 993-5443. Call ahead and they will pick-up golfers without transportation from the western side of the ferry.

Mini Golf; 9 mining-theme holes are open from 7 a.m. to 10 p.m., and are next to the restaurant already mentioned along the Klondike Highway. Tel. 993-5664.

The Paint Ball Game. Nothing else to do and feeling aggressive? The latest game in town lets you "kill" or get "killed", with little pain attached. Participants are let loose at each other on a Yukon River Island with guns that shoot paint balls. Call 993-5319 for more information. By the way - bears possibly encountered during the game are not qualified game participants.

Canoe or raft the Klondike River. Use your own canoe or rent one from the previously mentioned rental places in town. The river requires some skill to stay away from sweepers, but otherwise makes for a pleasant one hour or one day trip, depending on the point of departure. Most river runners will start at the Dempster Highway bridge for a 50 km / 31 mile float back to Dawson City, but many more put-in places exist closer to town for shorter trips. **River Klondike Rafting** organizes short 10 km / 6 mile rubber-raft trips down the Klondike River. Departures depend on demand for this two hour trip. Call them at 993-6973; $30 per person.

A BIT MORE ADVENTUROUS STUFF

Hike the ditch. This wilderness hike should not be taken lightly and preparations need to be thorough. Essentially, this trail connects the already described Fire Tower Dome with the western side of the Tombstone Range, about 50 km / 30 miles away. Various trails across the mountain range to the Dempster Highway can add a further 35 to 60 km, depending on which route is taken. The first part follows a partially washed out fire access road, which itself loosely follows the historic access road to the 12 Mile Power Plant. This power plant generated power to operate the gold dredges almost 100 km / 63 miles away. A very sophisticated system diverted water to the Klondike Gold Fields via wooden flumes, pipelines and ditches. This amazing feat of engineering was over 115 km / 72 miles long. Construction lasted from 1906 to 1908. By 1933, the whole water system was abandoned, and other systems took over to power the dredges.

The first 50 km of the trail, not only make good hiking, but mountain bikers and horseback riders will also find it to their liking. The trail reveals old camps, wrecked wooden flumes, power stations, and other historical leftovers of truly outstanding innovation - to carry a river of water from the mountains to the gold fields.

The outdoor guide '**Along the Dempster**', has more information and photographs about these and other hikes along the Dempster Highway. For topographical maps, go to the bookshop and for further information about the trail, check with the knowledgeable forestry officials at Renewable Resources above the post office. Before starting out, leave your estimated route and arrival time with someone you know - just in case you get in trouble. Various unmarked trails lead to the eastern side of the Tombstone Range and the Dempster Highway. The most popular is also the longest - via **Tombstone Pass** and **Divide Lake**, following the southern flank of the North Klondike River to the Tombstone Government Campground on the Dempster Highway. The Dempster Highway Section of this book provides more hike-in variations. This is one of the most spectacular hikes in North America, combining the history of a nearly 90-year-old engineering marvel, with that of a rugged mountain range, where sheer granite walls contrast beautifully with hidden, deep-blue, icy moraine lakes and the various greens of tundra vegetation. **Tombstone Mountain** is the highest point in the range at 2192 m / 7191 feet. If hiking the Tombstone Range, please consider all those who will follow; practice NO TRACE Hiking and Camping, and if possible carry out a bit more than was carried in, and definitely BE BEAR AWARE!

The Ridge Road Trail. This brand new trail (opened in 1996) was the first Territorial Government road constructed in the Yukon. Built in 1899, it connected Dawson City with the gold fields of Sulphur and Dominion Creeks. The remains of four roadhouses-hotels usually with a restaurant or bar- have been identified along the former road. The trail is 32 km long and can be hiked or biked. The trail begins in the Callison Industrial Area at the very end of Callison Way and follows ridges to as far as the King Solomon Dome; at 1234 m / 4048 feet - the highest hill in the Klondike area. It is easiest to hike or bike the trail from the Dome back to Dawson City - it's down hill all the way. Great views are always present along the trail, and there are two official tenting spots - obtain a trail map from the Visitor Centre.

Bike, hike or canoe to the former location of **Jack London's cabin on Henderson Creek**. A potentially interesting bike / hike combination over rough unmarked mining roads leads to a fascinating, unmarked and undeveloped historical site, where a young Jack London might have dreamt less of gold and more of stories to tell once back in San Francisco. Of the 50 books he later wrote, five were set in the Klondike. 'The Call of the Wild' and 'White Fang' are still beloved reading material for all ages, and have been translated into more than 50 languages.

Henderson Creek is about 130 km / 80 miles from Dawson City, and is reached by crossing the King Solomon Dome down into Sulphur Creek, and following mining roads to Henderson Dome. The northern arm of Henderson Creek flows off Henderson Dome and into the Yukon River, a short distance away. To get to the former cabin site, one needs to scramble down through dense underbrush toward an overgrown cat-trail, carved out of the valley by a road machine many years ago. The cabin site should be here - well, there is nothing there but hordes of mosquitoes waiting for just one more victim I am sending their way. One day, though, there will be marked trails leading to a re-built cabin with minimal facilities and a trail leading down to the Yukon River, allowing river travellers to hike up. Good topo and mining maps are needed to pick one's way through mining territory that includes crisscrossing roads built the way a spider weaves its web. The planned 'Coast to Coast Canada Trail' may pass through this valley.

'**Jack London's Cabin**' a booklet by Dick North, describes the history of the cabin and how it was found. The booklet is available at the Jack London Centre in Dawson City, at the hostel and at some gift shops. Dick North is the curator of the centre, and is always happy to answer questions about Jack London. Please see the Yukon River chapter, for how to get to the cabin if travelling by boat.

Canoe trips using Dawson City as a base: Various nearby rivers lend themselves for three to five day canoe trips beginning by car in Dawson City and returning by canoe. Most have already been mentioned - the combination McQuesten / Stewart River to the Yukon River will take between four and six days. Floats from either Pelly Crossing or Minto will allow stops in historic Fort Selkirk and on Stewart Island - a four to six day trip.

Leaving Dawson City by Canoe: One of the more popular floats from Dawson City is to the abandoned gold mining town of Fortymile. It allows the river traveller to stay within Canada, returning to Dawson City via the Fortymile and the 'Top of the World Highway'. Allow a minimum of two days. A pick-up from Fortymile must be arranged beforehand - check with the hostel or the Trading Post. Rent a canoe to Eagle, or Circle, in Alaska, from the hostel for a one-way trip. If you take your own canoe, it can be returned from Eagle to Dawson City on the 'Yukon Queen' for a fee of $65 per canoe. You are responsible for loading and unloading. Beyond the tiny river community of Circle, only one easy take-out point exists: about a week later at the Dalton Highway Bridge north of Fairbanks. If you have a couple of months, you can float all the way to the delta of the Yukon River.

SOUVENIRS TO BRING HOME

There is no better way to be remembered by your loved-ones back home than by returning with a genuine Klondike Gold Nugget for them. With gold mining still the strongest industry in the Klondike, gold abounds. Much of it, especially jewelry-sized nuggets, is being transformed into fascinating pieces of art. Gold can be worked into watch-bands, earrings, necklaces, rings, or just kept "pure", as a nugget straight out of the ground. The size depends entirely on your vacation budget. The largest selections can be found at the **Klondike Nugget and Ivory Store** on Front Street and Queen; at the **Ravens Nook** on 2nd Ave.; or at **Claim 33** on the Bonanza Road. Most other gift shops in town also sell gold nugget jewelry -often made by the owners during those long winter months. Look for the gold miner - old-timer who sells self-made gold nugget jewelry from the back of his pick-up, which is parked next to the Gazebo on Front Street.

Ivory: You might ask what ivory is doing in the Yukon, and how it got here in the first place. The answer: "Well, it came with the animals that carried the tusks". Mammoths and Mastodons roamed the hills and tundra of the Yukon up to 10,000 years ago, and with them were wild horses, arctic rhinoceroses, lions that were bigger than today's African lion, long-horned bison, short-faced bears and a whole cornucopia of other animals - all extinct today and making your hiking trips in the Yukon a wee bit less stressful!

Gold miners have been finding the bones and tusks from those animals ever since gold became the focus of human activity in this area. Ivory tusks of all sizes and qualities are being dug-up, season after season. Some of it is carved into quite appealing pieces of jewelry. It is somewhat ironic that ivory of an extinct animal is legally sold and carved into art objects, whereas the mammoths' cousin, the elephant, is being hunted almost to extinction. The Dawson City Museum has some impressive looking ivory tusks on display, and information about all those other exotic animals that used to call the Yukon home. Look for ivory jewelry in most stores selling gold.

WILDERNESS OPERATORS

Campfire Adventures. Tel. 993-5633, Fax 993-6801. Bag 5030, Dawson City, Yukon, Y0B 1G0. Organizes river trips, fly-in fishing and hiking.

Wylies Dog Camp. Bag 4080 Dawson City, Yukon, Y0B 1G0. Mobile radio 2M 4553, Mickey Channel. One week long dog team mushing trips in the Fortymile River area.

Trek Over The Top Adventure. Tours. Box 100 Dawson City, Yukon, Y0B 1G0. Fax 993-7423 / 2218. Snowmobile rental and tours.

Cultural Trekking. Box 1012 Dawson City, Yukon, Y0B 1G0. Radio phone JL3 6535. Customized trekking, with focus on survival skills.

Fishwheel Charters offers summer and winter tours. This company was mentioned previously.

ANNUAL FESTIVALS IN DAWSON CITY

Dawson City will keep a visitor busy for up to four days. Any of the many festivals, for which the city is known, might turn your stay into a longer one.

Undeniably, the very first celebration of a new season is the **break-up** of the Yukon River ice. Having been in the grip of a frozen river for approximately six months, there is no greater joy than watching the river's ice break-up and float out of sight downstream. This special day can be as early as late April, or as late as the end of May. It is the first chance to win a bundle in this gambling city of the North. As in many other Arctic communities, the inhabitants wager on the day and hour when the ice will go out. A wooden tripod in the middle of the river is attached by wire to the nearest building. The shifting ice will move the tripod, pulling a wire that stops the clock and sounds an alarm. A danger of flooding exists for a few days during and after break-up, and everyone is in a heightened state of alert. The Yukon River ferry usually will start its season 8 to 12 days after break-up, and the "Top of the World Highway" will be open by then.

Diamond Tooth Gerties Gambling Casino is always the first Dawson City attraction to open - usually by mid-May. The first night is always a party. There is nothing like "Gerties" and her Can-Can Dancers to draw out winter-shocked miners.

Third weekend of May. International Gold Show. Gold miners come from their creeks to check out the latest in gold mining technology. There are plenty of other exhibitions and other things to do. Call the Chamber of Commerce for more details. Tel. 993-6720. By the end of May, all Klondike attractions, from the museum to the Palace Grand Theater, should be open and so should most tourist-related businesses, from hotels to restaurants and campgrounds.

June 1st or the first Saturday of June. The Commissioners Ball - the social event of the year. Call 993-5575. The Ball is open to all, so long as you are dressed the-way-it-once-was. There are businesses in town renting (and making) period clothing. There is a charge for attending the Ball.

June 21st. The longest day of the year. Nothing official is going on, but the Midnight Dome is crowded with people who watch the sun disappear behind the mountains just after midnight - and wait for it to reappear a couple of hours later. Remember that public consumption of alcohol is against the law. The sad part is that from this day on, the sun will shine about 3 to 4 minutes less each day - until December 21st when the sun will barely give light for a few hours.

July 1st. Canada Day Celebrations and Yukon Gold Panning Championships. Tel. 993-5575. The winner of the Yukon Gold Panning Championships goes to the World Championships which, in 1996, were held in Dawson City. What is a Gold Panning Championship? Participants get the same measured amounts of gravel with between five and seven gold flakes embedded in the gravel. On "go", the idea is to retrieve the most gold in the least time - each missed gold flake will cost a time penalty. There is a Sourdough class and a Cheechakos class. Sourdoughs are old-time Yukoners and Cheechakos are the newcomers who have yet to see their breath curdle into ice fog at 40° below. That means YOU can compete. There are classes for different age groups, and the whole affair is rather fun to watch. Do not miss the Canada Day Parade and all the other things happening on this long weekend.

Third Weekend of July. The annual **Dawson City Music Festival** includes Rock, Folk, Pop, Native, New Age and Old Age - it's all there on this wild weekend. If you are unable to get one of those rare weekend tickets, do not worry, music can be found in abundance all over town, in free workshops, on street corners and outside the main tent. Tickets need to be reserved early. Write to: Dawson City Music Festival Association. Dawson City, Yukon, Y0B 1G0. Tel. 993-5584, Fax 993-5510.

Canadian Airlines International Dome Race. This 7.4 km / 4.6 mile foot race up to the Midnight Dome attracts runners from all over the world. Call 993-5726 or 993-6536. It is held on the Music Festival Weekend.

End of July. Klondike Placer Miners BBQ and Dance. There is a charge, but all are invited. If you want to rub shoulders with a genuine gold miner, this is the time and the place.

Discovery Weekend. Weekend nearest to August 16 and 17. This weekend celebrates the discovery of gold. There is a lot of family fun - parades, canoe races, games, a demolition derby and the arrival from Whitehorse of the participants in the Bathtub Race. Tel. 993-5434. It is around this time, in mid-August, when it starts getting dark again at night. The temperature is still summery, but the stars become visible and the first trees start changing colour.

Last weekend of August. Yukon Talent Night at "Gerties". Call 993-5575. Can you sing, act, play an instrument, tell a joke - or pretend to be doing any of the above? Then Talent Night is for you! Register at "Gerties", or by telephone a few days prior to the event. Off you go on the road to stardom. Remember, audiences can be cruel! Practice your act! Otherwise, this is a busy night at the gambling saloon - get there early. **The Annual 'Barmaids Race'** is held at this time. It's what one might expect - scantily dressed barmaids battle out who can serve drinks the fastest and with the least spills. It is organized by the Midnight Sun Hotel.

First weekend of September. The Great International Outhouse Race. Tel. 993-5575. There is not much to add to this one, is there? Teams of either serious minded racers or carnivalistic and / or goofily attired groups of either five males, five females or a mixed team, race a 3 km course through town. The outhouses, naturally, are on wheels and are not to be used either before, during or after the event. Local teams build their own contraptions, but visitors may rent their outhouse from the Visitor Centre - then decorate it to suit. Participants may win numerous prizes including best, funniest or most outrageous design. Some businesses already have closed for the season, and some others will close after the Outhouse Race Weekend. The **fall colours** are beautiful, especially along the Dempster Highway - and there are hardly any mosquitoes left! By mid-September, all attractions such as the theatre, the dredge and the museum, will have closed for the season. Diamond Tooth Gerties is usually the last one to shut its doors - by the last week of the month. By the beginning of **October**, winter will have given its first warnings. The ferry usually ceases its service across the river by the middle of October. During the winter months, Dawson City is busy with home grown theatre and concerts, curling bonspiels, downhill and cross country skiing, woodsplitting contests, and two major dog sled races that pass through town.

The "Annual Yukon Quest" dog sled race from Whitehorse to Fairbanks, or vice versa. The race passes through Dawson City in February, and it rivals the famous "Iditarod", in Alaska, in endurance and length. This 1600 km / 1000 mile race lasts for up to 14 days, and 36 hours of that time are spent in Dawson City as a compulsory rest stop for the dogs. In Whitehorse call 668-4711 for exact dates.

March is always a busy month with **Spring Carnival**, the annual **Percy De Wolfe Sled Dog Race** from Dawson City to Eagle and back, as well as a hugely popular annual **Snowmobile Jamboree** between Tok in Alaska, and Dawson City. The latter follows the snowed-in "Top of the World Highway". For all these activities, contact the Klondike Visitor Association for exact dates.

<u>Centennial Celebrations to 2004 - and beyond</u>.

1997. A world is told. News of the gold strike reaches the outside world - and the world reacts.

1998. The Great Gold Rush. 100,000 goldseekers stream toward the Klondike, many not making it. The Yukon Territory is born.

1999. The first school is built, and the Klondyke Mines Railroad begins operations.

2000. White Pass and the Yukon Railroad begins service, connecting Skagway with Whitehorse. Whitehorse turns 50.

Participants of the International Outhouse Race.

2001. The Great Building Boom in Dawson City. The city gains permanence.

2002. The Great Homecoming. A world-wide invitation to all descendants of the stampeders to revisit their roots. As plans for these Centennial Celebrations are developing, contact the Visitor Association for more information - or find it in updates to this book!

2003. Centennial of Mayo.

2004. Centennial of the arrival of Robert Service to the Yukon.

<u>A list of all centennial activities for 1997 and 1998 is at the end of this book.</u>

TRANSPORTATION - LEAVING DAWSON CITY

By bus to Whitehorse: Norline Bus every Mon., Wed. and Fri. at 16:00 from the Gas Shack at 5th and Princess; $72 one-way. Tel. 993-6010. Winter schedule is Wed. and Fri. only; from Sept. to the end of May. No credit cards are accepted.

To Inuvik: From Gold City Tours office on Front Street, every Tuesday and Thursday at 08:00; $198 one-way, $350 return. Arrive 20:00. Four passengers minimum. Tel. 993-5175.

The Dempster Highway as seen from mountain ridges (top).

Ogilvie Mountains (centre).

Hiking off the Dempster Highway (bottom).

Mountain stream in the Ogilvie Mountain Range (top).

Visitors to the Yukon trying their luck panning for gold.

To Tok in Alaska via "Top of the World" Highway: Alaska Direct Busline leaves Tok on Mon. at 8 a.m. and leaves Dawson City for Tok on Tues. at 9 a.m. About 4 to 5 hours each way, depending on the condition of the road; US $65 one way. Call them at 1-800-770-6652 for reservations. The driver will drop-off and pick-up passengers at the hostels in West Dawson and Tok. Larger groups can arrange trips on other days as well.

By rented car: Check under the rental car section.

By river: With the *Yukon Queen* every morning at 08:30 to Eagle in Alaska. The boat takes about 50 passengers for a four hour trip, and returns the same day to Dawson City; $90 one-way standby only. Front Street opposite Arctic Drugs. Tel. 993-5599.

By plane to Whitehorse: Air North daily except Sat. at 13:30 and 14:30. Call them at 993-5110. These are one hour flights for $195 one-way. Some flights go via Mayo.

To Fairbanks in Alaska: Air North on Tuesday, Thursday, Friday and Sunday at 09:35. Arrive in Fairbanks at 11:40 local time. Leave Fairbanks at 11:55 local time, arriving in Dawson City at 14:15; $195 one-way.

To Inuvik and Old Crow: Air North either flies to Inuvik direct, or via Old Crow. Every day (except Sat.) at 9:40.

Air North sells a 21 day Klondike Explorer Pass for $550, connecting six destinations - Whitehorse, Juneau, Dawson City, Old Crow, Fairbanks and Inuvik. For reservations call in Dawson City 993-5110, or toll-free 1-800-764-0407 from Alaska, and 1-800-661-0407 from the Yukon and B.C.

Bonanza Aviation flies charter to Inuvik, with a short stop at Eagle Plains. Leave Friday 12:45, arrive Inuvik at 15:30; arrive back in Dawson City at 19:45 the same day. Leave Sunday at 15:45, returning to Dawson City the same day at 19:45. One-way $219, and return $399. Call 993-6904 for more information. A minimum number of passengers applies. For scheduled flights from Eagle, in Alaska, to Fairbanks, see Eagle in the next chapter.

Distances from Dawson City: Anchorage, AK 828 km / 497 miles. **Fairbanks, AK** 631 km / 379 miles. **Tok, AK** 300 km / 180 miles. **Eagle, AK** 230 km / 143 miles. **Inuvik, NT** 766 km / 476 miles. **Prince George, BC** 2416 km / 1501 miles. **Skagway, AK** 716 km / 445 miles. **Vancouver, BC** 3191 km / 1982 miles. **Whitehorse, YT** 536 km / 333 miles. **Dawson Creek, B.C.** 2007 km / 1247 miles.

Two Royal Canadian Mounted Police Officers (RCMP or "Mounties") during the Discovery Parade in Dawson City.

Top of the World

Top of the World Highway, overlooking the Yukon River.

WEST DAWSON

A pack trail has existed between West Dawson and the gold mining district of Sixtymile near the Alaska border since 1891; the road was completed in 1953. It is the most northerly land entry into the USA.

km 0 / mile 0 Dawson City Yukon River Ferry, the *'George Black'*. The government ferry is free of charge. It shuts down for 10-15 minutes during shift changes and for re-fuelling at 6 a.m., 2 p.m. and 10 p.m. and stops every Wednesday morning between 5-7 a.m. for servicing. Otherwise, the ferry runs non-stop and on demand for 24 hours a day, between mid-May and mid-October. There can be up to a two hour wait late mornings and early evenings in July and August. Large RV's and motorhomes can quickly fill the ferry, the capacity of which is about 12 small cars or four to six motorhomes. Plan to leave early! If staying in West Dawson, and you are heading west into Alaska, fuel-up the day before your departure. Otherwise you might have to face two long waits! Cars with very low clearance may experience difficulties driving on or off the ferry. Call Dawson City at 993-5441 or Whitehorse at 667-5644 for information about the ferry.

West Dawson was first connected with Dawson City by a cable ferry in 1901. The old road still can be seen carved into the hillside. West Dawson during the Gold Rush was home to many cabins, farms and at least one "vacation" hotel. The ferry is built so that it can be pulled out of the river in late autumn and returned to the water in early summer. During freeze-up no access exists across the river, but temperatures to as low as -55°C quickly freeze the river, enabling even the heaviest truck to pass across the ice. To strengthen the ice road further still, water is sprayed on the "road" to thicken the ice.

km 0.1 / 320 feet A sharp left turn will get you to the **Dawson City River Hostel** with shared and single cabins, and tenting. Sorry, no space for RVs and motorhomes. Tel. 993-6823.

km 0.3 / 1000 feet Turn right into the Government Campground.

km 4.4 / mile 2.7 Left turn to the subdivision of **Sunnydale** and the **golf course.** During the early years of Dawson City, Sunnydale had many farms that provided fresh produce. Just past the turn-off watch, to your left, for a **viewpoint** overlooking Dawson City.

km 12.4 / mile 9 Rest stop with garbage cans.

km 15 / mile 9.3 Highway keeps climbing above tree line.

km 59 / mile 37.4 To your right (north) is an unmarked and barely maintained road (but it is okay to drive) to the former Cassiar Asbestos Mine of **Clinton Creek**, and to the former gold mining town of **Fortymile**. Asbestos was found in this area in 1957, and the town of Clinton Creek was built in 1967. When the mine shut down in 1979, it dealt a harsh blow to Dawson's economy. There are almost no traces left of the town site. The mining site is a few kilometres beyond the river bridge but, believe me, you do not want to go there! The Fortymile River Bridge is a take-out point for most river travellers who have started their journey in Alaska from points along the Alaska side of the 'Top of the World Highway'. A short distance before the bridge, a narrow road will swing to your right (northeast) leading to the Yukon River a few kilometres away. This Yukon River access point was built to accommodate salmon fishers who deliver their salmon to refrigerated trucks for transport to Dawson City.

FORTYMILE

This abandoned former gold town, can be found about one kilometre downstream, by either following the shoreline at low water, or by slugging it out through dense underbrush, at higher water levels. The town of Fortymile was established in 1887 as a trading post and supply centre for several thousand gold miners who were working the river as far upstream as Alaska. Gold was first found on the river in 1886, but even before that the river was named "Fortymile". Some rivers flowing into the Yukon got their name from the distance measured from Fort Reliance - a trading post established just below Dawson City in 1874, by Jack McQuesten and Alfred Mayo. Earlier names for Fortymile were "Shitando", "Chittondeg", "Ayonie's River", and "Cane Hill River". The town of Fortymile died a quick death just days after gold was found in the Klondike area. There are many buildings still standing, or barely standing. Please treat them with respect.

km 86 / mile 54.3 The road to your left (south) goes to the Sixtymile mining district. Gold was first discovered along the Sixtymile River in 1876, but not until 1891 were rich deposits found. Gold is still being mined there. There are no services along this road.

km 104 / mile 65 Rest stop with viewpoint.

km 107.8 / mile 67 Yukon / Alaska border at Little Gold Creek. Elevation 1258 m / 4127 feet. The border is open daily from the end of May to the beginning of Oct., from 9 a.m. to 9 p.m. from the Yukon side, and 8 a.m. to 8 p.m. from the Alaska side. It is illegal to cross the border at night; and there is a chain across the road. Since the Yukon River Ferry starts service earlier than the border officially opens, and may still run 3-4 weeks after the border has been closed officially for traffic, drivers are strongly advised to report to customs officials in either Dawson City or Beaver Creek. Snow can close the road at any time from the beginning of September.

km 108 / mile 67 Viewing platform and **rest stop**.

km 111.5 / mile 69.2 Boundary Lodge. Gas, food and lodging. Emergency phone. The airstrip is 640 m / 2100 feet long at an elevation of 896 m / 2940 feet.

km 127 / mile 78.8 Jack Wade Junction. Road to the Yukon River community of Eagle.

From the border, the "Top of the World" Highway #9 became the Alaska Highway #5 connecting Tok with Eagle. From this junction, it is 104 km / 65 miles to Eagle; to the Alaska Highway it is 154 km / 96 miles; and to Dawson City 127 km / 79 miles.

<u>the road to Eagle:</u>

km 127.5 / mile 79.2 Viewpoint and rest stop.

km 133.2 / mile 82.7 Steele Creek Dome is to your right. Elevation 1224 m / 4015 feet. The road is slippery when wet.

km 142.8 / mile 88.7 Viewpoint and rest stop. The road drops into the Fortymile valley.

km 154.2 / mile 95.8 Fortymile River Bridge and canoe launch for float trips to the Yukon River. A large part of the Fortymile River system has been declared a **National Wild and Scenic River.** For more information write to the Bureau of Land Management - Steese / White Mountain District, 1150 University Ave., Fairbanks, Alaska, 99709 - 3844. Tel. 1-907-474-2350, or visit their office in Tok.

km 155 / mile 96.3 Highway maintenance camp. Emergency services only.

km 174.8 / mile 108.6 Lodge with cafe and gas station.

km 184.7 / mile 114.7 King Solomon Creek Bridge campground. No facilities.

km 203.5 / mile 126.4 Road begins its descent into the Yukon River Valley.

km 229.4 / mile 142.5 Gas station.

EAGLE

km 231 / mile 143.5 Community of Eagle and end of the road.

For emergencies (health nurse, police or fire) call either 907-547-2300 or 907-547-2211. Eagle City, with Eagle Village 5 km / 3 miles further upstream, has a population of approximately 170 people. The elevation is at 250 m or 820 feet. Those arriving from Canada by canoe or plane need to report to **customs** (handled by the postmaster) - located at the **post office** (Tel. 1-907-547-2211) at the corner of Jefferson and 2nd. Eagle is a dry community; no alcohol can be bought or sold.

Gold discoveries in 1897 convinced 28 miners to settle here calling their "village" Eagle, because eagles were seen nesting on a nearby bluff. By 1898, Eagle had a population of about 1700, and in 1901 was declared the first incorporated city in the interior of Alaska. In 1905, Eagle made newspaper headlines world-wide as the city from which **Roald Amundsen**, the famous Norwegian Arctic and Antarctic explorer, announced to the rest of the world that he had found the Northwest Passage - travelling from the east to the west. Amundsen had to dog mush 1000 km / 650 miles from the whaling station on Herschel Island, in the northern Yukon, to the nearest telegraph station, here at Eagle. After World War II, the population dwindled to nine residents, but the construction of the Taylor Highway in the 1950s revived the village and gave it a permanent lease on life. The highway out of Eagle is not maintained during winter, and the first snowfall will effectively cut-off the community from the rest of the world - except for a year-round air service.

<u>Services in Eagle and where to stay:</u>

Eagle Trading Co. Lodge and RV Park. On 1st Street. Tel. 1-907-547-2220. Grocery store, gas station with repairs, propane, public showers and a coin laundry. Rooms from US$45. Eagle Trading runs a bus to the airstrip 3.2 km / 2 miles away.

Eagle B&B. Tel. 1-907-547-2264. Berry at 4th; from US$50.

The Yukon Adventure B&B. Tel. 1-907-547-2221; from US$50 to US$80.

Falcon Inn B&B. Tel. 1-907-547-2254. Fax 1-907-547-2255. On 220 Front St., rates from $65. No smoking. They also organize river trips and rent canoes.

Eagle Campground. 3 km / 1.8 miles from town near historic Fort Egbert. Follow 4th Street north.

The Village Store. Groceries, gas station, hardware store. On 1st Street at the south end of town. Tel. 547-2270.

For those arriving by canoe, almost no tenting spots can be found along the steep embankments separating the village from the river. The most convenient site to pitch a tent is on a small island facing Eagle. Paddling back and forth between the island and Eagle is not a problem. For further information call the **Eagle City Hall** at Tel 1-907-547-2282.

What to do:

There is a **walking tour through Eagle** every morning at 9 a.m., lasting between two and three hours and costing $3 per person over the age of 12. It leaves from the museum at the old court house, and more departures are possible throughout the day - depending on demand. Summer only. The store sells gifts, maps, books and some crafts. Contact the Eagle Historical Society. Box 23, Eagle City, Alaska, 99738.

Fort Egbert is a restored US Army Outpost built in 1899 to maintain law and order in this mining district. Many of the 37 military buildings constructed are still standing. The fort was abandoned in 1911. There is an interpretive centre with a photo gallery. It is open daily in summer.

The public library, at Amundsen and 2nd, shows videos of the old Eagle area every Monday at 8 p.m.

The National Park Service Center for the Yukon - Charley Rivers National Reserve is located at the northern end of 4th Street. Open daily in summer from 8 a.m. to 5 p.m. Telephone 1-907-547-2233. Address: Box 167, Eagle, Alaska, 99738. Topo maps of the area between Eagle and Circle are available.

Visit the Artist Co-op at Jefferson and 2nd.

Transportation to and from Eagle: The *'Yukon Queen'* arrives in Eagle Village, south of Eagle, every day at about 12:30 in the afternoon and returns to Dawson City at 14:00. This boat journey is mainly meant for Westours Grayline Alaska Bus Tours passengers, but vacant seats are sold on a first come - first served basis. The bus to and from Fairbanks will accept passengers depending on seat availability. One-way is US$197, with an overnight stay in Tok. Hotel accommodation in Tok is not included in the price. For further information call Grayline in Anchorage 1-907-277-5581, or Fairbanks 1-907-456-7741, in Whitehorse 1-403-668-3225 or in Dawson City 1-403-993-5599. An all inclusive three day tour: Fairbanks-Tok-Eagle-Dawson City-Fairbanks (bus-boat-plane) costs about US$700. The *'Yukon Queen'* has space for one or two canoes for the return trip to Dawson City. Loading and unloading has to be done by the owners.

By plane: There are at least two flights a day to Fairbanks, morning and afternoon. The Sunday flight to Fairbanks is routed via Circle, about 250 km / 155 miles downstream from Eagle.

Warbelow's Air Ventures leaves mornings Mon. to Fri. at 10:20, arriving in Fairbanks at 11:35; and Sat. at 11:25 arriving in Fairbanks at 12:55. The afternoon flights leave seven days a week (except Sat.) at 14:25. On Sunday's this flight is routed via Circle further downstream. From Fairbanks to Eagle, flights leave at 9:00 and 13:00 on the same days as previously mentioned. Call them in Eagle at 1-907-547-2212 / 2365, in Circle 1-907-773-1217 or in Fairbanks 1-907-474-0518. Fax 1-907-479-5054, or toll-free from Alaska only 1-800-478-0812. Also check with **Tatonduk Flying** in Eagle 1-907-547-2221 and in Fairbanks 1-907-447-4697. One-way is approximately US$80.

There are charter flights only, between Eagle and Dawson City, and it costs about US$500 for a three or four seater one-way.

Be adventurous - leave by canoe or raft:

Eagle Canoe Rentals. Call Mike Sager at 1-907-547-2203. One-way canoes to Circle are rented for US$160 for 5 days. The distance is about 265 km / 165 miles.

Charlie and Marla Charters rent boats to Circle. Tel. 1-907-547-2254.

Inflatable rafts can be rented from Mark and Angie for $60 a day. Renters pay for the return of the boat by plane. Tel. 1-907-547-2221.

A few words about the Yukon River between Eagle and Circle:

The **Yukon-Charley Rivers Park Preserve** covers over 80% of the total Yukon River distance between Eagle and Circle, and all the headwaters of the Charley River, for a total of 915,000 hectares or 2,260,000 acres. There are no services in the park, except for the **Slavens Roadhouse** at the riverside entrance to the park. The Roadhouse, a renovated river stop from paddle-wheeler times, offers bunk bed accommodation, a simple kitchen and solar powered showers, with cold water guaranteed on rainy-cloudy days. There is no charge for staying at the road house. An old road leading away from the river ensures good hiking past an old gold dredge, and to a former gold mining camp - now the ranger headquarters of the park, about 5 km / 3 miles from the river. For those who want to hike or raft the interior of the park, formidable preparations are necessary. For those just floating the Yukon River, between Dawson City or Eagle and Circle, the immediate area of the roadhouse and Coal Creek, with the dredge and the ranger station further inland, provide for some pleasant day hikes. There are several abandoned town-sites and cabins along the river, making this stretch of the Yukon River interesting not only for its wilderness value, but also for its rich history. Familiarize yourself with the heritage, and inquire about possible permits at the Park Headquarters in Eagle before setting out.

CIRCLE

Circle is the last canoe take-out point before the Yukon River spreads out onto the **Yukon Flats.** A hint for river travellers - Circle is not located on the main channel of the river, but on a western arm that can easily be missed if you are not careful. Watch the hills to your right (east)! If the hills obviously are flattening out, paddle to the left limit of the Yukon River and take the first channel to your left. That one should get you to Circle. Circle today has a population of less than 50, but before the 1896 gold discovery in the Klondike, Circle was a busy gold mining town of 2000 rough miners. The Gold Rush to Dawson City emptied Circle almost overnight, and it never recovered its former glory days. The beach facing Circle is not only the campsite, but also the beginning of the **Steese Highway to Fairbanks**, 261 km / 162 miles away. The airstrip crosses that road a short distance from the beach. The elevation of Circle is 186 m / 610 feet.

Circle Health Clinic call 1-907-773-7425, **post office** call 1-907-773-1220. There are two stores - **the Trading Post** has a cafe, lounge, post office, liquor store, gas, showers and a coin laundry; tel. is 1-907-773-1217. **The H.C. Company Store** sells gas, groceries and some gifts, tel. 1-907-773-1222. Both places together can be considered the "downtown" of Circle, less than a stone's throw from the beach! For those wishing to go on to Fairbanks, fly or hitchhike - no problem there - or return to Eagle by plane to pick up your car. **Warbelow's Air** flies from Circle to Fairbanks via Circle Hotsprings from Mon. to Fri. at 10:10, and Sat. at 10:30 (in the morning). The luggage max. is 40 lbs.

For those continuing their journey via the river, it is one week to ten day's of river paddling before the next road access point, at the Dalton Highway Yukon River Bridge. Enjoy your float, and may the weather be with you!

Back to the Jack Wade Junction for continuation of the Taylor Highway road description to Tok.

km 0 / mile 0 Jack Wade Junction.

km 6 / mile 3.7 Some non-maintained campsites near a tiny creek.

km 9 / mile 5.6 The old mining camp of **Jack Wade** that was in operation until 1940. This is still mining country and the whole area is staked. Please do not trespass.

km 15.5 / mile 9.6 The **gold dredge** next to the road began operations in 1934.

km 22 / mile 13.6 Walker Fork BLM (Bureau of Land Management) Campground. 16 sites, some with tables. Access point for the Fortymile River.

km 33 / mile 20.5 South Fork Bridge. Rest area with outhouses. Access point for the Fortymile River.

km 43 / mile 26.7 Lost Chicken Creek. Gold has been mined here since 1895.

km 44.2 / mile 27.5 BLM Chicken Field Station, with information about the Fortymile River National Wild and Scenic River System. Trailhead for Mosquito Fork Dredge Trail.

km 46.2 / mile 28.7 View of old town-site of Chicken. Private Property. Watch for chickens crossing the Highway - well - just kidding!

km 47 / mile 29.2 The Goldpanner. Free RV parking. Gas, groceries, gold panning.

km 48 / mile 29.8 Community of Chicken. With a human population of about 40, this really is New Chicken, but guided walking tours of Old Chicken can be arranged. Chicken, as the story goes, was supposed to be called Ptarmigan (a native wild bird similar to a chicken), but the early miners could not agree on the correct spelling of this bird (pron. TAR-mig-an) and settled on Chicken in frustration. Gold was first found in this mining district in 1886. "Downtown" Chicken offers a service station, cafe, store and saloon. The post office zip code is 99732. The book 'Tisha' by the late Ann Purdy is based on her life as a school teacher in Chicken. The Chicken airstrip is open year-round, with a length of 762 m / 2500 feet, at an elevation of 500 m / 1640 feet. The Fortymile River is accessible near the airstrip.

km 50.5 / mile 31.4 Mosquito Fork Bridge across the Fortymile. Boat access point.

km 72.7 / mile 45.2 Taylor Creek Bridge. Rough road to Kechumstuk Mountains.

km 74.7 / mile 46.4 Bridge over the **West Fork of Dennison Fork** of Fortymile River. Canoe access point.

km 75.1 / mile 46.7 West Fork Recreation Site, 25 tent sites, no water.

km 84.8 / mile 52.7 Logging Cabin Creek Bridge.

km 97.5 / mile 60.6 You are leaving Fortymile Mining District. The highway crawls up and down **Mount Fairplay** (summit 1689 m / 5541 ft) with steep grades up to 9%.

km 147 / mile 91.3 One km / 0.6 mile gravel **road to Four Mile Lake**; good fishing.

km 154 / mile 95.7 Tetlin Junction with the Alaska Highway; 40 mile Roadhouse has gas, diesel, some repairs and towing. It is 21 km or 13 miles west to Tok and 128 km or 80 miles east to the Alaska / Yukon border.

Dempster Highway

The Klondike River flowing through the Tombstone Valley. Tombstone Mountain is in the far right background.

INTRODUCTION

You may not have realized it before you left home, but this is the highway that is the true spirit of the Yukon, a forever continuing solitude of northern wilderness; this is the environment you hoped to encounter during your Yukon sojourn. The 736 km / 458 miles of narrow dusty or muddy gravel, as the case may be, winds its torturous way over otherwise untouched raw mountains and valleys, northern tundra and through waterlogged river deltas. Construction of the highway, which passes through a total of seven eco-regions, started in 1959 under a "Road to Resources" program initiated by then Prime Minister John Diefenbaker. It was 19 years before the highway opened

A view of mountain ridges and the distant Dempster Highway.

along its entire length. Discovery of oil resources in the Beaufort Sea during the latter stages of road construction sped up completion of the road. The first cars and trucks could travel as far as Inuvik by 1978. An upgrade of the highway was completed in 1988, turning this, the most northern Canadian highway, into one of the most adventurous driving experiences in North America. Be prepared! Carry plenty of spare gas (it costs over a dollar per litre north of the Dempster Corner), two spare tires, enough food to last a week, and warm clothing and camping gear if you're not in an RV or a camper / van. Rain can turn some sections of the highway into a slippery and dangerous mess - stop off the highway to wait it out. Snow can fall anytime at higher elevations, and vehicle problems can delay you for hours, if not days. Do not expect much traffic. There might not be another car to intrude on your solitude for an hour or two - you have the scenery all to yourself. If there are two or more cars at a time, it seems like rush hour! There is plenty of off-road parking. Take a hike, savour the quietness and the rich, clean air, and enjoy. Remove your garbage; there are not too many places like this left on our planet! The road is open year-round, call 1-800-661-0750 / 0752 for recorded messages about road conditions, ferry service and the weather.

The highway was named after Royal North West Mounted Police Capt. W.J.D. Dempster who, in the winter of 1911, found the bodies of a lost police patrol. The Canadian police forces during that time conducted regular dog team patrols of the north out of Dawson City. Read up on this tragic story in the book 'The Lost Patrol' by well known Yukon author Dick North. This road is not only a car traveller's dream, but more and more bicyclists brave this highway, and the Dempster has become a "must" for many extreme cyclists from all over the world. In these next pages I will try to accommodate cyclists by noting relevant facts such as sources of water along the road. Since few will cycle the highway twice, the favoured direction is south to north. Wilderness hikers, too, find the country left and right of the highway to their liking. There are no established trails (isn't that nice!) on either side and, for those who want to hike deep into the wilderness, precautions have to be thorough. Short, one or two day hikes onto the ridges on both sides of the highway can easily be done without losing sight of the gravel highway below, which is helpful to find your way back! Read again the section 'How to drive on gravel' in the Introduction chapter.

km 0 / mile 0 Klondike River Lodge at the Dempster Corner. It is 363 km / 226 miles to the next gas station at Eagle Plains. Fuel-up here and if you need a second spare tire, ask here or at any of the service stations in Dawson City if second-hand tires are for sale. Park your car here or at your place of accommodation in Dawson City if you want to continue by bike. The lodge is open from 7 a.m. to midnight daily year-round. Tel. 993-6892. There is a motel, RV parking, a cafe, store and car repairs. Stop at the information panels just before the Klondike River Bridge for historical information and other useful points about the highway.

km 0.3 / mile 0.2 Klondike River Bridge, one lane with wooden planks. Turn on your headlights! The road follows mainly rolling hills, gradually gaining in elevation to the Tombstone Campground, 72 km / 45 miles away. The North Fork of the Klondike River is to your right (east), hidden within the forest of spruce and poplars. Signs of forest fires are all around you - one in 1991 burned 2100 ha. / 5190 acres.

km 6 / mile 3.7 Narrow gravel roads branch off either side to the 1906-built **North Fork Ditch and Power Station;** until 1966 it provided water and power for Dawson City and the gold dredges.

km 15 / mile 9.3 The Antimony Mountain Range to the east has an elevation of up to 2040 m / 6693 feet. The Tombstone Range stretches to the west.

km 24.5 / mile 15.2 Glacier Creek.

km 29 / mile 18.2 Bensen Creek.

km 41 / mile 25.5 Pea Soup Creek was named in 1969 by a highway construction crew, when one of them fell into the creek. It has not been recorded if the person in question had been eating pea soup at that time, or if pea soup had been the staple fare at construction camps, or..... just make up your own history as you drive along!

km 48 / mile 29.8 Scout Car Creek was named in 1969 when a construction car got stuck in it.

km 51 / mile 31.7 Wolf Creek and Trappers Cabin are private. Two native elders, Joe and Annie Henry of the Han First Nation lived and trapped here for many years. Do not trespass.

km 59.5 / mile 36.3 Grizzly Creek. An unmarked trail (of sorts...) leads from this gravel pit up to Grizzly Valley, Mt. Monolith, Grizzly Pass and Twin Lake. This is the shortest entrance point into the Tombstone Range and beyond, and back to Dawson City. To your right (east) runs the Klondike River's north arm. Mt. Robert Service can be seen to the east.

km 61.5 / mile 38.2 Gravel pit. A 4 km/2.5 mile round trip hike from here heads directly west up the slope to the Cairnes Ridge; there are great views of Mt. Monolith, hidden lakes and mountain ridges.

km 63.7 / mile 39.6 Mike and Art Creek. Now - how could this creek have gotten its name?

km 65 / mile 40. The Klondike Highway Government Maintenance Camp is staffed year-round; emergency assistance is available. Fold Mountain (1973 m / 6472 feet) to the west, can be accessed from opposite the camp. Slog up the path of least resistance at the lower ends of the slope - then it gets easy; it is 6 km one-way. Take a tent and food, and stay a night on the ridge!

km 66 / mile 41 Follow the stream due west for about one kilometre to a small **waterfall**.

km 67.3 / mile 41.8 North Fork Klondike River Bridge.

km 71.5 / mile 44.4 T o m b s t o n e G o v e r n m e n t Campground; elevation 1034 m/3392 feet, 22 RV and tent sites, some are right next to the Klondike River. Shelter and firewood. There is an interpretive centre staffed with biologists who give talks on what is alive around you. The centre has a resource library, maps and information, as well as a record of what type of wildlife has been seen along the highway. You can contribute your sightings.

Mountain biking along the Dempster Highway.

The location of this campground is charming - and it's perfect for day or multi-day hikes onto the mountain ridges on both sides of the highway. One easy hike follows the Klondike River upstream on a well-established trail past fields of blooming fireweed. Keep on walking on this trail and soon enough you will notice what a teaser it was! Hiking up the Tombstone Valley following the Klondike River can be torture indeed - dense willow and alder underbrush seem like multi-armed octopuses hindering any step ahead. It is better to get your feet wet by crossing the river. There used to be a tree bridge off of the campground which went to the west side of the river. Otherwise, one needs to cross the river at the braided section further upstream. Once across, hike up the mountain side - straight up. Two to three hours later, the slope will slowly flatten out, revealing more and more stunning vistas and two beautifully pristine mountain lakes below. This can be a day-long hike, or an overnight trip, or the beginning of a week-long trek into the Tombstones. Enjoy and please practice NO TRACE HIKING and BE BEAR AWARE!

km 74 / mile 46 It is a long climb from the campground to the **North Fork Pass**. This rest stop offers one of the most breath-taking views along the highway. With the Klondike Valley below you, and the river twisting its way downward and out of sight to your left, look up and the Tombstone Mountain (2192 m / 7191 feet) sits right on top of the funnel shaped valley, about 28 km / 17 miles away. Hike to the rest stop from the campground!

km 75.5 / mile 46.9 There is a tiny creek, a sidearm of **Lil Creek**, that passes under the road in a culvert. Walk up this creek for a short distance and you will find a large section of slow-melting glacial ice - perfect for your ice-box. This creek runs off Goldensides Mountain, and the hike up to the summit is one of the easier treks because of the high altitude of the road at this point. Once on top, the hiker will find great ridge walking, great views, and even greater chances to observe caribou.

km 77 / mile 47.8   Lil Creek. There are three mountains west of the highway - on the left is **North Fork Mountain** (1830 m / 6000 feet); the furthest away and slightly to the north is **Whitecrown Mountain** (1968 m / 6458 feet); and to your right is **Incline Mountain** (1860 m / 6100 feet). All three are 5 to 7 km (3 to 4.5 miles) away, and combining them would be a several day-long hike. Approach by following the creek - there is plenty of wet tundra hiking until the base of the range is reached.

km 78.5 / mile 48.8   The Hart Pass Road (more of a trail, do not try driving it) leads to Hart Pass and to the Hart River beyond, which flows into the Peel River. The trail is easy hiking and offers wildlife observation. This area is named after Howard Hamilton Hart of Montana who crossed the Chilkoot Trail in 1884. He "struck it rich" on Bonanza Creek, mining Tagish (Dawson) Charlie's discovery claim. While heading to Seattle, Hart lost everything in a shipwreck.

km 81 / mile 50.3   North Fork Pass. Elevation 1289 m / 4229 feet. The highway crosses the continental divide. All rivers from this point on flow into the Arctic Ocean via the Peel and Mackenzie Rivers.

km 84 / mile 52.2   Angelcomb Peak to the east is 1740 m / 5700 feet tall.

km 89.5 / mile 55.6   Sheep Mountain to the east is 1740 m / 5700 feet high and the place to be on June 21, Solstice Day. To the north of Sheep Mountain all ridges are low enough to allow the midnight sun to be seen for a full 24 hours. To get to the summit is a bit of work, though. It's about 2 km one-way, and several knee-deep channels of the East Blackstone River have to be forded. Watch for Dall sheep in May and June, as well as eagles and grizzly bears. Please do not disturb sheep during lambing season in early summer.

km 91 / mile 56.5 Upper part of the **BlackStone River Valley**. Great bird watching.

km 95.5 / mile 59   Outfitter cabins to the east.

km 102 / mile 63.4 To Eagle Plains Lodge it is a further 261 km / 162 miles.

km 107.6 / mile 66.9   Rest stop with litter barrel.

km 115 / mile 71.4 The Road crosses the west fork of the **Blackstone River**.

km 116 / mile 72.1   A road sign commemorates the North West Mounted Police dog sled patrol, led by Inspector F.J. Fitzgerald. The party became lost in the winter of 1910-1911, and all four officers died of starvation. Sergeant Dempster, who recovered the bodies, died in 1964, one year after the highway was named in his honour. **Chapman Lake** is just ahead, with good fishing (as with most lakes along the highway) for grayling, char, northern pike, longnose suckers and inconnu.

km 117 / mile 72.7 Pilots Peak, elevation 1680 m / 5500 feet, is to the east of the highway. This volcano-shaped mountain was named by bush pilot Lionel Vines, who for many years had used this prominent peak as a landmark. Chapman Lake was named after a trader who operated a fly-in trading post here before the road was built.

km 124.4 / mile 77.3 Government Emergency Airstrip, 914 m / 3000 feet long at an elevation of 945 m / 3100 feet. The road is part of the airstrip.

km 138 / mile 85.7 The Blackstone River offers access for river travellers coming down the Blackstone to where it meets the Ogilvie River 130 km / 80 miles further downstream. At the conjunction of the Blackstone and the Ogilvie, where both rivers turn into the Peel River, river travellers have three choices - continue down the Peel, with potentially very dangerous rapids; make the rough slog out of the valley to the highway 8 km / 5 miles away; or ascend the Ogilvie River for about 60 km / 38 miles, until you come back to the highway.

km 146 / mile 90.7 The road leaves the Blackstone River Valley, climbing to **Windy Pass.**

km 153 / mile 95 Windy Pass, elevation 1060 m / 3480 feet. The treeless Windy Pass divides the Blackstone River Valley from Engineer Creek Valley. Wide open spaces provide great hiking from the pass to Mt. Distincta (1600 m / 5300 feet) to the south.

km 169.7 / mile 105.4 Engineer Creek at this point is a red-coloured, sulphurous, smelly mess. Iron-oxide in the soil is responsible, therefore don't drink the water.

km 194 / mile 120.5 Engineer Creek Government Campground, 15 RV and tent sites. The water must be boiled to purify it. Sapper Hill, to the east, offers a pleasant 4-5 km semi-strenuous round-trip hike past many interesting rock formations. "Sapper" is a nickname for army engineers and; obviously, the Canadian Armed Forces Engineers, who built the bridges in this section, named a few other sites as well.

km 195.7 / mile 121.6 Ogilvie River Bridge. The Native name, is "Gwazhal Nijik". William Ogilvie was a topographical surveyor for the Dominion of Canada between 1875 and 1898. He surveyed the Alaska / Yukon border in the Fortymile area in 1887-88, as well as the Klondike Gold Fields, and even the Dawson City town site. Ogilvie was made Commissioner of the Yukon Territory in 1898. In 1901, he rescued a young lady from drowning in Nome, Alaska, whom he later married. From the bridge, the highway closely follows the Ogilvie River. There are a couple of class II to III rapids, until the river leaves the highway 50 km / 31 miles later. If floating this stretch, do not miss your take-out point at highway km 243 / mile 151! The **Ogilvie Government Highway Maintenance Camp**, at the northern end of bridge, will assist in emergency situations.

km 214 / mile 133 There are some unusual rock formations along the highway called Tors; castle-like rock outcroppings that top the mountains. Steep cliffs might challenge a rock climber. At this point, if you look back, you will notice a hole in one of the rocky walls which was shaped by wind and water.

km 221.2 / mile 137.5 Rest stop next to the Ogilvie River.

km 243 / mile 151 The highway leaves the **Ogilvie River Valley**. Canoe travellers who want to paddle down into the Peel River need to be aware of dangerous white water canyons -the Peel has claimed several lives these last few years. Bicyclists need to stock up on water. From here to Eagle Plains, 126 km/78 miles away, are few, if any, conveniently located sources of water.

km 259 / mile 161 Rest stop with great views and a litter barrel. Cyclists! Do not tent near litter barrels. They are usually bear-proof, but will attract bears who might want to check out the delicious smell drifting out of them. For tenting, there are sheltered gravel pits at km 275 / mile 171; km 282 / mile 177.1; km 290 / mile 180; and km 297 / mile 184.9.

km 270 / mile 168 Beautiful open, rolling country above tree line.

km 321 / mile 199.5 The road doubles as an **airstrip**.

km 346 / mile 215 The Richardson Mountains become visible to the northeast. Those many arrow-straight lines cut through the tundra are seismic survey lines made during the 1950s and 1960s to explore for oil and gas. Not much was found, but part of the reason this highway was built was because of oil prospecting.

km 350.5 / mile 217.8 The road crosses **Big Timber Creek**.

km 369 / mile 229.3 Eagle Plains Hotel. Tel. and Fax 979-4187. Mobile radio HJL2 5889 Rat Pass channel. For ground to air radio, use channel frequency 122.80. The **landing strip** is at km 389 / mile 241.5. The hotel offers 32 rooms, RV parking and tenting with showers, coin laundry and a restaurant / lounge. The store offers some food items, a service station with car and tire repair, and propane. Public telephone. Room rates are: $90 single, $100 double, $110 triple. Visa, MC and Amex are accepted. Open Year-round. See the displays about the "Mad Trapper of Rat River" in the lounge. Cyclists and hikers can forward food supplies to Eagle Plains via the Gold City van-bus arriving here every Tuesday and Thursday around noon, from both Dawson City and Inuvik. If there are not at least four passengers, there is no bus!

km 378 / mile 235 Eagle River Bridge. See the information panels about the "Mad Trapper" at the southern end of bridge. Eagle Plains Hotel trucks all of its water from this river - a full time job! By canoe, it is about 380 km / 236 miles, or six to eight days, to Old Crow. Eagle River is a class I river; the biggest danger is that it can run out of water by late summer. You can charter a plane back to Eagle Plains, use regular scheduled services to either Inuvik or Dawson City, or keep on paddling down the Porcupine River to Fort Yukon, with daily air-services to Fairbanks and Circle.

OLD CROW

The population of Old Crow is about 270 people, and it is the only community in the Yukon with no road access. The traditional life of the native people of the Yukon was one of mobility, and the present village of Old Crow has only been there since 1911. The area around Old Crow is a treasure-chest for anthropologists, archaeologists and biologists, since proof of human existence in this area can be traced back almost 30,000 years. The Gwitchin people of Old Crow make a living from fishing, hunting, working for the government, and tourism.

There are few services:

Cho'oh Danjik B&B. Tel. 966-3008, Fax 966-3424. Box 25, Old Crow, Yukon, Y0B 1N0. One room with three beds $100 single, $150 double. Meals are served. Open year-round. **Nukon Cabin.** Tel. 966-3921. Camping is allowed in a designated area near the village. The Vuntut Gwitchin First Nation Office may also be able to help. Call them at 996-3261. There also is some accommodation available in private homes; check with the **Village Co-op** at 966-3241 or Fax 966-3507. Old Crow is a 'dry' village - no alcohol can be brought in for sale or consumption. **RCMPolice:** Tel. 966-5555. **Village nurse:**

Tel. 966-4444. **Canada Post**: Tel. 966-3419. **Banking** is by Toronto Dominion Bank, which is only open Tues. to Fri. from 12:30 to 2:30 p.m. There is a store with a cafe, public showers and coin laundry. Scheduled air services are offered by Air North from and to Dawson City and Inuvik.

Charters can be arranged from Old Crow to the newly declared **Vuntut National Park**, established in July, 1993. There are no services - it is just pure wilderness and home to the 80,000 sized herd of Porcupine Caribou. The park area covers 4,345 sq. km and borders to the west on Alaska, to the north on **Ivvavik National Park**, and to the east on the Arctic Wildlife Refuge. The park is mainly dedicated to the preservation of the caribou herd, the unique wilderness region, and the cultural heritage and life-style of the native people of Old Crow.

Four topographical maps are needed to cover this area: Old Crow 116-0 and 116 N, Davidson Mountains 117 B, and Blow river 117 A. Contact World Wide in Vancouver, or Jim's in Whitehorse.

The **Old Crow Flats** north of Old Crow is home to over 2000 lakes which are spread across 600,000 hectares. Those lakes are a prime breeding ground for scores of birds and ducks. Call the Canadian Wildlife Service in Whitehorse at tel. 393-6700, for more information.

Bordering to the north of the Vuntut National Park lies the 10,168 square km (3926 square mile) **Ivvavik National Park**, with the Herschel Island Yukon Territorial Park just off the coast. Access to these two parks is usually from Inuvik.

Continuing on the Dempster Highway:

km 389 / mile 241.7   Airstrip. The length of the runway is 762 m / 2500 feet, at an elevation of 721 m / 2365 feet. This is the main landing strip for supply flights to Eagle and Old Crow.

km 405.5 / mile 252   The Arctic Circle, latitude 66 degrees, 33 minutes north. Watch for a rope across the highway - well - just kidding! The imaginary line circling our planet is marked by picnic tables, outhouses, a marker, and sweeping views. The lowest point the sun reaches in the sky can be seen at 2 a.m. and, depending on where you are on this highway, the sun might appear and disappear behind distant hills just minutes apart - giving the viewer two or three sunrises and sunsets! Should you be at this point on December 21, forget about seeing any sun at all. And, yes, it has be mentioned! The Arctic Circle is not really where it is supposed to be - at least not for the moment. Look for the exact imaginary location 834 m or 913 yards north of where everybody says the line is. Why? Due to variations in the earth's rotation, the invisible line moves slowly in a northerly direction. It is predicted, though, that the Arctic Circle will move south again in due time - in 10,000 to 20,000 years.

km 407.5 / mile 253.2 A gravel pit gives tenters some shelter, should the weather be rough.

km 412.5 / mile 256.3 From this gravel pit, hike the ridge east to Mt. Hare (about 5 km away), the second highest peak in the Richardson Range at 1336 m / 4073 feet. There are many interesting ridge hikes for better midnight sun viewing, until about km 421 / mile 261. For those tenting, look for gravel pits that offer some shelter against strong winds; they are located at km 423 / mile 262.8 and km 427 / mile 265.3.

km 446 / mile 277.1   Cornwall River (Big River) Government Campground includes 17 RV and tent sites, with three sites for tents only. Water, shelter and firewood are available. The largest trees in the region grow in this sheltered canyon. Mosquitoes and black flies love it here too.

Captain Dick, and Pierre with his gold nugget studded hat- two Yukon characters.

Field of fireweed with an outhouse.

Unfold the adventure of exploring the frontier with an "International Travel Map"

km 465 / mile 288.9 Richardson Mountain Pass and Rest Stop is at 915 m / 3000 feet. This is also the **Yukon / Northwest Territories border, and the Continental Divide**. All western creeks flow into the Pacific Ocean; all eastern ones flow into the Arctic Ocean. The time changes - noon in the Yukon is 1 p.m. in NWT. The Richardson Mountains are named after the naturalist and surgeon Sir John Richardson. He was a member of the Franklin Party searching for the Northwest Passage in 1826. John Franklin died during his third journey in 1845. This mountain range is the most northerly extension of the Rocky Mountains. Weathering over the ages, and a ceaseless driving wind, have rounded the peaks. Vegetation is sparse, and trees are stunted, growing low to the ground and only in sheltered areas but, nevertheless, can be very old. The **Porcupine River** used to flow through this range into the Arctic Ocean, but glacial ice sheets 12,000 years ago forced the river to find a westward passage into the Yukon River. **Cyclists!**, there is no water until km 14 / mile 8.7. - The Dempster Highway #5 continues from this point as the NWT Highway #8, starting at kilometre post zero.

A few words about the Northwest Territories

The NWT has a landmass of 3,376,689 square km (1.3 million square miles), one third of the total size of Canada; or the size of India, or the combined size of Texas, Alaska, California, New Mexico and then some - and that is big! About 64,000 people live in a total of 63 communities, the capital being Yellowknife. Six national parks dot this huge expanse of tundra, lakes and rivers, forests, and mountains - but you can drive to only one; the Wood Buffalo NP, which the territory shares with Alberta. The people of the NWT speak 9 official languages, of which English is one. Five main groups of people share this land: the **Dene** of the northern forest; the **Inuit** of the northern islands and coast; the **Inuvialuit** who live along the Mackenzie Delta; the **Metis** who are the children of two cultures - the trapper, explorer and trader who married local women; and the **"Others"**, mainly Euro-Canadians. Oh yes - the North Pole is part of the NWT, and so is the Magnetic North Pole. The latter moves constantly (but slowly), which is why compass needles tend to be rather unreliable in the far north. Currently, the Magnetic North Pole is located northwest of Resolute Bay, near Bathurst Island.

The highest recorded temperature at 43°C/110°F was recorded in Coppermine in 1991; the coldest was in Shepard Bay at -57.8°C/-72°F. In the near future, the NWT will divide into two political entities, with the eastern half being called Nunavut with the town of Igaluit as the new capital. The western part will retain the name Northwest Territories or NT, and the capital will remain at Yellowknife.

---

km 479 / mile 297.6 (NWT km 14 / mile 8.7) James Creek Highway Maintenance Camp. Camping is okay at the creek, and so is fishing for grayling. A NWT fishing licence is required.

km 488.7 / mile 303.6 (NWT km 23.6 / mile 14.7) Wright Pass Summit at 853 m / 2798 feet. It is downhill from here to the Peel River, 51 km / 31 miles away.

km 509 / mile 316.3 (NWT km 44 / mile 27.3) Access road to Midway Lake - also the location of the annual Fort McPherson Music Festival, which takes place the last weekend in June.

km 514 / mile 319.4 (NWT km 49 / mile 30.4) Midway Airstrip; the length of the runway is 914 m / 3000 feet. During autumn and spring, when no ferry or ice road connects the communities to the north, aircraft are used as "ferries".

km 539 / mile 334.9 (NWT km 74 / mile 46) Peel River. The cable ferry, locally called Eightmile Ferry, operates from about the beginning of June to mid-October, daily from 9 a.m. to 12:30 a.m. No charge. Call 1-800-661-0752 for ferry information, road conditions, and weather. The Peel River is a major tributary of the Mackenzie River, and it was named by John Franklin after Sir Robert Peel (1788-1850), then Prime Minister of Great Britain. It is a slow and easy one day canoe trip from here to Fort McPherson.

km 540.6 / mile 335.9 (NWT km 75.5 / mile 47) Nitanlaii (Nutuilvie) Territorial Campground; 23 RV and tent sites, water, shelter, firewood. Please pay for an overnight stay at the NWT Information Centre next door. The centre has historical displays and sells NWT fishing licences.

NWT residents pay an annual fishing fee of $10. Other Canadian residents pay $20, or for three days $15. Non-Canadians pay $40 annually, or for three days $30. Anybody between the ages of 16 and 65 needs a fishing licence. Call 979-7247 for more information.

km 547.8 / mile 340.4 (NWT km 82.7 / mile 51) Fort McPherson Airstrip, length 1067 m / 3500 feet, and elevation 43 m / 141 feet.

FORT MCPHERSON

km 550 / mile 441.7 (NWT km 85 / mile 52.8) The community of Fort McPherson is mainly an indigenous community of about 700 people and is located on a hill overlooking the Peel River. The Gwich'in tribal name for the village is Tetl'it Zheh, meaning "House above the River". The village is named after an 1848 Hudson Bay Company chief trader, Murdock McPherson. The Gwich'in people inhabit a small corner in the Northwest Territories within the Peel River Delta.

A few important numbers: NWT has the same telephone area code as the Yukon, and that number also will change from 403 to 867, starting October 1997.

RCMPolice: 952-2551. **Health Centre**: 952-2586. **Airport**: 952-2121. **Post Office**: 952-2906, and for more information about the village call the **Village Office** at 952-2428. **CBC Radio** can be found on 690 AM.

Where to stay:

Tetlit Cooperative - Inns North and restaurant. Tel. 952-2417/2339, Fax 952-2602. Open year-round. 9 double rooms from $100 to $125. Visa, MC, Amex. Monthly rates. Service station, car and tire repairs. Grocery store. Also in town: a lounge, handicraft store and a community information centre.

Tetlichi's B&B. Tel. 952-2712 (9 to 5) or tel. 952-2356 after 5 p.m. Fax 952-2148. $75 for single or double.

Taxi services: Wolverine Cabs, tel 952-2660 and **Peterson Taxi**, tel. 952-2031. Both provide long distance travel, deliver goods, and operate 24 hours a day.

What to do:

Visit the graves of the "Lost Patrol"; the four officers of the North West Mounted Police who starved to death during a dog sled patrol in 1910-11, only 36 km / 22 miles from here.

The Tent and Canvas Factory is a large, native-run enterprise manufacturing canvas wall tents, teepees of all sizes, and other goods such as bags. The factory is open for tours weekdays from 9 a.m. to 5 p.m., and after hours and on weekends if pre-arranged. Tel. 952-2179, or write for a brochure to: Fort McPherson Tent and Canvas, Box 58, Fort McPherson, NWT, X0F 0J0.

For guided trips into the river delta and elsewhere: contact **Dempster Patrol Outfitters**, Tel. 952-2210/2039. **Keith Colin**, Box 103, Fort McPherson, NWT, X0F 0J0, organizes hiking day trips to the sacred Shildii Rock overlooking the Peel River, boat trips through the delta, visits to traditional fishing camps, and boat trips to the delta village of Aklavik.

CH II Adventure. Tel. 952-2424. Fax 952-2024. Daily walking tours through town with a traditional lunch and wilderness river boat tours.

AKLAVIK

The Community of Aklavik (Aktlaguik) "Place of the barren land grizzly bear", is totally surrounded by the Mackenzie River Delta. Aklavik can only be reached by air or by boat except in the winter, when boats are replaced by cars, with a winter ice road connection to Inuvik. The remains of the "Mad Trapper" Albert Johnson are buried here. Aklavik was first established in 1910 as a trading post, and today's population stands at about 850 - of which only 8% are non-native. The village is located 58 air-km. west of Inuvik, and Aklavik only offers 6 km. of unpaved roads.

A few words about **Albert Johnson** - Books have been written and movies have been made about the 'Mad Trapper of the Rat River'. During the winter of 1931, one of the coldest in recorded history, the whole world knew about the 40 day-long manhunt for Albert Johnson, a reclusive trapper who had run afoul of the law, shot at police officers and finally was cornered and shot to death. It had been the first time in criminal history that an airplane was used in tracking down a suspected criminal.

<u>Aklavik has two B&Bs</u>:

Bessie Boarding B&B. Tel. 978-2215, Fax 978-2815. Bessie Erigaktuk. Box 116, Aklavik, NT X0E 0A0. Guests may use the kitchen.

Daadzaii Lodge B&B. Tel. 978-2252. General Delivery, Aklavik, NT, X0E 0A0. Kitchen facilities.

There is one cafe: **The Caribou Cafe**. Telephone 978-2528.

Arctic Wings out of Inuvik has scheduled flights to Aklavik. Their tel. is 979-2220 and fax 979-3440. Call 978-2727 for **F E S Greenland's Bus and Taxi** services, or **Arey's Taxi and Tours** at tel. 978-2358.

<u>Two interesting festivals:</u>

Pokiak River Festival. With traditional games, canoe races and a music festival. Always held at the end of June.

Aklavik Dizzy Daze. Carnival type activities, with all kinds of fun games. Beginning of September. Call 978-2340 for information on both festivals and for more information about Aklavik, call the **Village Office** at 978-2351 or by Fax 978-2434.

THE DEMPSTER HWY. FROM FORT MCPHERSON TO THE MACKENZIE RIVER

km 587.6 / mile 365.1 (NWT km 123 / mile 76.4) Frog Creek rest stop offers fishing for grayling and pike. The water is okay for drinking, but boil or treat it anyway. Water also can be found at NWT highway km 108 / mile 67.

km 606.8 / mile 377 (NWT km 142.2 / mile 88.4) Rest stop next to Mackenzie River. Shelter, picnic tables, firewood.

MACKENZIE RIVER

km 608.2 / mile 378 (NWT km 143.6 / mile 89) Mackenzie River. The ferry operates daily from 09:00 to 00:30, leaving the Fort McPherson side of the river at 9:25, 10:25 and so on, with the last ferry at 12:25 a.m; leaving from the Inuvik side of the river for the first run of the day at 9 a.m., and on the hour after that with the last ferry at midnight. From the village of Arctic Red River, the first ferry leaves at 9:45, at 10:45 etc. with the last one leaving for the Inuvik side of the river at 12:45 a.m. The ferry runs from mid-June to about early October. There is no charge. The ice bridge is usable from late November to the beginning of May. The ferry connects both shores of the Mackenzie River, with one further stop at the village of Arctic Red River, which is located further upstream at the confluence of the Arctic Red and Mackenzie rivers. Tell the ferry crew if you want to go to Arctic Red River.

The Mackenzie River is one of the mightiest rivers in the world, draining the whole eastern side of the Rocky Mountains from latitude 52° N. The length of the Mackenzie, not including Great Slave Lake, is 1800 km / 1120 miles, but it approaches over 4000 km / 2500 miles when adding the Slave and Peace River systems. Its total watershed equals 1.7 million square kilometres, or 656,000 square miles, making the Mackenzie the second largest river in North America and the 10th largest in the world. If you are looking for a very long and continuous canoe trip, this is it! Alexander Mackenzie, in 1789, was the first White man to canoe the entire length of the river - it took him 21 days from where the river spills out of Great Slave Lake at Wrigley Harbour, to the delta, and 31 days to paddle back! With this journey, and the subsequent building of trading posts along the entire river, this huge area became company land of the North West Trading Company. Two fur trading companies vied for business and the favour of the native inhabitants of Western Canada and the Western Arctic. The Hudson Bay Company had been given most of Canada by the crown in 1670, and the North West Trading Company was its major rival. Almost all communities in western and northern Canada started out as company stores and / or trading posts. Today, there still is "The Bay", a large chain of department stores represented in many Canadian cities.

Below the ferry crossing, the river fans out into a huge 12,000 square km (4634 square mile) delta of countless winding river channels, and islands equal in number only to the population of mosquitoes and biting black flies. In late summer, the swampy, grassy, tundra turns into a multi-coloured patchy mosaic of brown, red, orange and various shades of green. The river carries tons of silt and vegetation of all kinds into the delta, continuously changing, shifting and altering the channel system, and extending the land base of the river further and further out into the Arctic Ocean.

ARCTIC RED RIVER

Community of Arctic Red River. (Tsiigehtchic) This small and beautifully located village of about 140 inhabitants was established at its present location in 1868. First a trading post, it soon expanded into a Roman Catholic mission and school. The people of this village call themselves Gwycha Gwich or "People of the Flat Land", and the Village of Arctic Red River has officially been renamed Tsiigehtchic, which means "Mouth of the Iron River". Fishing, trapping, government work, and tourism are the mainstay of the village's economy. In 1993, the Arctic Red River was designated a Canadian Heritage River.

There are limited services in Arctic Red River:

Sundog Enterprises. Tel. 953-3904, three rooms with a total of eight beds. Full breakfast provided, all other meals on request. Also offers boat and fishing tours.

Sunshine Inn. Tel. 953-3003, Fax 953-3906. Two rooms with four beds each and full kitchen facilities provided. $75 single, accepting Visa and Master Card. Cafe / store / gift shop.

Hilltop Restaurant. Open 9 a.m. to 9 p.m. Mon - Fri. and weekends from 1 -6 p.m.

The Tire Shop is open daily and on call. Call 953-3311.

The village also offers RV parking and camping, showers, coin laundry, a restaurant, craft shop, and wilderness tour operators. For the latter check with: **Red River Incorp. Band Ltd.** Tel. 953-3003, Fax 953-3906, General Delivery, Arctic Red River, NT, X0E 0B0. Daily and weekend boat tours and canoe pick-up with transport to Inuvik. Snowmobile and cross-country tours are organized from the village. The local **craft shop** and **Information Centre** are open daily from 10 a.m. to 8 p.m.

Continuing on the Dempster Highway...

km 643 / mile 399.5 (NWT km 173 / mile 107.5) **Rest stop** with picnic site and good fishing.

km 650 / mile 404.4 (NWT km 178 / mile 110.6) Cyclists do not usually love this - a 21 km / 13 mile long straight-as-an-arrow stretch of highway.

REINDEER RESERVE

km 679 / mile 422 (NWT km 206.5 / mile 128.3) **Mackenzie Valley Reindeer Grazing Reserve.** The story of how this reindeer reserve came about is a fascinating one. Due to over-hunting by whalers and hunters (see section on Herschel Island), caribou, the local food supply, was severely depleted. In 1935, the Canadian Government decided as an emergency measure to buy a herd of 3500 domesticated reindeer, which are closely related to the caribou, from western Alaska. A Finnish Laplander with his crew of native Alaskans took five years to herd them a distance of 5000 km / 3100 miles to the Mackenzie delta. Only 2400 animals survived the trek, but today there are about 10,000 reindeer in this huge reserve. The economy of many communities depends on them to a large extent. The Yukon author Dick North has written a fascinating account of this reindeer drive in his book - 'The Arctic Exodus: The Last Great Trail Drive'.

km 686 / mile 426.3 (NWT km 221 / mile 137) **Caribou Creek Territorial Campground,** 12 RV and tent sites. Firewood is not always provided. Boil the creek water. Outhouses.

km 696.5 / mile 432.8 (NWT km 231.5 / mile 143.9) **Viewpoint across Campbell Lake.** Hiking is possible to the cliffs that are the highest points in the vicinity.

km 709 / mile 440.6 (NWT km 244 / mile 151.6) **Cabin Creek Picnic Site.** Outhouses, and fairly good fishing - in the creek!

km 712 / mile 442.4 (NWT km 247 / mile 153.5) **Campbell Creek Picnic Site.** Boat launch and fishing.

km 724 / mile 450 (NWT km 259 / mile 161) **Access road to Inuvik Airport.** Elevation 68 m / 224 feet. The road is paved the last 10 km to town - doesn't it feel good to leave the gravel behind!

km 725.8 / mile 451 (NWT km 260.8 / mile 162) Service station, motel, restaurant and store.

km 730.6 / mile 454 (NWT km 265.6 / mile 165) Chuk Territorial Campground, 38 RV and tent sites, and 20 pull through's with electric hookups. Showers and firewood; $10 per site. Pick the Chuk (cranberries) in mid-August.

INUVIK

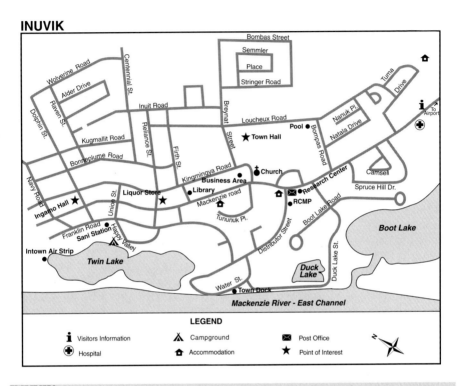

INUVIK

km 734.4 / mile 456.3 (NWT km 270 / mile 167.8) Inuvik. You have arrived at the end of the Dempster Highway. Turn left onto **Mackenzie Road** which heads downtown. **Finto Motor Inn** is at this junction, and it is 1 km / 0.6 mile further to downtown. You will pass the hospital and the **Visitor Centre,** and when you come to a stoplight (yes, a stop light!) you will be very close to the **Post Office** and the **RCMP**. Most other necessary businesses, such as a supermarket, coin laundry and the Boreal Bookshop, as well as the Igloo Catholic Church, are on the Mackenzie Road. In the Inuit language, "Inuvik" means "Place of Man", but this city of about 3200 people has only been here since 1955. Before that, Aklavik, the town in the middle of the river delta, was the regional administration centre. Constant flood and erosion dangers necessitated a new site. The construction of Inuvik was completed by 1961; discoveries of oil and gas in the Mackenzie Delta and off the coast created economic growth in the '70s. Inuvik is the transportation hub for many smaller communities scattered along the coast, and for northern Arctic islands like Banks and Victoria Island. It is also blessed with 24-hour daylight from May 14 to July 24; however, there are 30 days in December and January when the sun does not rise above the horizon.

A special notice: By October 1997 the area code **403** *will change to* **867**, *not only for the Yukon but also for the western part of the North West Territories. The Eastern Territories, called Nanuvut, area code will be 819. The first three digits of* **ALL** *Inuvik telephone numbers will change. Presently these numbers are* **979**, *but by Oct. 1997 they will change to* **777**. *Call Northwest Tel at 1-800-663-5266, for further information. If in doubt about a telephone number call toll-free 1-888-777-1867.*

A few telephone numbers:

RCMPolice: 979-2935. **Hospital**: 979-2955. **Road and Ferry Report**: 1-800-661-0752, in Inuvik call 979-2678. To report a **forest fire**: 1-800-661-0800. To report an **oil spill** call collect: 920-8130. Inuvik has a fully equipped community hospital, and full dental care is available at the **Clark Dental Clinic** on 22 Reliance Street, tel. 979-3008.

NWT Tourism Arctic Hotline, from Canada and the USA call toll-free 1-800-661-0788. **Tourism Association in Inuvik,** call tel. 979-4321 or fax 979-2434. The **Visitor Centre** is located opposite the hospital on Mackenzie Road. It is open from the third week of May to the middle of Sept., from 9 a.m. to 9 p.m. daily. Call them at 979-4518. For **weather** information, call 979-4183. **Radio**: CBC and local stations. There is one weekly newspaper, **The Drum**, and their office can be found on 65 Mackenzie Rd., tel. 979-4545 or fax 979-4412.

Bank services in Inuvik:

Bank of Montreal is on 147 Mackenzie Road. Open Mon. to Thu. from 10 a.m. to 4 p.m., and Fri. from 10 a.m. to 6 p.m. Tel. 979-3311 or Fax 979-3191. Their 24 hour ATM accepts Mastercard with the Cirrus and Interac logos.

CIBC is opposite the Bank of Montreal. Opening hours as above, except opens Friday at 11 a.m. Their ATM is only accessible during banking hours, and accepts Visa with the Interac and Plus System logo. Tel. 979-2848.

Where to stay:

Happy Valley Territorial Campground. $10 per site. End of Franklin Street, close to river and downtown, 32 RV and tent sites, electric hook-ups, showers, firewood.

Hotels and B&B's:

Eskimo Inn. Tel. 979-2801, Fax 979-3234. Full service hotel, dining room and lounge. All major credit cards. $115 single, $125 double.

Finto Motor Inn. Tel. 979-2647, Fax 979-3442. Full service hotel, dining room, all major credit cards. $115 single and $125 double.

Mackenzie Hotel. Tel. 979-2861, Fax 979-3317. Full service hotel, coffee shop, lounge, all major credit cards. Rates from $110 a night.

All three hotels are open 24 hours a day, year-round and are located in the downtown area.

Gardiner Guesthouse. Tel. 979-4408, Fax 979-3155. 22 Kingmingya Road, four rooms with seven beds. Open year-round, room rates from $65. Close to stores and downtown. Visa and MC accepted.

Robertson's B&B. Tel. 979-3111, Fax 979-3112. 41 Mackenzie Road. Year-round, no smoking, Visa and MC accepted. Rooms from $65.

Hillside B&B. Tel. 979-2662. 68 Reliance Street, four beds in two rooms. $75 single, $85 double, year-round.

Arctic Chalet. Tel. 979-3535/2230, Fax 979-4443. 25 Carn Street, 3 km outside town; transportation provided. $65 single, $72 double, $150 for a three bed cabin. Weekly rates. German, Spanish and Norwegian spoken. Open year-round.

Polar Bear B&B. Tel. 979-2554. Fax 979-3668. In the downtown area and open year-round.

Eastbranch B&B. Tel. 979-4529. 7 Centennial Street. No smoking and open year-round.

Restaurants

There are a number of restaurants in town but, as you may have noticed, the prices went up almost at the same rate as the miles driven the further north you went. There are few bargains in Inuvik but do not despair - everything will become cheaper from now on as you will be going south again.

Restaurants in Inuvik: Chicken Chef, on 124 Mackenzie Road, tel. 979-3272, serving the obvious - chicken. **Peking Garden,** on 288 Mackenzie, tel. 979-2262 and **The Roost,** on 106 Mackenzie, tel. 979-2727 serving Chinese and Canadian / International food. For a quick meal, check out the **To Go's Take Out,** on 71 Mackenzie, tel. 979-3030 or the **Northern Quick Stop,** on 160 Mackenzie, tel. 979-4714. All major hotels have a restaurant / cafe and a lounge / saloon on their premises.

For taxi services call: Inuvik Arctic Taxi, tel. 979-3434. **Inuvik-Delta Caps,** tel. 979-2525 / 2121. **United Taxi,** tel. 979-5050. **Co-Op Taxi,** 979-2244.

What to do in Inuvik:

"Our Lady of Victoria" Roman Catholic Church definitely is a landmark in this otherwise very modern city. Designed by Father Joseph Adam and Brother Joseph Larocque, with interior artwork done by the Inuvialuit artist Mono Thrasher, and built in 1960, the church represents the winter home of a wandering people, right down to the lines on the outside wall representing snow blocks. The doors of the Igloo Church are open, and guided tours can be arranged.

The Ingamo Hall Community Centre. This social and recreational centre was built with 1,020 white spruce logs that were cut far to the south and floated down the Mackenzie River. Inquire about festivities, which include native drum dances, special celebrations and feasts.

Inuvik Research Centre. Open to the public, and visitors are welcome.

Boreal Books. Tel. 979-2260, Fax 979-4429. A huge selection of northern books, local music tapes and CDs, topo maps, marine and air charts, as well as federal government publications. A mailing list is available from Boreal Books, Box 1070, Inuvik, NT, X0E 0T0. Open daily, at 181 Mackenzie Road.

Northern Images. 115 Mackenzie Road. Tel. 979-2786. Fax 979-4430. Native art from across the territory.

Inuvik Bowling Centre is located on 175 Mackenzie, tel. 979-2891, open daily and all year.

Inuvik Centennial Public Library is easy enough to find on the Mackenzie Rd., open daily, tel. 979-2749.

Liquor Store: 54 Mackenzie Road. Opening times vary - call 979-2355.

Information about **Ivvavik National Park** in the northern Yukon, and the **Aulavik National Park** on **Banks Island,** can be found in the same building as the post office, on the corner of Mackenzie and Distributor Street. Or write to Parks Canada Box 1840 (EK), Inuvik, NT, X0B 0T0. Tel. 979-3248, Fax 979-4491.

A few tundra hikes can be undertaken right out of Inuvik. Ask at the Visitor Centre for trailheads and routing for the **Three Mile Lake Hike** (6 km one-way); the **Hidden Trail Hike** (1 km one-way); and the **Boot Lake Trail,** which passes through the **Jimmy Adams Peace Park** at the southern end of town.

A bicycle store is located on Distributor Street near the river, which sells parts and outdoor gear, and performs repair work. **Inuvialuit Sporting Goods LTD** can be reached at tel. 979-3102 or fax, 979-2190.

Rental Companies:

Krystal Klean Outfitting. Tel. 979-3535. Fax 979-4443. Rents kayaks, canoes and fishing gear. Dog-sledding tours during the winter.

Western Arctic Adventures. Tel. 979-4542. Fax 979-3103. Canoe and snowmobile rental.

Annual Festivals in Inuvik:

May - Break Up Break Down Weekend. No fixed date. Call 979-2476. Music Festival to celebrate the break-up of the ice on the river.

June - 21st. Midnight Madness. Traditional music and games to celebrate the longest day of the year. Call 979-2067.

July - first weekend. Taste of the Arctic. Food festival celebrating northern foods and wild game, such as moose, hare, caribou and char. Served by professional chefs, banquet style. Call 979-4321 for details.

July - mid-month. Park Canada Day at Happy Valley Campground, with food, fun and games.

July - last weekend. Annual Great Northern Arts Festival. One of NWT premier arts festivals. Call 979-3536.

October - first week. Delta Daze. Delta Prince and Princess competition, dance and BBQ.

January - around the 5th. Sunrise Festival. After a month without sun, townsfolk celebrate the first sunrise with bonfires and fireworks. Call 979-2607 for the date.

Late March/Early April - Muskrat Jamboree. Tel 979-3813. Spring Carnival with snowshoe races, muskrat skinning and more.

Tour Companies:

Western Arctic Nature Tours. Tel. 979-3300, Fax 979-3400. Next to the Igloo Church. Information and booking centre for boat and air tours, also wildlife and cultural displays, slide shows and an art gallery.

Arctic Tour Company. Tel. 979-4100. Fax 979-2259. Tours to Herschel Island, wildlife tours, and others.

Eagle Tours. Tel. 979-3465. Boat tours and visits to native fishing camps.

There are many other tour companies - check with the Visitor Centre.

OUTLYING COMMUNITIES

Tuktoyaktuk or "Tuk". 'Tuk' is located 130 km / 80 miles north of Inuvik, on the shores of the Arctic Ocean, and a visit there is the most popular boat and/or flight day-trip out of Inuvik. The native name for "Tuk" is Tuktuujaartuq; which means "resembling caribou". For a short period of time, off-shore oil drilling gave this community of about 1000 people a powerful economic boost. Oil is still there, but the boom is gone. For ages, these beaches facing the frigid waters of the Beaufort Sea were a whale hunting location for native hunters, and only in 1934 was a more permanent community built here. The area around 'Tuk' is home to a large number of pingos and the **Pingo Canadian Landmark National Reserve** is located near Tuktoyaktuk. See below.

PERMAFROST AND PINGOS

Permafrost is exactly what the name implies; a permanent layer of ice - ground that remains frozen all year round. It strikes many first-time visitors to the North as preposterous to be told that the forest, the tundra and, yes, the road one is travelling on, is resting on a thick layer of ice. The road builders of the Alaska Highway discovered permafrost the hard way. Removing the top layer of growth and topsoil, adding layers of gravel and asphalt and - bingo - you get a road that will work in the South. In the Arctic, this meant that by removing the insulating layers of topsoil, the thick layers of ice beneath it could thaw during the short but intensely hot summers. That meant mud, and mud forever. Today's northern highways are built on top of all vegetation, with layer upon layer of gravel added - which is why northern highways always seem to be so much higher than the surrounding land. You are still skeptical? Find a layer of moss within a treed area, carefully lift the moss, and the ice might be only a hand width away. This also explains why along the Dempster (and other roads) one gravel pit seems to be chasing another, and why road crews never seem to run out of work. The layers of permafrost continue to melt, thanks to the warmth generated by the gravel on top - but more slowly. Those bulges, wrinkles and slippings, that northern car travellers are all too familiar with, are caused by a highway floating on top of permanent ice.

Pingos are part of this phenomena. A few can be seen along the northern sections of the Dempster Highway, but there are many more, especially in the Mackenzie River Delta. Driving northern roads your car has made acquaintance with many mini versions of pingos, jarring the axles, spilling your coffee and, generally, keeping drivers alert and awake. Essentially, a pingo is a huge frost heave; which can be up to 50 m (164 feet) high and nearly 200 m. around. Water that collects under the asphalt in summer will freeze in winter, expand and push the asphalt upwards, causing a less than perfect driving experience for those who like to speed. A pingo has been created the same way, just on a much larger scale.

In this vast land of marshy-wet terrain, the unfrozen, saturated layer of soil above permafrost (called talik) will freeze from both directions. The core freezes solid during the long winters because it is exposed to subzero temperatures from above, and touching the permafrost below when it freezes, it pushes up to form dome shaped mounds. As the top layer of soil erodes, the ice is exposed, causing the pingo to slowly melt during the short but hot Arctic summer.

There are three Hotels in Tuktoyaktuk:

Hotel Tuk Inn. Tel. 977-2381, Fax 977-2566 and a restaurant in-house. Visa, MC, and Amex are accepted.

Pingo Park Lodge. Tel. 977-2155. Cafe, shop. Visa is accepted.

Sauna Tuk Fishing Lodge. Tel. 977-2348, Fax 977-2257. Visa, MC. Package fishing tours only.

If tenting, ask at the village office for permission. For taxi services call **Joannes' Taxi** at tel. 977-2474.

Most tours include a walking tour, a visit to local craft shops, and an optional Arctic Ocean "toe dipping" ceremony which includes a certificate for having gone "swimming" in the Arctic waters. If anything should go wrong, please remember Capt. Dick's Sourtoe in Dawson City - he will certainly be happy to take any frozen-off toes off your, ah, hands. A four hour round trip can be had for about $150 - try various tour operators or airlines.

Aklak Air: Tel. 979-3777, Fax 979-3388; and **Arctic Wings**: Tel. 979-2220, Fax 979-3440. Both airlines operate out of Inuvik, with scheduled flights to Fort McPherson, Tuktoyaktuk, Paulatuk, Sachs Harbour and Aklavik.

Tour organizers out of Tuktoyaktuk:

Anderson River - Nature's Best. Tel. 977-2415. Week long dog team trips for groups of up-to 6 people.

Ookpik Tours. Tel. 977-2170. Fax 977-2399. Boat tours, river rafting and dog sledding.

Coastal Community of Paulatuk. "Soot of Coal". This village of 250 inhabitants is located 500 km / 310 miles east of Inuvik at the south end of Darnely Bay and near the Hornaday River Delta. Coal seams nearby that have been smouldering for thousands of years have given this village its name. People here live off of hunting, fishing and trapping.

Paulatuk Hotel and Meals. Eight rooms. Tel. 580-3612.

Paulaken B&B. Tel. 580-3531 / 3232. Fax 580-3703. Five people in two rooms, with use of a kitchen.

There is a brand-new National Park southeast of Paulatuk. **Tuktut Nogait National Park**, established in 1996, and initially this park will cover over 16,000 hectares, protecting the calving grounds of the Blue Nose Caribou. The park is accessible only through Paulatuk, and no visitor facilities are available. Park permits are obtained from the Western Arctic District Office of Parks in Inuvik. Call Jerry Kisoun at 979-3248.

The community of Sachs Harbour is located on Banks Island, 700 km / 435 miles northeast of Inuvik. The native name is Ikaahuk, meaning "where people cross sea-ice from land to land".

Kuptana's Guest House. Tel. 690 4151. Room for 16 guests.

Wolkies B&B. Tel. 690-3451. Six guests in three rooms. $80 per person with full meals included. Tours can be arranged for guests, including overnight stays in a wilderness cabin.

Icicle Inn. Tel. 690-4444. Fax 690-4433. Open May to October, with 10 rooms and a cafe.

Tour organizer out of Sachs Harbour:

Banks Island Tundra Tours. General Delivery. Sachs Harbour, NT, X0E OZO. Tel. 690-3705. Boat and ATV fishing, photographic and nature viewing trips.

Aulavik National Park is accessible through Sachs Harbour. The park is located north of the coastal village of Sachs Harbour, and includes archaeological sites dating back 3400 years. There are no visitor facilities within the park. For more information and permits, check with the Parks Canada office in Inuvik.

IVVAVIK NATIONAL PARK AND HERSCHEL ISLAND TERRITORIAL PARK

Ivvavik National Park in the northern Yukon was established in 1984, and its creation was a direct result of the widely publicized Mackenzie Valley Pipeline Inquiry in the 70's. There are no visitor facilities within the park. Individually organized trips by one or more persons into the park is somewhat difficult due to the extensive planning that has to be done. Inuvik is the closest point to organize treks into the park; Dawson City is second closest. Inuvik is close enough for organized day trips into the National Park, with maybe a quick side trip to the **Herschel Island Territorial Park**. Only by spending at least one or two nights here, can you really experience the awesome and grand wilderness of this northern corner of the Yukon. Boat trips to Herschel Island and to Ivvavik National Park can also be organized out of Aklavik. Wilderness tour operators out of Whitehorse undertake float trips down the Firth River, one of the principal rivers of the National Park, and most rafting trips will also include stays on Herschel Island. Whatever you decide - you are in for a very special treat. This over 10,000 square km (3926 square miles) National Park is almost untouched by human activities. It preserves significant numbers of grizzlies, wolves, foxes, caribou, and countless other equally important species. The first hunters left early evidence of human occupation over 5000 years ago - mainly along the coast. This treeless expanse of tundra, low growing willows, and birch trees, expresses an almost poetic beauty. The miles and miles of clear-rolling rounded hills and mountains, usually showing beautifully against a clean blue sky, contrast with the ocean, which is most of the year, covered with floating, glaringly white ice.

Tours:

Arctic Tour Company. Box 2021 - Y5, Inuvik, NT, X0E 0T0. Tel. 979-4100, Fax 979-2259. Naturalist and Cultural Tours to Banks Island, Ivvavik National Park and Herschel Island.

Ecosummer Yukon Expedition. Box 5095, Whitehorse, Yukon, Y1A 4Z2. Tel. and Fax 663-8453. Rafting and hiking trips through Ivvavik National Park and Herschel Island, with a focus on the natural history.

Herschel Island Yukon Territorial Park. Herschel Island is located about 130 km / 80 miles west of the Mackenzie River Delta. A treeless, wind-swept and almost flat island, its long, narrow sand-spits nearly touch the mainland shoreline of the Ivvavik National Park. This 100 square km / 62 square mile island carries the native name of "Qikiqtaryuk", which means "Island". For thousands of years, indigenous Inuvialuit hunters and gatherers used this island as a staging point for hunting trips, and native families from the delta still do so. In 1826, Sir John Franklin became the first White explorer to set foot on this island, naming it after John Herschel, a British astronomer and chemist.

American whalers followed in the late 1800s, after having depleted more southern waters of their prey. The whaling season in far northern waters only lasted from about the middle of June to late August. Most whaling ships wintered over in various settlements along the coast, with Herschel Island one of the favourite spots to spent a nine month long winter. During the winter of 1895-96, about 600 sailors, and an equal number of native helpers and hunters, shared this small island. With little to do but to stay out of trouble in a harsh environment, interesting past-times were developed. Some historical accounts mention the formation of theatrical groups, complete with auditions and female roles being played by shipboys. Further entertainment was furnished by a seven-piece orchestra with two violins, two guitars, a drum, one mandolin, and an accordion; with music written by a German whaler/violinist. Boxing exhibitions were held (often getting out of hand), and baseball, soccer, and other games were played on the frozen waters off the island - weather permitting. During one baseball game, a sudden snowstorm created white-out conditions, and five players could not find their way back to the ships. They were found frozen to death only minutes after the brief but icy storm had settled. Before 1907, up to 1500 whalers lived on the island, and, generally speaking, it can have been no paradise, with so many rough-living sailors of many national backgrounds concentrated on such a small island in this huge northern expanse. The native peoples lives were changed drastically with the influx of guns, alcohol, tobacco, western foods and maybe not the most civilized of manners. Imported diseases such as tuberculosis, measles and the common flu killed up to 80% of some aboriginal groups.

Missionaries and the establishment of police posts brought some health care and law and order, but only the almost total depletion of the bowhead and beluga whaling stock, with the resulting collapse of the whaling industry, returned the island and the coast to native use. By 1907, most of the whalers had gone, and only the police and the missionaries remained. In 1964, even the RCMP closed its post. The island became the Yukon's first territorial park on July 30, 1987. Many of the original buildings at Pauline Cove, the centre of human occupation, are still standing. The Park is open to the public from May to September. There are tenting spots behind driftwood shelters, but there is only a limited amount of drinking water.

All visitors have to register with park staff. More information is available from the Yukon Department of Renewable Resources. Box 2703, Whitehorse, Yukon, Y1A 2C6. Tel. 667-5648; or from the Heritage Branch, Yukon Department of Tourism, Box 2703, Whitehorse, Yukon, Y1A 2C6. Tel. 667-5811.

For more information about national parks in the north contact:

Parks Canada Information Centre for all of the Northwest Territories - 45 Forks Market Road, Winnipeg, Manitoba, R3C 4T6. Tel. 1-204-983-2290. Fax 1-204-983-2221.

For the Pacific and Yukon Region only - 300-300 W. Georgia Street. Vancouver, B.C., V6B 6C6. Tel. 1-604-666-0176. Fax. 1-604-666-3508.

<u>**Leaving Inuvik**</u>: Those who drove their own vehicle have no choice but to return the way they came - but I'm sure most of you are looking forward to a few more days on the Dempster Highway. Bicyclists have three choices: cycle those 800 km back again; go by plane directly to either Dawson City, Whitehorse, Yellowknife or points beyond; or go by transport truck. The Tue. and Thurs. mini bus, leaving at 08:00 to Eagle Plains and Dawson City, does not take bikes, unless you can make them small enough to fit into a backpack. Transport trucks can take bikes for $30-$50 to either the Dempster Corner or Dawson City, and it will cost more to Whitehorse or points further south. Check the notice boards at the post office, visitor centre, or campgrounds for those that might offer cyclists a ride south. Of course, you also could sell your bicycle - there always seems to be demand for 'cheap' bikes. Commercial barges connect most delta communities with the southern Mackenzie River town of Hay River, with access to highway #35 and Alberta to the south. These barges can handle almost any sized vehicle - for a price. Another alternative would be to fly from Inuvik to Norman Wells,

about 500 km to the south, and then hike the Canol Road Trail back into the Yukon. Williams Aero / Arctic Airlines out of Norman Wells, flies this route: Tel. 587-2243. Fax 587-2335.

For any type of research, may it be wildlife, archaeological or any other topic, contact the Science Liaison Office in Inuvik, tel. 979-4029 or fax. 979-4264. Access restrictions exist in many areas because of Land Claim settlements; call 1-800-661-0788 for more information. Visiting pilots can request the **Air Tourist Information - Canada** package by calling toll-free 1-800-661-0788. Pilots calling toll-free 1-800-463-6377, will be put in touch with a flight service specialist who then will connect the visiting pilot with a pilot who has northern flying experience for a specific area; or call 873-4049 in Yellowknife; 979-2522 in Inuvik **(area code 403 changing Oct. 97 to 867)**; or in Vancouver 1-604-666-9403.

For any other type of visitor information concerning the NWT, call toll-free 1-800-661-0788 from the USA and Canada, or Fax 1-403-873-0294, or write to: Box 1320 (EX), Yellowknife, NT, X1A 2L9.

One last suggestion - if you are not burdened with heavy gear, and if you have enough time AND sufficient funds - just keep on flying; to Inuvik, Sachs Harbour, Holman (charter), Cambridge Bay and so on. There are over 20 local airlines with scheduled flights connecting all NWT communities. First Air, out of Ontario (toll-free 1-800-267-1247 or Tel 613-839-3340. Fax 613-839-5690) even has a scheduled flight from Frobisher Bay (Iqaluit) to Nuuk on Greenland - and you are almost in Europe! Have fun, be safe, enjoy, and I am certain to see you again in the Yukon, and soon.

A happy camper along the Dempster Highway picking a good bye tune.

A GLOSSARY OF MINING AND OTHER YUKON RELATED TERMS

Abandonment - having given up title to a mining claim or prospecting lease, either by design or default.

Above - if the claim number is before 'above' it indicates a claim upstream from the "Discovery" Claim.

Alchemy - before there was chemistry there was alchemy- the science of turning base metals into gold. It has so far been unsuccessful.

Alloy - a mixture of metals, usually created artificially. For example, silver is added to gold to make gold harder. Gold comes in various colours depending on in what part of the world it is found, and with what other metals it has naturally alloyed. Gold can range from a pale yellow (a high percentage of silver) to quite red-looking (a high copper content).

Alluvial - sand and clay that has been gradually deposited by moving water, as in a river delta, or a constantly shifting and changing island within a fast flowing river.

Amalgam - mercury and gold fused together.

Amalgamation - recovering fine gold with the help of mercury. A very simple but, if care is not taken, potentially quite unhealthy and dangerous way to recover gold. Mercury has the ability to attract and absorb gold (also silver and platinum) into a ball-like substance, rejecting sand, gravel and other materials. It's a frequently used method used by gold miners worldwide; including the Yukon.

Apron - part of a gold recovery contraption used to trap very fine gold.

Aqua Regia - will dissolve gold and platinum if added to the mixture of one part nitric acid, to three parts hydrochloric acid. Do not try this at home with your wedding ring!

Assay - to determine the worth of a mining claim by testing small samples. Puts a dollar and cent value to mining property.

Assessment Work - annual work that has to be done on a mining claim to legally retain ownership.

Auriferous - other metals containing gold, or mining operations where gold is only a smaller by-product.

Bar - a sand bar or gravel bar either above or below the water line.

Barren - ground where there never was any gold, or which has been mined out.

Base Metals - copper, tin, aluminium, lead, zinc and others. Gold, silver and platinum, in contrast, are precious or noble metals.

Bedrock - the solid rock foundation beneath creek beds, ancient stream beds or valley floors. Placer gold deposits were generally best just above bedrock. Everything above bedrock is called overburden - topsoil, trees, gravel, and other materials have to be removed to recover gold.

Bench - a flat, level area above a creek or stream.

Bench Claim - a gold claim located on a bench.

Black Sand - if you have it in your gold pan, gold can not be far behind! Black sand consists of magnetite, hematite, and other heavy metals which are almost as heavy as gold.

Bonanza - a Spanish term for instant wealth and riches; a creek or gold vein with incredible amounts of gold.

Bullion - raw gold that has been melted for easier storage, or readied for transportation.

Cache - wilderness cabins have them, and hikers should build themselves one for their food. A cache can be a high, above ground, bear-proof, food storage or a place to hide your gold.

Carat, also karat - a metric measurement jewellers use. Pure gold is 24 carats, but it would be too soft for use in a ring. Ten or 18 carats, alloyed with copper or silver, are more common. One carat is equal to 200 milligrams. Pure gold also can be called 1000 fine, your ring stamped 921 would contain 921 parts per thousand of gold. The other 79 parts are other metals.

Cemented Gravel - or false bedrock, can be rich in gold.

Claim - a typical claim is 1000 feet by 500 feet (305 m by 152 m) in size, and must be used for the sole purpose of mining for minerals within this claim.

Claim jumper - a person who illegally uses, works or mines a previously staked claim.

Clean-Up - the fun part of working in a gold mine. Accumulated gold, or concentrate, is removed from either dredges, sluice boxes or your gold pan.

Coarse Gold - rough nuggets that have not travelled for long distances in a creek; otherwise they would be smooth.

Colours - smaller than nuggets. Small specks of gold, from invisible to barely visible.

Concentrates - what is left in the gold pan after a thorough panning, or in a larger gold recovery contraption - usually a mixture of black sand, gold and other heavy particles.

Conglomerate - various types of gravel that have been cemented together naturally; often by volcanic activities.

Deposit Area - two types of placer gold deposits exist. The eluvial location is found near the vein, and the alluvial location is a fair distance away due to water action.

Discovery Claim - the first claim that has been staked on a creek or stream. This claim can be up to three times larger than all later claims.

Dredge - a dredge can be of any size; it scoops or sucks gold-bearing gravel out of creek beds, river sandbars or artificial ponds.

Drifting - the tunnelling of horizontal shafts that follow veins or seams of gold. In the Yukon, this used to be done during winter when the ground was frozen enough to allow less problematic drifting through unstable ground.

Dust - also called flour gold. Finest particles of gold, which are difficult to recover, but are of the highest purity.

Eldorado - Spanish for "the golden place" and in gold-producing areas it means a fabulously rich creek.

Electrum - naturally occurring alloy of gold and silver.

Flake Gold - tiny flat pieces of gold.

Flume - an artificial sloping waterway which carries water over long distances to a mining operation.

Fool's Gold - can be pyrite or mica, which only looks like gold to the untrained eye.

Fraction area - can be a small piece of land between two claims, which is caused by an error in measurement. Some of the tiny fractions on Bonanza Creek were richer than neighbouring full sized claims. Re-measuring other peoples claims to find fractions has made some people rich, but does not make friends.

Gold - a fusion of gases, liquids and trace elements from out of the molten core of our earth, pushed up over millions of years through cracks in the planet's crust and hardened into veins or lodes. It then breaks up into tiny particles and is washed off into the oceans by water: or not so tiny particles - the largest nugget found in the Yukon weighed over 2.2 kg (72 oz.) and was nearly 15 cm (6 inches) long. The Greeks called the bright yellow material "Au", after their goddess of dawn, Aurora. Gold - the noble and eternal, the bringer of youth and, in the Middle Ages, said to cure the sick. Gold is a very soft metal, one gram of gold can be drawn into a continuous thread over 500 m long. Gold has uses beyond our wildest imagination - from the use in microchips, to window coverings, to preserve heat, to capping teeth, and not to forget - the "golden heart", which makes some humans so lovable!

Gold Pan - a dish-like shallow contraption made from metal or plastic; it is used to wash gold- bearing gravel. New metal pans are covered with a fine film of oil to prevent rusting. This oil has to be burned off in a red-hot fire before use. They also can be used as a frying pan; for washing your socks in; as a head-rest; or as an ashtray, once back home, for smokers.

Gold Panning - the technique of washing gravel to search for gold.

Grains - a unit of weight. One grain = 64,798.91 mg, 24 grains equal one pennyweight, 20 pennyweight make one troy ounce which is 31,103.48 grams.

Grizzly - a strong screen used in front of a sluice box to keep large rocks out of the box.

Hardrock Mining - opposite of placer mining; gold that is within layers of rock.

Haematite/hematite - an iron ore that is red in colour.

Hidden Values - gold too small to be seen with the naked eye.

Hydraulic Mining with a Monitor - water under great pressure is used to wash overburden off a hillside.This process is very destructive to the environment, drowning fish in the sediment washed into the streams.

Ice Bridge - a road built across rivers and lakes during the winter.

Ingot - a bar of gold or silver, for easier stacking!

Jade - a prized semi-precious stone, green in colour and found in northern BC.

Jig or Jigger - a screen that is used to shake concentrate, in order to sort gold by size.

Limit - looking downstream to describe the left or right side of a river or stream. Left limit versus right limit.

Lode or Mother Lode - the original source of placer gold.

Long Tom - a gold sluicing box built to capture very fine gold.

Low Grade - small deposits of gold not worth mining.

Magnetite - also lodestone or black sand. A magnetic form of iron. A magnet will help to separate black sand from gold.

Malleable - a soft metal that can be hammered thin without breaking.

Marcasite - white iron pyrite used in jewellery.

Mercury or Quicksilver - used to recover gold; this metal comes in liquid form, is very heavy, very toxic to the environment, and has a low melting point.

Mica - a mineral that crystallizes into thin layers. It can be mistaken for gold, except that mica will crumble between your fingers.

Moss - a cryptogamous plant that grows on wet, moist surfaces. A very good insulator; old-time cabin builders used it as insulation between logs.

Muskeg - swampy wetland, a bog. Terrible hiking territory.

Non-ferrous - a mineral containing no iron.

Nugget - can be gold, silver, copper or platinum. A nugget can be picked up with one's fingers. The largest nugget found to date was nearly 90 kg (200 lb.).

Open Cut or Open Pit - surface mining as done in the Yukon.

Ore - any mineral or metal worth mining.

Overburden - soil barren of gold; the topsoil and gravel above the bedrock that has to be removed.

Paydirt - if it contains gold it's not dirt any more, it's paydirt.

Paystreak - a very rich layer of paydirt.

Permafrost - overburden that is frozen year-round in the Arctic north and most everywhere in the Yukon.

Pingo - A donut shaped mound of earth usually with ice in the interior; basically a giant frost heave, 50 to 200 metres in circumference. They are created by underground water freezing in the fall; the ice expands and raises the surface to form a dome, which usually collapses is the centre.

Peter Out, Play-out - a claim that has been worked out.

Placer - any sand or gravel containing gold.

Placer Mining - recovering gold from placer deposits; the process depends largely on the use of water.

Platinum - a very rare malleable metal that is harder than gold. It can be found by itself, or in combination with gold, and was once considered to be worthless.

Pocket - a heavy concentration of gold in a crevice or under a rock at the downside of a creek.

Poke - a bag or pouch to carry your gold in.

Pup - a very short creek.

Prospecting - a prospector searches for gold or any other valuable metal. The moment a prospector recovers gold, he or she becomes a miner. Most miners try to sell lower grade mining properties to large companies.

Pyrite - a compound of various metals which contains sulphur or arsenic. It can be mistaken for gold, especially copper pyrites, but it will break if hit with a hard surface - gold will not.

Quartz - gold lodes are usually compressed within veins of quartz. Quartz is pure silicone dioxide and it can be from transparent to opaque, from colourless to coloured. It may be worth checking small pieces of quartz to see if gold is embedded in it.

Riffles - an obstruction, usually built out of steel, put into a sluice box to create the same conditions as in a wild running creek, in order to capture gold in pockets.

Royalty - what a miner pays to the state as taxes.

Rusty Gold - gold that has been naturally coated with other minerals.

Sluice Box - a large downward-pointing trough, usually built out of steel, with riffles on the bottom of it. The gold bearing gravel is fed into the wide opening on top, and fast flowing water will wash the gravel down the sluice box. Sluicing means the washing of gravel in order to separate gold.

Sourdough - someone who has spent a winter in the Yukon, or fermented bread dough, or someone who did not have enough "dough" to leave, turning "sour" in the process. Early miners were called sourdoughs because sourdough bread was their staple food.

Stake - either to mark a claim with wooden claim stakes, or to have accumulated enough "cash" to start a new operation, or to retire on the wealth generated through mining.

Strike - a large discovery of gold which becomes a "Rush".

Sweeper - a tree leaning over the river.

Tailings - after all the gold has been taken out, or almost taken out, what is discarded as piles of gravel, rocks and debris is the tailings. Modern miners with better machines might work through tailings still finding gold.

Tributary - a creek, a stream, or a river that runs into a larger body of running water.

Unalloyed - a metal that is not alloyed with other metals.

Unconsolidated Deposits - loose rock, gravel, sand, clay, etc.

Vein - a deposit of gold that is longer than it is wide.

Wet Placer - a deposit of gold located under water.

BOOKS TO READ ABOUT THE YUKON

KLONDIKE - the last great Gold Rush. Pierre Berton. An historical account by the author, who was born in Dawson City. An excellent rendition of the Gold Rush.

GOLD AT FORTYMILE CREEK - early days in the Yukon. Michael Gates. A well written account of pre-Klondike Gold Rush mining activities in the Yukon.

I MARRIED THE KLONDIKE - by Laura B. Berton. The mother of Pierre Berton and her account of her life as a teacher in a Yukon mining camp.

THE WHITE PASS - GATEWAY TO THE YUKON - By Roy Minter. An historical account of the construction of the White Pass & Yukon Railway. Roy Minter died at age 79 in February, 1996.

CALL OF THE WILD, WHITE FANG - or any other story written by Jack London based on his time spent in the Yukon during the winter of 1897 - 1898.

THE MAD TRAPPER OF RAT RIVER, THE LOST PATROL, ARCTIC EXODUS, and to be published in 1997, **CABIN FEVER - JACK LONDON IN ALASKA AND THE YUKON.** Four interesting historical accounts by the Whitehorse writer, Dick North.

LAW OF THE YUKON - A pictorial history of 100 years (1895 - 1995) of the NWMP - RCMP in the Yukon. By Helen Dobrowolsky.

GOLD & GALENA - By the Mayo Historical Society. The Mayo District- from the Gold Rush in 1883, to the discovery of silver in 1903, to the present.

THE GOLDFIELDS OF THE KLONDIKE - By John W. Leonard. A reprint of the authors 1897 first-hand account of the Gold Rush.

REPUBLIC OF RIVERS - Edited by John A. Murray. Three centuries of nature writings from Alaska and the Yukon.

THE BEST OF ROBERT SERVICE - By Robert Service. All the popular verses by this great Canadian poet. Nobody explains the mystic of the Northland better than Robert Service. Do not miss the Robert Service Poetry Readings, held in his original Dawson City cabin. You have not really 'been' to the Yukon until you have read (or listened to a rendition) 'The Shooting of Dan McGrew' or 'The Cremation of Sam McGee'.

MARTHA BLACK - By Martha Black. The true story of a woman who came across the Chilkoot Trail during the Gold Rush, and later became the Yukon's first woman member of Canada's Parliament.

WOMEN OF THE KLONDIKE - By Frances Backhouse. An account of women's accomplishments during and after the Gold Rush.

LIFE LIVED LIKE A STORY - By Julia Cruikshank. A book of traditional stories as told by three Yukon Elders.

PART OF THE LAND, PART OF THE WATER - By Catherine McClellan. A history of the Yukon First Nations.

BOOKS TO READ ABOUT THE WESTERN NWT

ARCTIC ORDEALS. The journal of John Richardson who, from 1820 to 1822 was the surgeon / naturalist with the Franklin Expedition.

A WALK ON THE CANOL ROAD. By S. R. Gage. From history to present day hiking conditions.

BARRENLAND BEAUTIES- By P.M. Burt. Plants of the Arctic coast.

CANOEING CANADA'S NORTHWEST TERRITORIES -By M. MacCreadie. A guide to the northern rivers.

A HISTORY OF THE ORIGINAL PEOPLES OF NORTHERN CANADA.-By Keith Crow.

NAHANNI, RIVER OF GOLD, RIVER OF DREAMS- By N. Hardling. The history as well as a guide to the South Nahanni River.

PEOPLE AND CARIBOU OF THE NWT- By Ed Hall.

TO THE ARCTIC, AN INTRODUCTION TO THE FAR NORTHERN WORLD- By Steven Young. Everything about the north - geology, weather, wildlife and northern people.

AIR AND MARINE CHARTS AND TOPO MAPS CONCERNING THE NWT

Tgit Geomatics Ltd. Box 244, Yellowknife, NT. X1A 2N2. Tel. 873-8448. Fax 873-8439. Request a free copy of index 2 (western territories) to determine which maps are needed. 1:25,000 and 1:50,000 are available.

World Wide Books & Maps (ITMB) out of Vancouver, B.C., also carries most NWT topo maps. Contact them at tel. 1-604-687-3320, fax 1-604-687-5925.

For Hydrographic Charts:

Hydrographic Services. Box 6000, 9860 W. Saanich Rd. Sydney, B.C. V8L 4B2. Tel 604-363-6358. Fax 604-363-6841.

SOME INTERNET AND OTHER COMPUTER ADDRESSES / FORUMS

- **CompuServe:**

- **The Travel Forum (GO TRAVFOR)** has one message section & one library dedicated to Canada.

- **The Canada Forum (GO CDNFORUM)** dedicates a section to The Territories.

- **Klondike Gold Rush Centennial events.** E-mail: yukonann@mail.klondike.com and Internet: http:IIwww.Yukonweb.wis.net//

- **Canada's Internet Directory.** http://www.canadas.net/Maple-Square

- **Tour Canada without leaving your desk.** Information on places and events, as well as how to reach most provincial, territorial and municipal tourism agencies:

http://www.cs.cmu.edu/Web/Unofficial/Canadiana/Traveloguo.html

- **Parks Canada. Addresses, phone numbers and information about each National Park in Canada.**

http://parkscanada.pch.qc.ca/park/npdemo.html

- **Bed and Breakfast Guide to Canada.** http://www.achilles.net/-bb/index.html

- **Via Rail. Schedules, fares, reservations, maps.** http://www.viarail.ca

- **Air Canada. Flight schedules, Aeroplan information, promotions.** http://www.aircanada.ca

- **Canadian Airlines. Flight schedules, airport maps and more.** http://www.cdnair.ca

- **BC Ferries.** http://bcferries.bc.ca/ferries

- **Tourism Yukon.** http://www.touryukon.com. E-Mail: yktour knet.yk.ca

- **White Pass and Yukon Route.** E-Mail ngauge 73 @ aol.com www.whitepassrailroad.com

- **Haines Junction and Kluane Country.** Homepage: http:\\www.Yukonweb.wis.net\community\kluane\ and E-Mail vhainesjet @ hypertech.yk.ca

Klondike Visitor Association. E-Mail: kva @dawson.net

CENTENNIAL EVENTS

Yukon Anniversaries 1997 Calender of Events - The World Finds Out!

(**For regular annual events check under individual communities in this book**)

February:

From Feb. 7 to Feb. 17 - **Satch Carlson's Rally of the Lost Patrol.** A 8000 km / 5000 mile auto rally from Seattle to Inuvik and back. The rally is billed as the longest, coldest and toughest winter rally in the world. This is not a high speed event. Contact: Satch Carlson at 1-907-345-1195.

March:

From March 01 to March 25 - **Re-Creation of the 1905 Stanley Cup Challenge** between a Dawson City and an Ottawa hockey team. In 1905, eight Klondike hockey players, the 'Dawson City Nuggets' travelled overland to take on the Ottawa 'Silver Seven' in a pre-NHL Stanley Cup Challenge. Not only was the journey remarkable, but also how the Dawson City team lost - with scores of 9-2 and 23-2. A one-eyed Ottawa player by the name of Frank McGee shot 14 goals, setting a record for the most goals in a single Stanley Cup final game. The record still stands today. The historical journey will include a trip by dog sleds from Dawson City to Whitehorse, as well as a combination of ferry, bus and train to Ottawa. Contact: Pat Hogan at 1-403-993-5803.

March 14 and 15 - The **Whitehorse Snowmobile Expedition** will follow the 1898 route of the Gold Rush Trail between Carcross, Tagish and Whitehorse. Contact: Peter Greenlaw at 1-403-668-6935.

From Skagway between March 20 and 22. **Buckwheat Classic Ski Race.** A 10, 25 and 50 km race following the historic train tracks from Log Cabin to Lake Bennett, and part of the Chilkoot Trail between Lake Lindeman and Lake Bennett. Contact: Buckwheat Donahue at 1-907-983-2544.

From March 21 to March 23 - **Atlin Fun Days.** Weekend activities with family entertainment, friendly races and First Nation dancers. Contact: George Holman at 1-250-651-7717.

May:

May 01 to August. **The Klondike All Canadian Centennial Exposition.** This is a multi location event between Edmonton and Dawson City re-enacting the historical 3100 km trek to the Klondike gold fields. Contact: Douglas Clute at the Lakehead University in Edmonton, tel. 1-705-945-5838.

May 15 to Nov. 15, in Anchorage, Alaska. **Gold Fewer in the North: The Yukon / Alaska Gold Rushes.** A 5000 square foot exhibit about the gold rushes in the North, covering the era from the 1880s to the 1910s: the Klondike, Nome, Fairbanks and Iditarod. Contact the Anchorage Visitor Information Centre.

May 16 to May 18. Canadian National Youth Dart Championships - in Whitehorse. Contact: Phil Robertson in Whitehorse at tel. 1-403-667-5763.

May 18, in Dawson City. **Gold Poke 5 Kilometre Run.** Race through Dawson City with gold as prizes. Contact: Roger Hamburg at 1-403-993-6474.

May 30 to June 01, in Dawson City. **Dawson School Reunion '97.** Did you ever attend school in the Dawson City area? Then you are invited. Contact: Myrna Butterworth at 1-403-993-5353.

June:

June 01 to June 25. **Panama - Alaska Rally 1997.** This is a long distance touring rally for pre-1970 vehicles passing through Dawson City. Contact: Malcolm Wilson 1-604-580 1222 or Fax 1-519-638-5049.

June 14, in Dawson City. **Howdy Neighbour Scramble Golf Tournament.** A theme golf tournament where the prizes are gold. Contact: John Kostelnik at 1-403-667-1472.

June 15 to June 30. **Dyea to Dawson City Centennial Race to the Klondike.** Re-enactment race over the historic Ckilkoot Trail from Skagway to Lake Bennett, followed by a canoe race from Bennett to Dawson City. Open for 50 teams of two people each. The 1997 race is open for residents of Alaska and the Yukon only. The same race has been scheduled for 1998, but only for international hikers and canoeists. There are strict rules for those who want to participate - like carrying 50 pound packs! Contact Jeff Brady in Skagway, tel. 1-907-983-2354 or tel. 983-2854, fax 983-3854.

June 21 to June 30. **Flotilla from Dawson City to Eagle, Alaska.** One-Hundred years ago, 28 miners left Dawson City by river, discovering gold near present day Eagle and founded a new townsite, which grew to 1000 residents. Contact: Cassie Richter in Eagle, tel. 1-907-547-2230.

June 21 to June 22. **Real Midnight Sun Golf Tournament.** Held in Dawson City, and limited to 44 players, with prizes paid in gold. Contact: John Kostelnik, tel. 1-403-667-1472.

July:

July 01 to July 31, in Whitehorse. **Waterfront Days.** Students will dress in period costumes, adopting identities from the Klondike Gold Rush. They will engage in walking tours and numerous other activities along the Whitehorse waterfront. Contact Denise Lafontaine, tel. 1-403-667-5901.

July 04. 4th of July Celebrations and Gold Panning Contest, in Eagle, Alaska. Contact: Elva Scott 1-907-547-2230. Skagway also has a great 4th of July Parade and Celebration - the 1997 theme is 'Trails and Transportation'.

July 05 to July 19. 'Ton of Gold' Re-enactment of Klondike Miners Arrival in Seattle. In Dawson City, Skagway, Alaska and in Seattle, Washington. On July 14, 1897, the steamer Excelsior arrived in San Francisco and on July 17th, 1897, the steamer Portland arrived in Seattle, both carrying over a ton of gold from the Klondike Goldfields. These events sparked the Gold Rush. In Skagway the re-enactment will arrive by train on July 12, and the Gold and Millionaires will board the SS Portland the following day, July 13. Ports visited will be Juneau, Haines, Sitka and Ketchikan, and the arrival in Seattle is scheduled for Saturday, July 19, 1997. Contact: Jeff Brady in Skagway, tel. 1-907-983- 2354 or call 983-2854, fax 983-3854.

July 05, in Skagway. **J. Bernard Moore Homestead Dedication.** Moore was the original settler and founder of Skagway and his homestead, on the corner of 5th and Spring, has been restored by the National Park Service. Tours through the building will be available daily starting in 1998. Call -1-907-983-2921 or fax 983-2046 for more info.

July 05 to July 06. **Watson Lake Rodeo,** sanctioned by the National Rodeo Association. This year there will be special events to honour the centennial celebrations. Contact: Ralph & Katie Grunow at 1-403-536-2272.

July 09 to July 10. **Phil Temple Rodeo in Haines Junction**. The rodeo commemorates the 1997 Anniversary of the Dalton Trail, which was a alternate route to the Klondike. Contact: Barb Eikland at 1-403-634-2514.

July 10 to July 13 in Whitehorse. **'Ton of Gold' - Ton of Fun Festival.** The festival will celebrate the Year of Transportation with storytelling, theatre, a parade with antique cars and a welcome party for the 'Ton of Gold Re-Enactment' on its way from Dawson City to Seattle. Contact: Marilyn Margeson at 1-403-668-8665.

July 11 to July 13, in Whitehorse. **Yukon Rodeo**. From bull riding, team roping to, as a special for the centennial celebrations, pack horse races. Contact: Debbie Brewster at 1-403-863-6524.

July 13, in Skagway. **'Ton of Gold' and Dedication of Skagway's Centennial Statue and Park.** In Wayfinding Park on the waterfront; the statue will depict a Native packer and a prospector heading for the Chilkoot Trail.

July 18 to July 20. **Dawson City Music Festival.** An annual festival eagerly awaited by music lovers all across the west. This year there is also going to be special musical workshops dedicated to music from a hundred years ago. Contact: Jennifer Edwards at tel. 1-403-993-5584.

July 25, in Dawson City. **K.P.M.A. Miner's Ball.** This annual event brings together the placer mining community of the Klondike and other mining regions of the Yukon for a BBQ and dance. There will be special celebrations this year and in 1998.

July 30 to August 31, in Dawson City. **Klondyke Scramble,** a theme golf tournament with 'named' holes and prizes paid in gold. Contact: John Kostelnik, tel. 1-403-667-1472.

August:

August 09, in Carmacks. **Back to the Future Celebration.** Grand opening celebration of the recently restored Carmacks Road House Heritage Site. Contact: Village of Carmacks, tel. 1-403-863-6271.

August 15, in Dawson City. **Tr'ondek Hwech'in Culture Day**. This day will reflect the culture of the Han Nation through a variety of activities, such as theatre, jigging, and traditional food and games. Contact: Jackie Worrell tel. 1-403-993-5385.

August 15 to August 18 in Dawson City. **Discovery Days Festival.** An annual event with all kinds of activities. Be in Dawson City for the Discovery Days Festival in 1998 - when the Gold Rush stampede swamped the Klondike, creating Dawson City. Contact: Peter Menzies, tel 1-403-993-7409.

Discovery Days Festivals are held in many other Yukon communities.

August 16 to 17, in Dawson City. **The Discovery Festival Country Jamboree is held** only in 1997. **The Discovery Festival Gold Field Relay** is a 50 km / 5 person team event through the goldfields of Bonanza and Hunker Creeks. For the former, contact Joe Magee, tel. 1-403-993-5000; and for the latter, contact Roger at tel. 1-403-993-6474.

September:

Sept. 17 to 21, in Dawson City. **Jack London Festival**. 100th Anniversary of Jack London's trek to the Klondike. This festival will include a film festival and a trek to the site of his original cabin on Henderson Creek, south of Dawson City. Contact: Denny Kobayashi, tel. 1-403-993-5575. Email: kva@dawson.net.

Sept. 17 to 21. Sept. 19 to 20. **Klondike Trail of '98 International Road Relay**, from Skagway to Whitehorse. This is an annual team relay race with a special historical twist for 1997 and 1998.

100 Year's Gold Rush - Centennial Events planned for 1998:

February:

Satch Carlson's Rally of the Lost Patrol; from Seattle to Inuvik and back. **Yukon Quest International Sled Dog Race**; from Fairbanks via Dawson City to Whitehorse. **Yukon Hot-Air Balloon Festival**, in Whitehorse. **Annual Klondyke Centennial Ball**, in Dawson City.

March:

Percy DeWolfe Memorial Mail Race. Sled Dog Race from Dawson City to Eagle in Alaska, and back. **Buckwheat Classic Ski Race,** in Skagway. **International Gold Rush Bonspiel**, in Whitehorse.

April:

Yukon / Alaska Kiwanis Gold Rush Stampede Spring Conference. In Whitehorse.

May:

Kluane Mountain Festival, in Haines Junction. Dawson City International Gold Show, held in Dawson City the last week of May.

June:

Alsek Music Festival, in Haines Junction. **Dyea to Dawson City Centennial Race to the Klondike-** Across The Chilkoot Trail on foot and by canoe to Dawson City. **Yukon International Storytelling Festival**, in Whitehorse. **1998 Gathering of the Clans and Celtic Festival, in Whitehorse.**

July:

Yukon Gold Panning Championships, in Dawson City. **Square Dance Festival,** in Whitehorse. **20th Anniversary Dawson City Music Festival,** in Dawson City.

August:

Scouts 'Gold Rush' Jamboree, in Dawson City and Whitehorse. Discovery Days Festival, in Dawson City. **Tríondek Hwechíin Culture Day,** in Dawson City.

September:

International Sourdough Reunion, in Dawson City. **Pioneer's of the Alaska Klondike Trek**, in Dawson City.

No dates have been set for events listed for 1998 and beyond. For further information contact: Yukon Anniversary Commission, Bag 1898 - 1998, Whitehorse, Yukon, Y1A 4K8, Canada. Tel. 1-403-668-1998. Fax 1-403-667-4939. Email: yukonann@mail.klondike.com. Visit their Internet site at: /www.yukonweb.wis.net/ special/goldrush/calendar

Index

INTERNATIONAL TRAVEL MAPS
DIVISION OF ITMB PUBLISHING LTD.
The following travel reference maps and guide books are published by ITM:

WORLD/CONTINENTAL
World Travel Adventure Map 2nd. Edition 1997
Antarctica Travel Reference Map 1st. Edition 1997/99
North America Panorama Physical Relief Map 5'x4'

AFRICA
Botswana Travel Reference Map 1st. Edition 1997/99
Eritrea Travel Reference Map 1st. Edition 1997/99
Ethiopia Travel Reference Map 1st. Edition 1997
Ghana Travel Reference Map 1st. Ed. 1996/99
Kilimanjaro Tourist Map, Tanzania 1998
Malawi Travel Reference Map 1st. Edition 1996/99
Namibia Travel Reference Map 1st. Edition 1997/99
Mount Kenya Tourist Map 1st. Edition ITM/OS
Rwanda/Burundi Map 1st. Edition FUTURE TITLE
Senegal/Gambia Map 1st. Edition 1995/99
Sierra Leone Travel Reference Map 1st. Ed. 1997/99
Southern Africa Travel Reference Map Edition 1998
Uganda Travel Reference Map 1st. Ed. 1996/99
Zambia Travel Reference Map 1st. Ed. 1997/99
Zimbabwe Travel Reference Map 1st. Ed. 1995/98

ASIA, AUSTRALIA, AND NEW ZEALAND
Australia Travel Reference Map 2nd. Ed. 1996/99
Bangladesh Map 1st. Edition - FUTURE TITLE
Beijing, China, Traveller's Map 1st. Edition 1995/97
Cambodia Travel Reference Map 1st. Edition 1995/98
China Travel Reference Map 2nd. Edition 1996/99
Hanoi and Region Travel Map 2nd.Edition 1997/99
India Travel Reference Map 1st. Edition 1997
Indonesia Travel Reference Map 1st. Ed. 1996/99
Japan Travel Reference Map 2nd. Ed. 1994/98
Laos Travel Reference Map 1st. Ed. 1996/99
Mongolia Travel Reference Map 1st. Ed. 1995/98
Nepal Travel Reference Map 1st. Ed. 1994/98
New Zealand Travel Reference Map 2nd. Ed. 1997/99
Saigon/Ho Chi Minh City (Vietnam) 1st. Ed. 1996/99
Shanghai, China, Traveller's Map 1st. Ed. 1995/98
South East Asia Map 2nd. Edition 1996/99
Thailand Travel Reference Map 1st. Ed. 1996/99
Tokyo, Traveller's Map 1st.Edition 1993/96
Vietnam Travel Reference Map 2nd. Ed. 1997/99

CARIBBEAN
Ambergris Cay, Belize, Tourist Map 1st. Ed. ITM/OS
Bahamas Travel Reference Map 1st. Ed. 1994/97
Barbados Travel Reference Map 1st. Ed. 1996/99
Bermuda Travel Reference Map 1st. Ed. 1994/97
British Virgin Islands Tourist Map 1st. Ed. ITM/OS
Cayman Islands Travel Reference Map 1st.Ed. 1996/99
Cuba Travel Reference Map 1st. Ed. 1996/99
Dominica Tourist Map 1st. Edition ITM/OS
Dominican Republic Map 1st. Edition 1994/98
Jamaica Travel Reference Map 2nd. Ed. 1995/98
Puerto Rico Travel Reference Map 1st. Edition 1997
Saint Lucia Tourist Map 1st. Edition ITM/OS
Saint Vincent and the Grenadines 1st. Edition ITM/OS
Virgin Islands (British and American) Map 1st. Ed.

EUROPE
Armenia/Azerbaijan Travel Reference Map 1997/00
Cruising the Mediterranean FUTURE TITLE
Georgian Republic (Georgia) 1st. Edition 1997/99
London Map Guide 1st. Edition 1998/00
Prague (Czech Rep.) Traveller's Map 1st. Ed. 1995/98
Scotland Travel Reference Map FUTURE TITLE

MEXICO, CENTRAL AMERICA, AND SOUTH AMERICA
MEXICO
Mexico Travel Reference Map 2nd. Edition 1994/97
Mexico: Baja California Travel Map 3rd. Ed. 1997/99
Mexico S.: South Coast Travel Map 2nd. Ed. 1995/98
Mexico NW: Sonora/Copper Canyon FUTURE TITLE
Yucatan Peninsula Map 5th. Edition 1996/99
CENTRAL AMERICA
Central America Map 4th. Edition 1997/99
Belize Travel Reference Map 3rd. Edition 1997
Costa Rica Travel Reference Map 2nd. Ed. 1994/98
El Salvador Travel Reference Map 1st. Ed. 1996/99
Guatemala Travel Reference Map 2nd. Edition
Honduras Travel Reference Map 1st. Ed. 1996/99
Nicaragua Travel Reference Map 1st. Ed. 1995/99
Panama Travel Reference Map 2nd. Ed. 1996/99
SOUTH AMERICA
Kevin Healey's South America Map Memorial Ed.
South America: North West Map 2nd. Edition, 1996
South America: North East Map 2nd. Edition, 1996
South America: Southern Map 3rd. Edition, 1997
Amazon Basin Travel Reference Map 2nd. Ed. 1993/98
Argentina Travel Reference Map 1st. Ed. 1993/98
Easter Island Travel Reference Map 2nd. Edition 1997
Ecuador Travel Reference Map 1st. Ed. 1996/99
Falkland Islands Travel Ref. Map 1st. Ed. 1996/99
Galapagos Islands Map 2nd. Edition, 1997/99
Rio de Janeiro, Brasil Traveller's Map 1st. Ed. 1994/97
Uruguay Travel Reference Map 1997/00
Venezuela Travel Reference Map 2nd. Ed. 1997/99
NORTH AMERICA
Western Canada Map 1st. Edition 1998/00
British Columbia Travel Map 3rd. Edition 1997/99
Prairie Provinces Map 1st.Edition FUTURE TITLE
Yukon Travel Reference Map 2nd. Edition 1996/99

BRITISH COLUMBIA SECTIONAL ROAD MAPS
Cariboo Country Regional Road Map 1st. Ed. 1996/99
Cranbrook and Region Topographic/Recreation Map
Fraser Valley: Langley to Hope Topographic/Rec Map
Garibaldi Region Topo/Rec Map Revised Ed. 1997
Gulf Islands, Southern, Topographic Map 2nd. Ed.
Invermere and Region Topographic/Recreation Map
Lower Mainland Region: Vancouver /Pemberton
Okanagan Region: US border/Kamloops to Merritt
Queen Charlotte Is./Haida Gwaii Topo Map
Saltspring Island Topographic/Recreation Map
Stein Valley Wilderness Hiking Trail Vancouver Island
Travel Road Map 2nd. Ed. 1997/99
Vancouver Citymap/Guide For Visitors 1995/97 Ed.
Vancouver's Northshore Hiking Trails 1st. Ed., 1994/96
West Coast Trail Wilderness Hiking Map 2nd. Edition
Whistler and Region Recreation Map 3rd. Ed. 1995/97

UNITED STATES OF AMERICA
Alaska Travel Reference Map 2nd. Edition, 1996/99
Florida Keys Travel Reference Map 1st. Ed. 1996/99
Mount Baker Region Topographic Map 1994/97
San Juan Islands (WA) Recreation Map, 4th. Ed. 1997

GUIDE BOOKS
Alaska's Inside Passage Traveller 1996
Northern Califonia Travel Adventure 1997
Prague and the Czech Republic 1996
RVing in Mexico and Central America 1996
Yukon Travel Adventure Guide 1997

Don't Get Lost! Get A Map!

345 WEST BROADWAY
VANCOUVER, B.C. CANADA V5Y 1P8
Ph. (604) 879-3621   FAX (604) 879-4521
Web site http://www.nas.com/travelmaps

About the Author

Dieter Reinmuth is a Yukoner. For over 20 years he has lived in Dawson City and made a living gold mining in the Klondike. He has travelled throughout the territory, not only by car, but by bicycle, and has floated the length and breadth of the Yukon River from White-horse to the Bering Strait. His world-wide travelling has been even more extensive. For 15 years he toured the world with a simple pre-mountain bike style bicycle, covering over 100,000 km, while working and living in countries such as Australia, Japan and Costa Rica- to name a few. One of his many passions, photog-raphy, has been

The author at the historic gold mining town of Fortymile.

turned into a business- 6 of his postcards are Dawson City scenes, and so are 5 distinct greeting cards depicting not only Yukon wide animal scenes, but also the ill-famed SOUR-TOE- the human pickled toe that Captain Dick of Dawson City has turned into the 'sour-toe cocktail'.

Dieter is also the builder, owner and manager of the Dawson City River Hostel; since 1992 the only affiliated Canadian Hostel in the Yukon. The hostel provides cabins and tenting sites on the banks of the Yukon River, right across from Dawson City. His contacts with travellers of all nationalities have been numerous, and some information contained in this book has been gathered from hostel guests who have canoed, biked, hiked and driven in every nook and cranny of this huge territory. Thanks to them this book has been made possible, and the author dedicates these pages to them and all future travellers of this northern wonderland.